French Modernisms
Perspectives on Art Before, During, and After Vichy

French Modernisms: Perspectives on Art Before, During, and After Vichy examines the period 1937 to 1968 by looking at the margins of official art history. The author focuses on underreported exhibitions of modern French art, atypical visual artifacts, aberrant art criticism (Fascist or Vichy-inspired but also anti-establishment). Her Benjaminian approach uncovers surprising continuities in the French attitude toward the "other": a hybrid of anti-foreigner, anti-Semitic, anti-American protectionism, and little resistance to cultural narcissism.

Cone's analyses demonstrate that France attempted to safeguard the integrity of indigenous traditions in painting, sculpture, and the decorative arts not only during Vichy but throughout the period under consideration. Cone also argues that the French art establishment may have caused its own downfall after World War II by continuing to privilege an art of national identity and national tradition based on outmoded concepts of beauty. Thus, she concludes, postwar French modernisms could not compete with either the so-called invasion of American Abstract Expressionism in the 1950s or American Pop art in the 1960s.

Michèle C. Cone is the author of the groundbreaking text *Artists under Vichy: A Case of Prejudice and Persecution*. Dr. Cone has written widely on French art and society in the 1940s, contributing to the *Art Bulletin*, the *Art Journal*, *Art in America*, and *Yale French Studies*. Her essays have also appeared in *Picasso and the War Years*, *Fascist Visions*, *The Jew in the Text*, and *The Art of the Everyday*. She is on the board of the Art Critics' Association (AICA-USA) and a long-standing faculty member at the School of Visual Arts.

French Modernisms

Perspectives on Art Before, During, and After Vichy

Michèle C. Cone

CAMBRIDGE
UNIVERSITY PRESS

PUBLISHED BY THE PRESS SYNDICATE OF THE UNIVERSITY OF CAMBRIDGE
The Pitt Building, Trumpington Street, Cambridge, United Kingdom

CAMBRIDGE UNIVERSITY PRESS
The Edinburgh Building, Cambridge, CB2 2RU, UK http: //www.cup.cam.ac.uk
40 West 20th Street, New York, NY 10011–4211, USA http: //www.cup.org
10 Stamford Road, Oakleigh, Melbourne 3166, Australia
Ruiz de Alarcón 13, 28014 Madrid, Spain

First published 2001

Printed in the United States of America

Typeface Aldus 11/14 pt. *System* Quark XPress[R] [GH]

A catalogue record for this book is available from the British Library.

Library of Congress Cataloguing-in-Publication Data

Cone, Michèle C., 1932–
French modernism – perspectives on art before, during, and after Vichy / Michèle C. Cone.
p. cm.
ISBN 0-521-78350-X
1. Modernism (Art) – France. 2. Art – Political aspects – France – History – 20th century.
3. Art, French – American influences I. Title.

N6848.5M63 C66 2001
709′44′0904 – dc21 00-040328

ISBN 0 521 78350 X hardback

For Terry

Contents

List of Illustrations

Acknowledgments

I would first like to thank Beatrice Rehl, my editor at Cambridge University Press, whose positive outlook on this project has been extremely heartwarming. Françoise Bartlett, my project editor, is to be thanked for her excellent work and personal interest in the outcome of the book. My thanks go to the editors of the publications in which chapters of this book first appeared as articles and essays. Finally, I would like to recognize the smart and helpful work of the anonymous readers who were asked to give their specialists' opinions on this book's contents. Thank you very much, all of you.

French Modernisms
Perspectives on Art Before, During, and After Vichy

Introduction

Art, Nationality, and National Tradition in France from 1937 to 1968

> Dates and places keep and preserve history: they protect against commemorative history and at the same time maintain the possibility of another history, of other anniversaries. So that to give their physiognomy to dates, to restore their faces, to tie them to the events they recall, is truly to make them live all over again, to picture them, to fix their image.
>
> – Françoise Proust, *L'histoire à contretemps: le temps historique chez Walter Benjamin*

PAROXYSMS of racist protectionism such as Lucien Rebatet writing in the Parisian weekly *Je suis partout*, "The beautiful tree of French art is threatened by a nasty virus, and the Jewish vermin responsible must be destroyed" mark a horrendous moment of the French past: the period when France lay under the Nazi boot and a pro-Nazi French government headed by Marshal Pétain operated out of the provincial town of Vichy. Although the author of this ugly piece of art journalism was not your average banal art critic but a famous pro-Nazi ideologue who, with his colleague Robert Brasillac, was condemned to death by Liberation tribunals, it is figures like him that have given the Vichy years their most damning image. And it is why the Vichy period in France has long been viewed by the French as a temporary aberration, a parenthesis, totally separate from the period that preceded it, the Third Republic, and from the Fourth and then the Fifth Republic that followed it.

Even so, in recent years, a number of historians have come to the conclusion that among the policies attributed to Vichy some were in fact republican in origin (Gérard Noiriel), that virulent anti-Semitism already prevailed in France in the thirties (Ralph Schor) and, more generally, that there was a "Vichy before Vichy" (Pierre Laborie).[1] In the realm of artistic policy and practice, there might have been not only a Vichy before Vichy, but a Vichy *after* Vichy. The premise underlying Rebatet's defense of the beautiful tree of French art, namely that art rooted in national soil, national traditions, and national know-how is superior to art infiltrated by modes and ideas foreign to the French sensibility dies hard in France. Resistance to artistic isolationism often goes unrewarded and, after World War II, even May '68, the most critical moment of opportunity for change to a more internationalist outlook leaves an ambiguous trace.

Without occulting the specificity of the Vichy years, I will show here that the French state attempted to safeguard the integrity of indigenous traditions in painting, sculpture, and the decorative arts not only during Vichy but under the Popular Front, and throughout the postwar period. I also will argue that the French art establishment may have caused its own downfall after World War II by continuing to privilege "painting in the French tradition," an art of national identity based on outmoded concepts of beauty for that time. Such postwar French "modernisms" could not compete in the fifties with the so called "invasion" of American Abstract Expressionism.[2] Nor, as revealed in my epilogue, could *new figuration (la figuration narrative)*, a French vanguard of the sixties with an anti-American art agenda, compete with Pop art, its American counterpart.

The materials under scrutiny in this text are drawn from the margins of mainstream art history – underreported exhibitions of modern art, long-neglected pieces of art criticism, rarely displayed furniture and decorative objects, rarely seen artworks, posters, and art books. These materials have not been observed as works of art but as "image-objects worthy of interest for bearing witness" (Marc

Ferro).[3] Or put in the words of Donald Preziosi, the author of *Rethinking Art History: Meditations on a Coy Science,* art history is used here "as a chance for reflection, a place to see seeing."[4] Though most of my essays first appeared in art historical publications, their primary intent was, as will become apparent, neither connoisseurship nor canon revision.

To "see seeing" and to "bear witness" have meant bringing to the forefront of art history image-objects that go against the construction of a memory that glorifies the nation, finds alibis for its faults, or, when that is impossible, banalizes guilt. "To write history," Walter Benjamin proposed (in a brief passage of his *Fragments on Baudelaire*), "is to give their physiognomy to dates." To do so has meant exposing the agenda behind the chronology of exhibitions commemorating the art of the period between the Popular Front and May '68 in France, and proposing new dates tied to the events they recall. Of course, events fleetingly come into and go out of memory, and whoever retrieves them only speaks in the present tense: "The event is not imbedded in memory to be preserved, archived, and commemorated. On the contrary, it is deposited there so it can come back over and over again, like a ghost asking for justice" (Françoise Proust).

In 1981, the Pompidou Center hosted an exhibition entitled *Paris–Paris 1937–1957,* the last of a series of exhibitions on the theme of artistic interaction between world capitals. In 1981, there were quite a few taboo subjects still buried in official French memory. The Pompidou exhibition avoided the subject of the thriving decorative arts industry in France and the fomenting of the cult of personality at the national manufactures during Vichy; it finessed showing examples of painting in a neoromantic style and a palette "after Corot" that Lucien Rebatet, the art critic of *Je suis partout* during the Occupation years, praised for being "between the Jew and the Pompier." It remained silent on the sculpture caricaturing the Jew at the exhibition *Le Juif et la France* held at the Palais Berlitz in 1941. And, as far as the curator of the exhibition was concerned, the "sinister gleam" that had blemished the August 25, 1944, liberation of Paris was Hiroshima. "The longed-for bright light of the liberation of Paris, 25 August 1944, would be shadowed a few months later by the sinister gleam of Hiroshima."[5]

Although the *Paris–Paris* exhibition used 1937 as a starting date, it presented the end of the thirties in terms of imminent closure, a period haunted in Paris by fascism and energized by the moral stand of detractors of fascism, Picasso, and the surrealists. One of the authors of the catalogue did note that a conservative chauvinistic French art bureaucracy was in charge of divvying up major commissions to artists in 1936–37, and of distributing aid to unemployed artists.[6] But he made no mention of the transformation of this "national preference" into a policy of exclusion on the basis of place of birth and religion, the policy applied in an officially sponsored exhibition of modern French art that was held in Nazi Berlin in 1937.

I show in my first chapter, "Collaboration Foretold," centered on this 1937 exhibition, the extent to which the French government was already willing in 1937 to sacrifice its talented non-French and Jewish artists so as to appease the Nazi government. I raise the possibility that the artists who participated in the Berlin exhibition, many of them dependent for their livelihood on commissions from the state, were good candidates for future use by fascist governments in France or in Nazi Germany. And I show in the next two chapters, "Decadence and Renewal in the Decorative Arts Under Vichy" and "Lucien Rebatet: Anti-Semitic Art Criticism During Vichy" that the 1937 Berlin exhibition anticipated in important respects the agenda of Vichy.

Continuity between the Vichy years and the postwar period is officially admissible in the realm of the French decorative arts. An exhibition held near Paris in December 1998 displayed furniture and accessories produced in France by twenty-one interior architects active from the late thirties to the end of the forties, which was entitled *Les Décorateurs des années 40*. In a chapter headed "Wartime Gilt," I hint that this arresting though elitist style of furniture thrived during the Occupation years and beyond, with the help of the French government, and even after it became clear that a luxury approach to interior décor had become irrelevant to the needs of the average French home.

In the fine arts, however, the idea of a brilliant new awakening *after* the defeat of Vichy dominates European thought from the sixties on. This view was expressed by Germain Viatte in his contribution to the catalogue of *Paris–Paris* when he wrote of "une bouleversante explosion de création au lendemain de la guerre.[7] It was also made clear in the division of presentations at the exhibition *Face à l'Histoire* at the Pompidou Center in 1997. And it is signified by the use of the date 1945 as a favored point of departure for analyses of modern art. Typical are *L'Art vivant 1945–1955*, an exhibition at the Fondation Maeght in 1966; *Art et Idéologies: L'Art en Occident, 1945–1949*, an anthology based on a symposium and published in 1978; *L'Art en Europe: Les Années décisives 1945–1953*, an exhibition at the Musée de St-Etienne in 1987; and the memorable *Paris Post War: Art and Existentialism 1945–55*, held at the Tate in London in 1993.

There is no question that the war changed the climate of the art world. But I propose that in France, several events that took place in 1943 are more meaningful signifiers of changes than 1945. In the midst of war, in February 1943, the first exhibition of semiabstract *bleu-blanc-rouge* painters, including Jean Bazaine, Maurice Estève, and other pillars of the postwar Ecole de Paris, takes place at the Galerie de France. In November 1943, the René Drouin gallery holds a retrospective of Jean Fautrier, including examples of his new antiform style and possibly examples of his *Hostage* paintings; and in December 1943, despite interdictions on displays of Picasso's art, an illustrated *Picasso Album* is published by a half-Jewish publisher, with a text by Robert Desnos, the surrealist Resistance poet, inspired by existentialist philosophy.

In 1943, ideological distinctions that will get lost in the postwar shuffle are clear and important. The tricolor painters, abiding by the idea of national tradition, attempt the synthesis of a tradition that includes Henri Matisse and Georges Braque but excludes Soutine and the surrealists. They find allies in the Vichy government, in the official Paris press, and even in the Paris-based Nazi press. On the contrary, Fautrier's expressionist art, influenced by Chaim Soutine and by prehistoric cave painting, is ruthlessly condemned by the fascist critic Lucien Rebatet and defended by Jean Paulhan, the Resistance author who contributes the introduction to his catalogue. As for Picasso, he is accused by the fauve painter Maurice Vlaminck of betraying the French tradition and of being nothing but a pasticheur.

Three of my chapters deal with these issues: "'Abstract' Art as a Veil: Tricolor Painting in Vichy France"; "Jean Paulhan and His Artist Friends"; "The Picasso Album: A Landmark of Artistic Resistance."

The selection of 1945 as the key moment for the birth of new energies sends a message that is as clear as it is misleading. What is declared is that in France, the end of World War II made a definite break with the recent past not only in politics with the return of democracy but in art with new forms of expression. Indeed, using the year 1945 as a starting date avoids lifting a veil on the art made during a murky period, but, more important, it banalizes the difference between an anti-Vichy visual culture that bears witness in an expressionist – some would say "existentialist" – mode (Sartre's *Being and Nothingness* was published in 1943) and a formalist culture of cubo-abstract painting that simulates an anti-Vichy stance while remaining loyal to the idea of French tradition.

Thanks to the use of 1945 as the date of change and discontinuity, the cubo-abstract *bleu-blanc-rouge* painters, Bazaine, Estève, Manessier, and Le Moal, can emerge in a golden light from the dark age of World War II, successfully competing with the expressionism of Fautrier's *Hostage* paintings, of Picasso's skull images, and other visual testimonies of suffering and death. Although in 1952, in his text *L'Art autre,* the French critic Michel Tapié de Celeyran had already detected an international trend (Picasso, Fautrier, Wols, Jean Dubuffet, Henri Michaux, Pierre Soulages, Georges Mathieu, Germaine Richier, together with English and American expressionists) that clearly stood against the abstract formalism of the Bazaine group; the two groups continued to be thrown together in group exhibitions organized in France after the war. In fact, by reading tragedy behind the cheerful look of tricolor painting, and hope behind the anguished watercolors of the Jewish expressionist Wols, the French historian Jean Laude in a 1976 text attempted to permanently blur the difference between the two groups.[8] One must await 1993 and the Tate exhibition *Paris Post War: Art and Existentialism 1945–1955* for Fautrier and Picasso to become separated from the school of national tradition (my expression) on philosophical grounds.

There is, however, less of a consensus about the end of this alleged new élan in French art than there is about its beginning. For the English art historian Sarah Wilson, writing in the catalogue of the 1993 exhibition *Paris Post War: Art and Existentialism 1945–1955*, 1955 marks "an epistimological break in the languages of art and society in France."[9] Indeed 1955 coincides with Maurice Merleau-Ponty's formal attack of Jean Paul Sartre and with the publication of *Tristes Tropiques* by Claude Lévi-Strauss and of Alain Robbe-Grillet's important novel *Le Voyeur,* all of which point to the emergence of new antiexistentialist theory. But from the point of view of expressionist artists such as the mature Germaine Richier and the young César, who are the subjects of my chapter "The Mature Richier, the Young César: Expressionist Confluences in French Postwar Sculpture," the crucial hinge is not 1955 but later in the decade. I show how Richier veered away from her postwar expressionist sculpture toward abstract, sometimes painted sculpture at the end of her career in the late fifties (she died in 1959), while the young César abandoned the expressionist vision of his *Seated Nude Pompei* for a hands-off approach, using American technology to turn car carcasses into rectangular blocks of mangled steel, the first of which was exhibited at the Salon de Mai of 1960.

Other dates that have been used to signify the end of an alleged postwar élan are 1951 (Jean Laude) and 1953 (Bernard Ceysson). These dates, coinciding with the increasing presence of new American art in Paris, barely conceal a profound anti-American agenda. The fact that several of the American artists were Jews made them doubly foreign. The aforementioned Jean Laude, influential French mentor of several generations of French cultural historians, argues that the turning point was the 1951 exhibition *Véhémences Confrontées* in Paris, an exhibition that included Pollock and de Kooning, along with Wols, Mathieu, and Riopelle. Ignoring the theorizing on Action Painting and abstract expressionism that was taking place in New York, this partisan of painting in the French tradition (Bazaine, Manessier, Estève) claimed that the new American art produced a situation in which art could no longer be judged through "normative" judgments based on "concepts of harmony, beauty, and delectation," but only through the criterion of novelty. In 1976, he was still dreaming of "a history of art that would not limit itself to distributing innovation certificates but would evaluate those inventions and only recognize them as inventions through the use to which they had been put."[10]

As for Bernard Ceysson, the curator of *Les Années décisives: L'Art en Europe 1945–1953*, he suggested that 1953 was a key signpost, marked by the triumph of American art in Europe and its irresistible attraction to European museums. Rehashing an argument already found in Serge Guilbaut's thesis in *How New York Stole the Idea of Modern Art*, he wrote: "The esthetic reorientation that takes place around 1953 in Europe and leads museum people to substitute American art for European art on their walls, is a perfect manifestation of the success of a promotional enterprise, remarkably organized, during the cold war by official U.S. services."[11]

I concur with Pierre Restany ("Pierre Restany: Postwar Remnants of Cultural Pétainism Exposed") that the aggressive presence in Paris of abstract expressionist painting is more an alibi than an explanation for why Paris lost the battle of modern art in the postwar years. According to this critic, the Parisian art establishment itself, ensconced in the national-tradition idea that it had successfully defended during World War II, was loath to make a change in the postwar years and continued to defend the group formed in 1943 by Bazaine, Manessier, and Estève and then their cubo-abstract followers, renamed Ecole de Paris. Not until the end of the fifties, when *affichistes* and *nouveaux réalistes,* influenced by Marcel Duchamp, by American art, by modern life and by technology, made themselves heard, was the issue of national tradition put on a back burner in Paris.

However, as I show in my epilogue, "Hitler Equals de Gaulle in a May '68 Poster," in the sixties, hostility to the inroads made in Europe by American art resumed, directed this time at American Pop art. In *La Figuration narrative,* a French figurative mode with an anarchist agenda examplified in the paintings of the Icelandic expatriate Erro, Pop art strategies were used in a mocking tone, and American capitalism derided along with Soviet communism.

Whatever merit there is behind the desire of a proud nation to protect its national indigenous culture, in France the memory of Vichy renders the idea of cultural protectionism suspect. An agenda denying the continuity of a protectionist – at times xenophobic – attitude to culture is unfortunately part of a larger crisis that has made even longtime admirers of France uneasy if not disillusioned. Readers of French literature have only recently been told of compromises and cowardice in the ranks of the literary elite during Vichy that did not foreclose (with rare exceptions such as Robert Brasillac) thriving careers afterward. Revelations have recently come out concerning the anti-Semitic behavior during the Vichy years of the then president of the society for the protection of authors' rights (SACEM), whose son is now in charge.[12] And of course, Maurice Papon, a high functionary during Vichy, went on winning honors in the French official hierarchy until the nineties, when he was finally put on trial for his role in the deportation of Jews during World War II.

A Break in 1937

1

Collaboration Foretold

French Art of the Present in Hitler's Berlin

On June 5, 1937, an exhibition of French modern art, *Ausstellung Französischer Kunst der Gegenwart* (French Art of the Present), opened at the Preussische Akademie der Künste in Berlin.[1] It featured works by, among others, Henri Matisse, Maurice de Vlaminck, Georges Braque, and Fernand Léger – painters officially designated "degenerate" by the Nazis. Hermann Göring attended the opening of the show, and Adolf Hitler visited it in the company of the French ambassador to Germany, André François-Poncet.

On the surface, such an event, cosponsored by the French and German governments, appears astonishing. The Preussische Akademie der Künste, responding to Nazi directives, had recently expelled its "degenerate" members (including Ernst Barlach, Otto Dix, Ernst Ludwig Kirchner, and Oskar Kokoschka). That same year the Nazis' notorious exhibition *Entartete Kunst* (Degenerate Art) opened in Munich. And the artists so courteously received by Nazi

First published in the *Art Bulletin,* Vol. 53, no. 3, September 1998.

officials in Berlin in 1937 had had their works removed from the German museums that owned them, starting in 1934.[2]

On closer examination, the apparent contradictions of the exhibition disappear. Documentation shows that each government used the occasion of an outwardly cordial gesture to further its own propagandistic ends. The French ultimately hoped to interest Germans in visiting the costly *Exposition Internationale des Arts et Techniques* scheduled in Paris for the spring and summer of 1937 (it opened May 24, 1937), while presenting a "healthy" all-French image to their frightening neighbor. The Germans sought a quid pro quo – an exhibition of German sculpture to be held in the prestigious venue of the Jeu de Paume – as well as to demonstrate to their populace the harmlessness of the French as potential foes and, by contrast, the vigor of the German national racial tradition. *Ausstellung Französischer Kunst der Gegenwart* thus contributes a new perspective on the Socialist government of Léon Blum and sheds new light on the Nazi reception of non-German modern art.[3]

French officials viewed the exhibition as a testing group for *rayonnement culturel,* or cultural radiance, the French answer to the aggressive propaganda tactics that totalitarian regimes, particularly Nazi Germany, were using so successfully as a weapon for their cause.[4] "For its defense, a country cannot depend exclusively on an army. Its rays can shine abroad through the press, the radio, the word, or natural beauty," reads a report by the *député* Ernest Pezet to the French Chambre des Députés dated March 28, 1935.[5] During the rule of the Popular Front, the Socialist government led by Léon Blum from May 1936 to June 1937, the "defense and illustration" of French culture became a focus of the government's attention. *Rayonnement culturel,* with its connotations of spiritual enlightenment, remains one of the legacies of the Popular Front to this day.

Jean Zay, French minister for national education in the Blum government and the moving force behind *rayonnement culturel,* conceded the political dimension behind it:

> In the realm of what is called "propaganda" – a word to be proscribed – the Ministry for National Education, with the *Action Artistique,* organized in collaboration with the Ministry of Foreign Affairs . . . extensive theatrical tours . . . exhibitions of French art . . . the shipping of books to universities in foreign capitals,

etc. . . . Many other decisions were taken, whose character might seem purely technical, and yet had a political dimension.[6]

In several respects, *rayonnement culturel* was a new term for an old idea, for there had always been a cultural dimension to colonialism. What gave the concept a new urgency was the context. In 1937, the European democracies suffered from economic depression, high unemployment, and political turmoil, their political values threatened by competing forms of government – Communism, Fascism, Nazism. All these factors placed them on the defensive. Thus, for France, at least in theory, the political aims of *rayonnement culturel* were caught up in defending democracy against totalitarianism, using democracy's most vital symbol, freedom of expression in art and literature.

The exhibition in Berlin, however, presented a rather different view of French art. In hindsight, *Ausstellung Französischer Kunst der Gegenwart* strikes us as cautious and conservative (see Appendix). It managed to avoid all the signs of what the Nazis termed decadence: no distortion, no abstraction, no figures inspired by African statuary. The human form was idealized in both the painted portraits on view, such as *Portrait of a Blond Woman* by André Derain and *Portrait of Mme Othon Friesz* by Othon Friesz (Fig. 1), and the figurative sculpture by Aristide Maillol and Charles Despiau (Fig. 2). Many of the landscapes, in styles ranging from Impressionism to naive, depicted regions of France: *The Seine near Champagne* by Henri Verge-Sarrat, *View of Avignon* by André Planson, *Brittany Landscape* and *Basque Landscape* by Roland Oudot, *Snow in the Doubs* by Jules Zingg.

Genre scenes included upper-class pastimes (*Golf at St. Tropez* by André Dunoyer de Segonzac, *Regatta* by Raoul Dufy), work and leisure activities (*Fair [Brittany]* by Lucien Simon, *Camping* by Gaston Balande), and family life, including an example by Edouard Vuillard. In this last group, *Departure* by Roger Chapelain-Midy (Fig. 6) and *Children's Vespers Bread* by Maurice Asselin, could easily have found a place in an exhibition of Nazi-approved art, alluding respectively to duty to the homeland and duty to the family.

A drawing by Bernard Naudin showing a stern couple and their teenage daughter dressed in Victorian clothes for a visit to an art exhibition was used for the cover of the catalogue (Fig. 3).[7] Finally, a few allegorical paintings were shown, including *Leda* by Marie Laurencin,

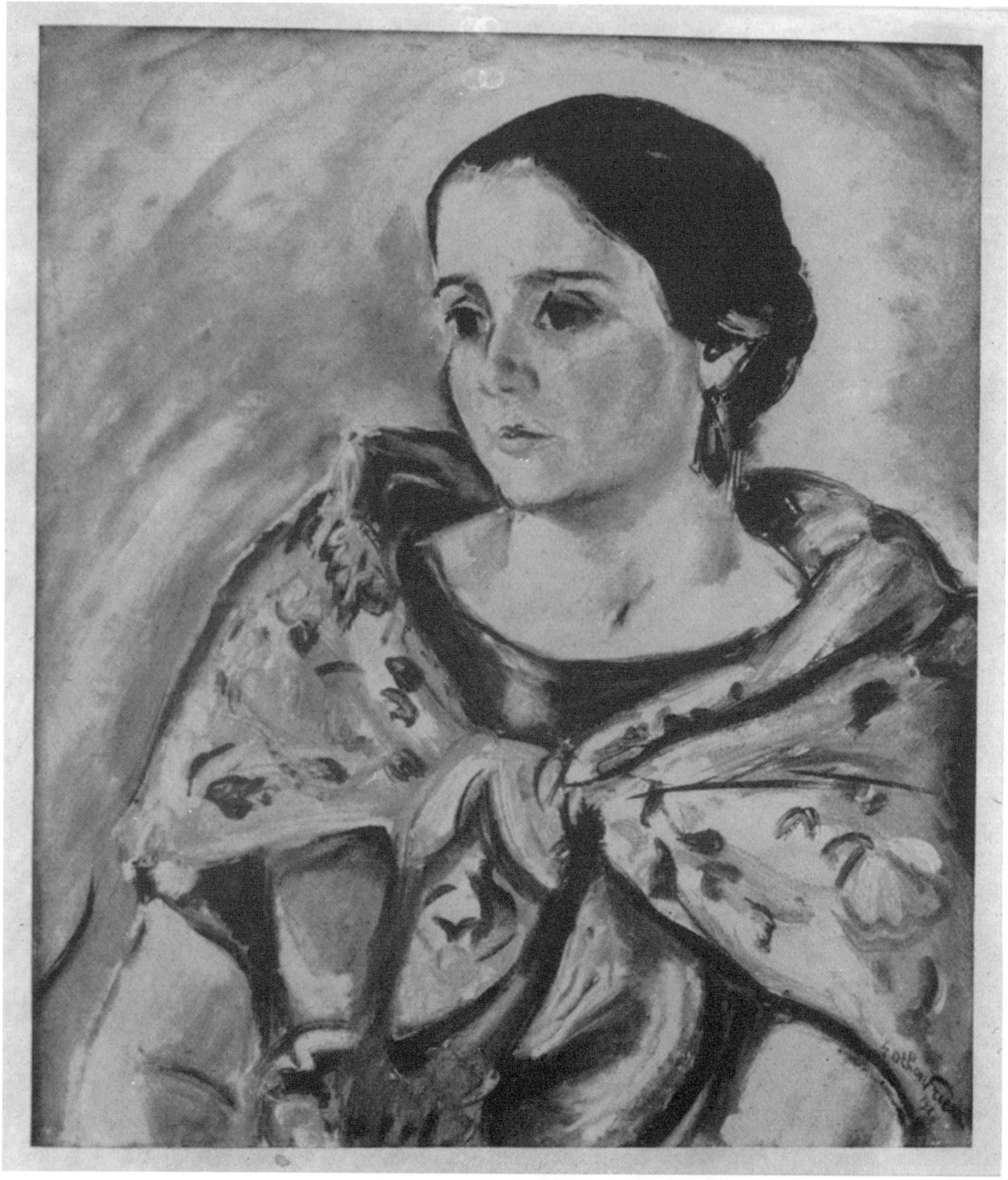

1. Othon Friesz, *Portrait of Mme Othon Friesz.* Date, location, and dimensions unavailable (first reproduced in *Ausstellung Französischer Kunst der Gegenwart,* exh. cat., 1937; photo: Frick Art Reference Library, New York).

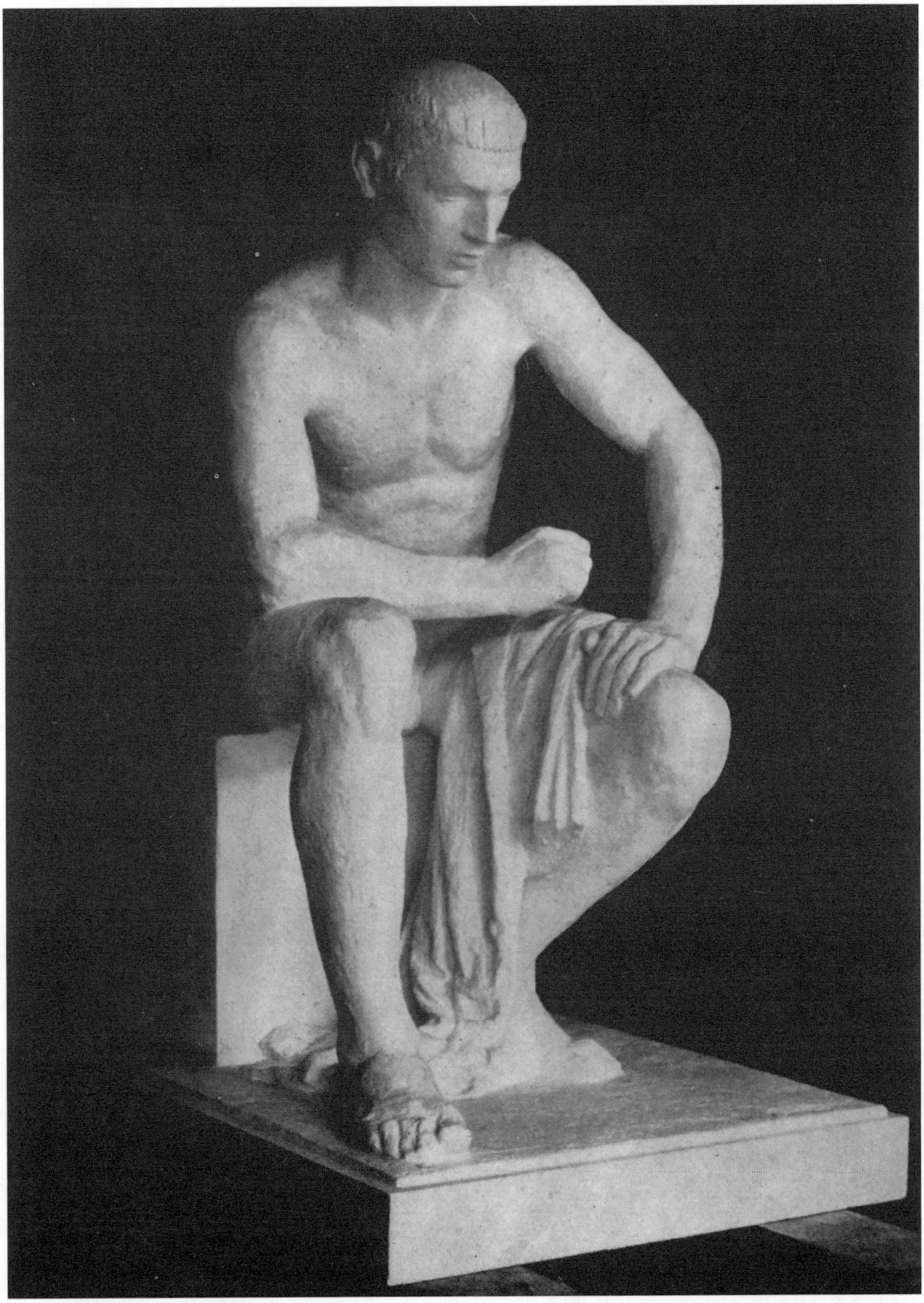

2. Charles Despiau, *Figure for a Monument*. Date, location, and dimensions unavailable (first reproduced in *Ausstellung Französischer Kunst der Gegenwart*, exh. cat., 1937; photo: Frick Art Reference Library).

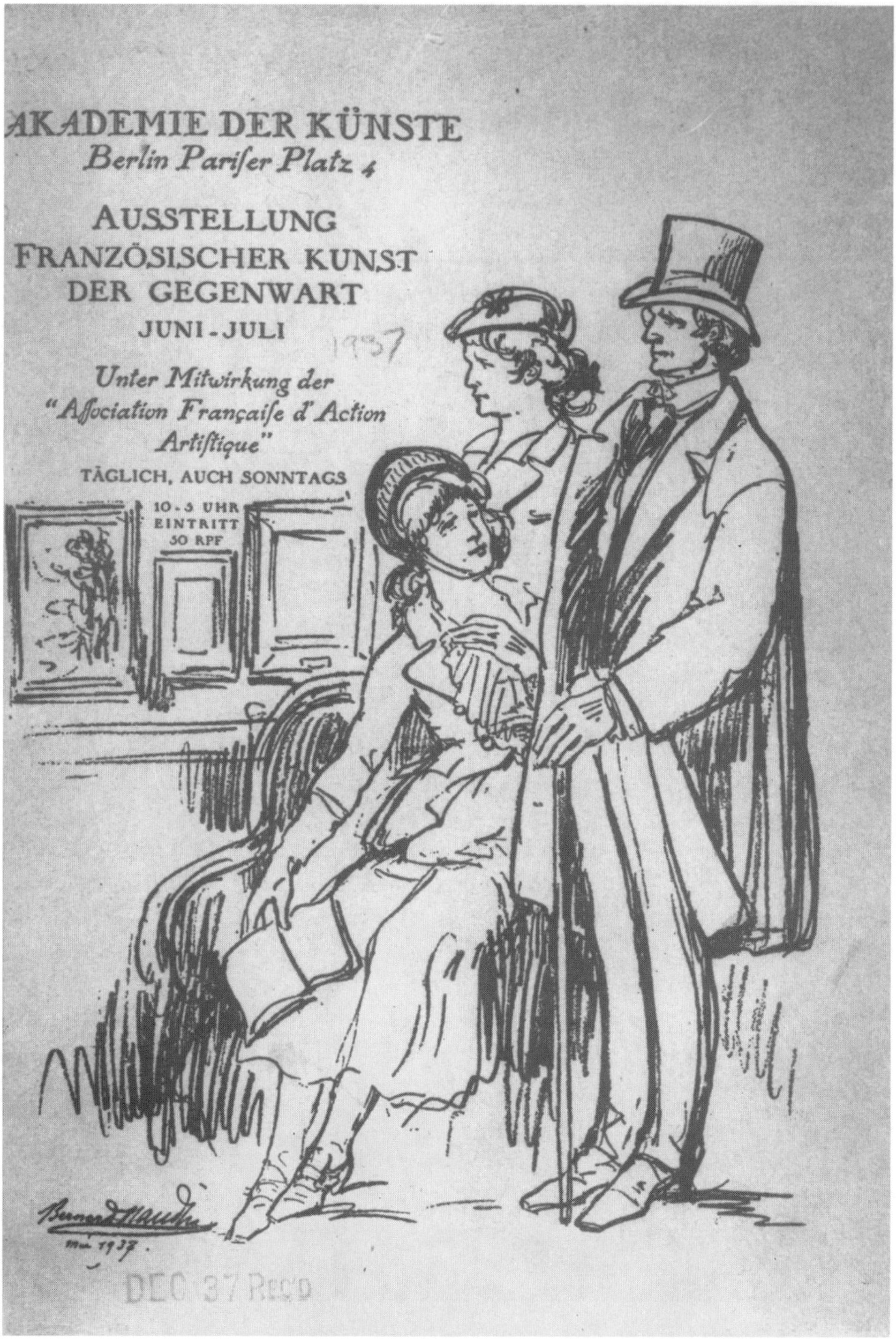

3. Cover for *Ausstellung Französischer Kunst der Gegenwart*, exh. cat., 1937 (photo: Frick Art Reference Library, New York).

Judgment of Paris by Raymond Brechenmacher, and *Adam and Eve* by Georges Desvallières.

Although the exhibition displayed works by many modernists once associated with the French avant-garde, particularly the Fauves, a comparison with a list of artists who participated in the exhibition *Maîtres de l'Art Indépendant 1895–1937* held in Paris in 1937, also sponsored by the French state, reveals that many more controversial artists had been left out. The modernists included in the Berlin show had come to prominence at the beginning of the century, and their styles were familiar. The works by these artists placed on view in Berlin seemed to have been chosen for their inoffensiveness. Matisse was represented by three paintings, including his 1914 *Branch of Lilacs* (Fig. 4), Vlaminck by three paintings, including the landscape *Huts* (Fig. 5). There were three works by Charles Camoin, three by Henri Manguin, three by Albert Marquet, three by Derain, three by Dufy, five by Dunoyer de Segonzac, two untitled drawings by Léger, and *Mandolin and Vase* by Braque.

In light of the reputation of the Popular Front as the first French government to demonstrate serious interest in helping the cause of avant-garde art, and of Léon Blum's personal affinity for the work of Robert and Sonia Delaunay, a bolder selection might have been expected. However, the involvement of François-Poncet helps to explain the visual conservatism of the works on display in the Berlin exhibition. A close reading of his correspondence makes it clear that he had a different conception in mind for *rayonnement culturel* than Blum's ambition to defend and illustrate art from France in its "inclusiveness *[sa globalité]*" and "continuity."[8] He was using it to promote the image of a "healthy" art. With their emphasis on leisure activities for different social groups – regattas, golf, camping, going to art exhibitions – on a daily life oriented toward healthy family values, and on a figurative style understandable by all, the selected works illustrated values dear to Socialist governments rather than articulating freedom of expression under the Popular Front.

The presentation of the artists in the catalogue, however, suggests a more complex agenda than does the visual text alone, and also answers other questions raised by the Berlin show. On several points, the exhibition catalogue was very specific on details while, on one

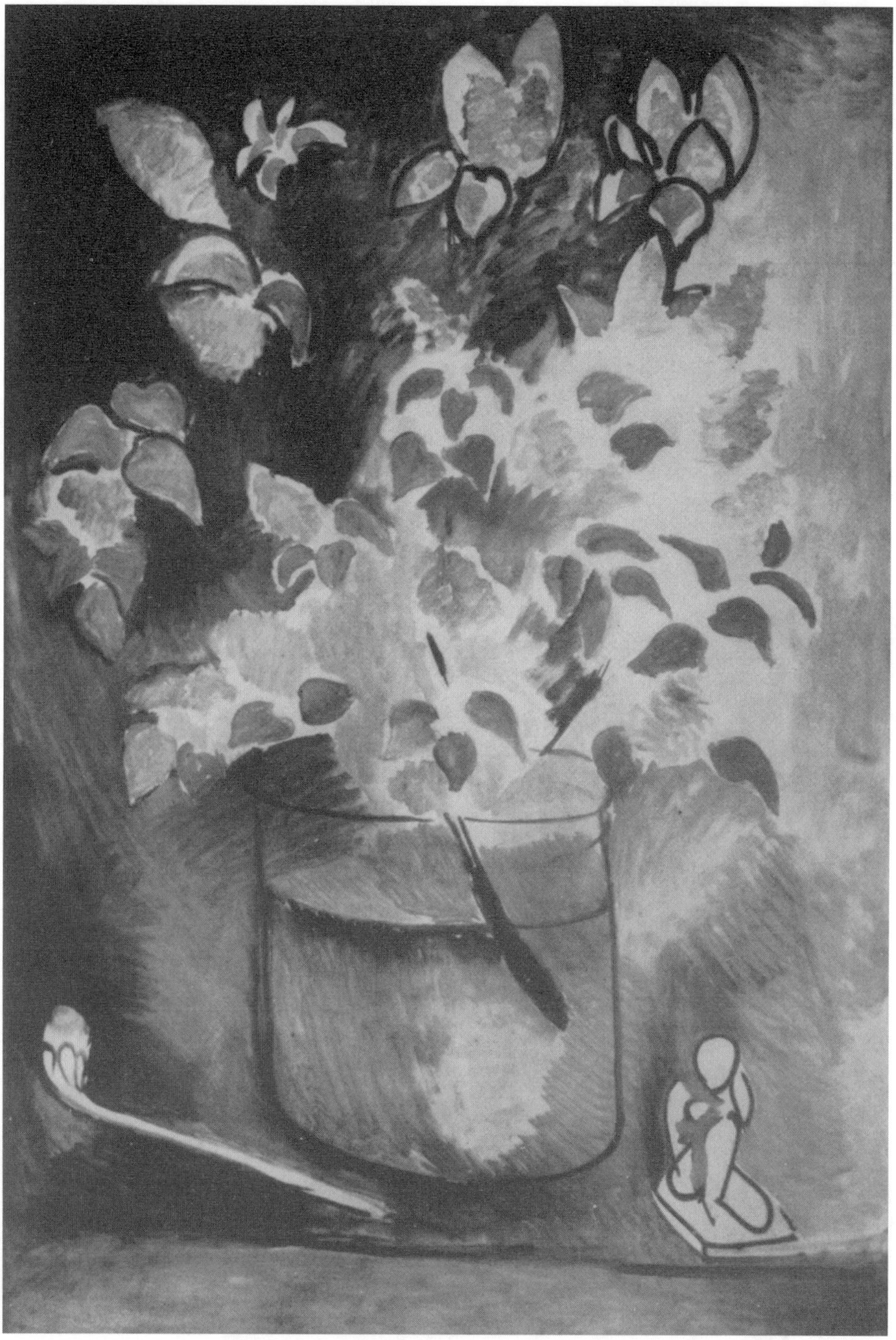

4. Henri Matisse, *Branch of Lilacs,* 1914. Location and dimensions unavailable (photo: Frick Art Reference Library, New York).

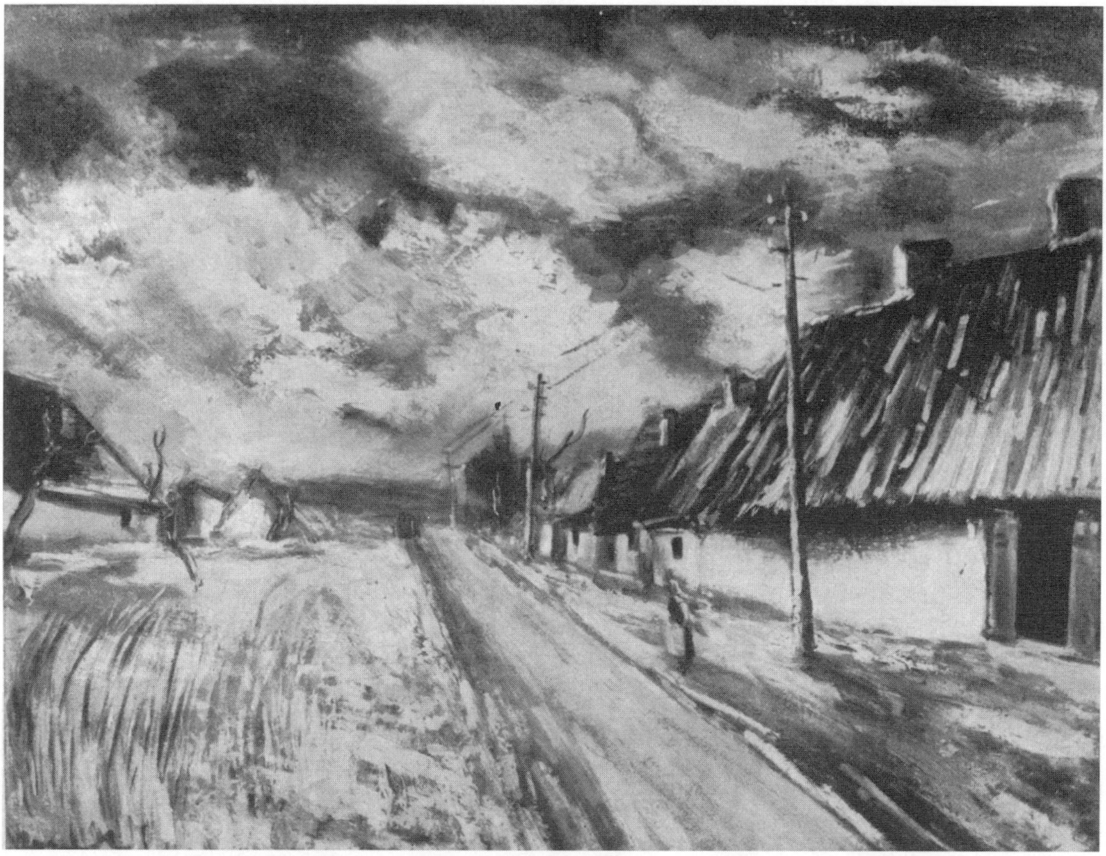

5. Maurice de Vlaminck, *Huts.* Date and dimensions unavailable; formerly Musée du Luxembourg, Paris (photo: Frick Art Reference Library, New York).

point, it remained pointedly silent. Next to Pierre Bonnard's name in the catalogue, for example, was the following notice: "Born in 1867, in Fontenay-aux-Roses. Decorative paintings for the Theatre of the New Palais du Trocadéro at the International Exhibition 1937."[9] Yves Brayer was presented as a recent recipient of the Prix de Rome working in the Pavillon Thermal; Alfred Courmes is described as working in the "Pavillon des Manufactures de Sèvres" (probably the display for la Manufacture de Sèvres in the Pavillon de la Céramique); Raoul Dufy as working for the Palais de l'Electricité; Jean Aujame, Georges d'Espagnat, Marcel Gromaire, André Lhote, and Maurice-Georges Poncelet were said to be working in the Palais de la Découverte; Pierre Ladureau in the Pavillon du Centre Régional des Flandres; Adrienne Jouclard and Henri Verge-Sarrat in the Pavillon de l'Enseignement. The special mention of the involvement of a number of the artists in the decoration of public buildings in Paris raises the possibility that an economic agenda – to sell the artists' experience in the adornment of public buildings to Nazi Germany – accompanied the idealistic agenda of *rayonnement culturel.*[10]

The catalogue description also meticulously entered the birthplace of all the artists following their names. Every single one of the artists showed roots in the French soil. No artist not born in France who had made France a permanent home was included. It appears that Jewish artists were not considered French even if they had been born in France. Thus, before Vichy, under Republican government, a narrow criterion of nationality is already in place in this exhibition. Although making a distinction between foreigner and French-born artist, between Aryan and Jew, was a common practice in France during those years, it did not apply to every official exhibition of modern French art at that time. *Maîtres de l'Art Indépendant 1895–1937,* an exhibition with a similar agenda organized by Raymond Escholier for the city of Paris at the Petit Palais that same year, included a far wider selection, as can be observed by comparing the list of artists in the two exhibitions (see Appendix). Had the French and German co-organizers of the Berlin exhibition reached a consensus not only on aesthetics but also on issues of nationality? Is it a coincidence that the chosen representatives of "French art of the present" could demonstrate "pure" racial lines, from the German point of view?

While the exhibition catalogue for the Berlin exhibition gave precise information on birthplace and public works, it supplied the scantiest of information in the matter of the lenders. Since this was an exhibition cosponsored by the French government alone, the works that came from French museums were clearly identified.[11] The provenance for the other works was either omitted or in specific instances listed as "private."[12] In at least one case, *Branch of Lilacs* by Matisse, investigation proved that the work had been lent by the artist himself.[13] Such discretion on the part of lenders, like the continued silence of French historians on the subject of the exhibition, raises the possibility that the show was perceived as politically problematic from its inception.[14]

Before the experiment in *rayonnement culturel,* the cultural activities of the French state had essentially fallen to the fine arts department (Direction Générale des Beaux Arts) of the Ministry for National Education. With the new policy, French diplomats working for the Ministry of Foreign Affairs became involved, looking for opportunities to display and sell French culture in the countries where they were posted. Thus, it is hardly surprising to find the name of the French ambassador to Nazi Germany as cosponsor of the exhibition.

Until François-Poncet became involved in the Berlin show of modern French art, little is known about his taste in modern art. He had had his portrait painted by an official portraitist of those years, Lucien Jonas. This portrait figured in the Berlin show. Named ambassador to Germany in 1931, two years before the advent of the Third Reich and five years before Léon Blum came into office, François-Poncet kept his post after the arrival of Hitler and during the Socialist government of Blum. He was known as a perennial appeaser.[15]

Born in 1887, François-Poncet began his career as the director of an economic research institute. He wrote an essay on the ideas of German youth in 1911 and later published a book on Goethe.[16] Clearly fascinated by German culture, the French ambassador spoke fluent German and had many private conversations with Hitler. "He was the only Western diplomat at Hitler's court able to understand the Führer without an interpreter's help and to talk to him and his lieutenants in fluent German," states the foreword to his memoirs.[17]

Writing about his feelings on leaving Nazi Germany for Fascist

Rome in 1938, François-Poncet, the instrumental figure behind the defense and illustration of French culture in Nazi Germany, admitted to an obsession for Hitler's regime: "I was obsessed by this regime, by its methods and language and mystery and police, by its tyranny and pride and songs and parades, by its clicking of heels and hallucinating thud of boots along the streets."[18]

Ausstellung Französischer Kunst der Gegenwart, the exhibition of modern French art associated with the name of François-Poncet, must have been organized in great haste. In an overlooked series of letters to and from the ambassador, it appears that the first discussions of the exhibition occurred at the beginning of 1937.[19] The first mention of an exhibition of modern French art in Nazi Berlin is found in a letter dated Berlin, January 28, 1937, from François-Poncet to the French Minister of Foreign Affairs, Yvon Delbos:

> In the course of a recent conversation with M. Goebbels, I had the opportunity to talk to him about the eventual organization in Berlin of an exhibition of modern French painting. The Minister for Propaganda opined that such an event would probably be a success and that it might have as its counterpart an exhibition of German sculpture in Paris. During my last trip to France, I had already broached the subject with the Direction Générale des Beaux Arts, which seemed very favorable to that project.[20]

Although the letter is ambiguous about who first raised the subject of a show of modern French painting in Berlin, the French ambassador or the German minister of propaganda, it indicates that the French ambassador had broached the possibility of such a show while in Paris, prior to the oral exchange with Goebbels. It also seems that the Nazi minister for propaganda was quick to seize on the opportunity that such a show might provide, namely, the display of Nazi-approved German sculpture in a Paris museum. From the start, the Nazis attached a quid pro quo with respect to the propaganda efforts of the French government.

The letter to Delbos goes on:

> Modern German painting is rather weak. In any event, it is far from capable of presenting an ensemble of names and canvasses of the first rank as ours does. On the other hand, there is in the

> Berlin public a real taste for painting. An exhibition of modern French art would have a good chance of success. . . . This event would constitute a happy prelude to our 1937 Exhibition [Internationale des Arts et Techniques], and would possibly help to attract the German public there if, as I hope will be the case, an agreement can take place on the question of foreign exchange.[21]

A display of modern French painting in Berlin, the ambassador tells his superior, would accomplish two goals at once. It would enhance the prestige of France by showing Germans the superiority of French art over German art – fulfilling the goal of *rayonnement culturel* – and it would act as publicity for the international exhibition about to open in Paris. From the start, propaganda and publicity goals were considered complementary rather than contradictory.

In the letter to Delbos, the ambassador also raises the issue of a venue for the two shows, proposing the Akademie der Künste in Berlin and the Jeu de Paume in Paris. The choice of the Jeu de Paume for a show of new German sculpture made sense to the extent that that institution was devoted to exhibitions of art of foreign origin. Even so, offering a prestigious venue in Paris to Nazi-approved German sculpture would have meant carrying appeasement policy to the point of legitimating the Nazi approach to art. For that reason, perhaps, the show did not occur in Paris in November 1937 as initially scheduled.[22]

As for the Akademie der Künste, it had not had an exhibition of French art since before World War I. Rarely noticed until now is the fact that since 1933, the program of the academy alternated between shows imported from abroad and shows of German artists, suggesting that the exhibition of French art may have been part of a larger cultural project. In 1933, a survey of recent Belgian art had taken place there, followed in 1935 by an exhibition of contemporary art from Poland.[23] In 1936, the academy had held a jubilee celebrating one hundred and fifty years of its existence. Just before the June–July 1937 exhibition of modern French art, there had been a spring exhibition of German painting and sculpture with work by, among others, Georg Kolbe, Gerhard Marcks, and Arno Breker. A show of modern Italian art was scheduled for November 1937. Though the academy appeared a proper place for the display of modern French art, the fact that it had recently expelled its "degenerate" members – Ernst Barlach, Rudolf Belling, Otto Dix, Ernst Ludwig Kirchner, and Oskar Kokoschka – should have given pause to the French ambassador (unless he condoned these artists' dismissal).[24]

At France's Ministry for National Education, the response to the ambassador's proposal seemed hesitant. Scheduling was a problem and the project needed further analysis.[25] It was thought that the show of German sculpture in Paris should be postponed until November 15, "because shows of Catalan, Austrian and American art were scheduled until the autumn season."[26] As for the exhibition of French art in Berlin in the spring, it was approved with some reservations.[27] Delbos, the minister for foreign affairs, however, was enthusiastic.[28]

Usually, this type of exhibition would have been financed by the Association of d'Expansion et d'Echanges Artistiques, a private group of dues-paying wealthy art patrons, whose director was also the director of the Service d'Action Artistique à l'Etranger.[29] In 1937, the director was Robert Brussel. For reasons that can only be surmised – disagreement among its members? – the association refused to finance the exhibition,[30] and the required sum of one hundred thousand francs had to be found elsewhere. The French Ministry of Foreign Affairs appropriated the necessary funds.[31] And, at the end of March 1937, while an exhibition of new German art, *Grosse Deutscher Kunsthausstellung,* was being prepared for Munich and the French curator Raymond Escholier was working on the exhibition *Maîtres de l'Art Indépendant 1895–1937* for Paris, German officials approved the Berlin show of new French art – *Ausstellung Französischer Kunst der Gegenwart* – for a June opening.[32]

According to the telegram to François-Poncet dated March 4, 1937, a French curator had to be chosen who "would go to Berlin so as to organize with the French Ambassador and the German authorities the conditions under which this event could be prepared to which a sculpture exhibition would answer in Paris."[33] This phrasing is worth noting not only for its convoluted wording but because of its implications. The French curator would have to defer to the French ambassador and to the German authorities, who, in practical terms, could veto any art or artist that did not meet their approval. René Huyghe apparently declined under these conditions.[34] The assignment fell to Robert Rey, who in 1941, during the Vichy period, published *La peinture moderne ou l'art sans métier*,[35] a text the fascist polemicist Lucien Rebatet would approvingly call in his review for the newspaper *Je Suis Partout* "a sort of fascist treatise on the condition of the Fine Arts."[36]

At the time of the French show, Rey had recently been named to the post of inspector general of the fine arts, an important position created by the Blum government to improve the quality and performance of provincial museums. An enigmatic figure of the art world of his day and a friend of Georges Huisman, general director of fine arts in the French government, to whom he dedicated his 1938 monograph on Edouard Manet, he shared with Huisman an abhorrence for abstract art that he formulated at length in his book *Contre l'art abstrait*.[37]

While in Berlin in April 1937, Rey collected information on the conditions under which the show of modern French painting would take place and transmitted them to the Ministry for National Education, which forwarded it to the Ministry of Foreign Affairs. The date of the opening was confirmed as well as the Akademie der Künste as the locale for the exhibition. Of note is the fact that the catalogue and the poster were going to be paid for and produced by the "German organizers." Specified in the conditions was the fact that the show would have to take place without the participation of public and private Berlin collections.[38] Their holdings in modern French art were in the process of confiscation by the Hitler regime. Having agreed to these conditions, the French organizers were allowed to include a few pieces of sculpture to what was originally to be a show of paintings only.

A telegram dated Berlin, June 5, 1937, from François-Poncet to Delbos described the opening of *Ausstellung Französischer Kunst der Gegenwart*, claiming the presence of Nazi officials as a great triumph for Franco-German relations:

> This morning at noon in Berlin, the exhibition of French art was inaugurated in the locale of the Prussian Academy of Fine Arts. The ceremony took place under the best of conditions, and the German authorities had neglected nothing to make it a brilliant event. Göring was there in person, although a recent fall from his

> horse obliges him to use a cane. He was accompanied by M. von Neurath, M. Schacht, and the Minister of Public Instruction, M. Rust. . . . A large crowd of guests filled the rooms. Speeches were made by a President of the Academy, Prof. Schumann, by me, and by Minister Rust. The latter spoke in very flattering terms about our country and its art, and declared himself very happy about this event. The Academy offered a lunch in honor of the French curator. . . .[39]

Three days after the opening of *Ausstellung Französischer Kunst der Gegenwart,* François-Poncet wrote again to Delbos. In this very long letter, he first cautioned Delbos that expectations should not be too high: "One should not have too many illusions on the scope of this event. It will not change much in the atmosphere of the relations between France and Germany. They are dominated by problems that transcend cultural events." Then he explained the dual goals that he hoped the exhibition would achieve. On the one hand, he said, "It will have shown to the Germans that it is false to represent France as enclosed in an insurmountable antipathy vis-à-vis Germany, in an attitude of wall-like negation and aversion reaching down to hatred. It has, on the contrary, fully revealed the feelings of humanity and understanding that are ours." At the same time, he claims, "It is also an opportunity to show to some Germans whose opinions are still wavering, that there is a way to conceive of life other than that honored in the Third Reich."[40]

In reality, the goals of turning Germans who were still hesitant about Nazism toward democracy – *rayonnement culturel* in action – and improving relations with a country whose every propaganda move was aimed at converting Germans into full-fledged Nazis were mutually incompatible. One of the goals of the Berlin exhibition had to eclipse the other. The next sentence of the ambassador's letter gives away his priority: "It [the exhibition] will have made them [the Germans] feel our presence; it will have reminded them of the existence of a great neighbor [France] . . . a neighbor whose face has been wrongly depicted [as hostile] by tendentious [Nazi] press campaigns, and one whose culture and whose art are neither decadent nor in regression." He would deem the Berlin exhibition of French art a success not for turning hesitant Germans toward freedom of expression but for representing France as a friendly neighbor to Nazi Germany, one that echoes Nazi sentiment on decadence in modern culture and shares with Nazi Germany a healthy artistic culture that should *not* be perceived as decadent or in regression.

While the French ambassador reveals his agenda in this long informative letter to Delbos, his analysis of the German reception of the exhibition in the same letter points to another major puzzle of the Berlin exhibition, the motivation of the host country in accepting the presence of art it had officially attacked. Although the reception of the show was overwhelmingly positive, François-Poncet told Delbos, he noticed a certain reticence in *Angriff*, the party's official voice. "Visibly, they wish to avoid giving the Party militants the impression that they have fallen into the guilty errors of the Weimarian epoch when . . . admiration for French art was dogma."[41] The speeches of German officials at the opening were also very courteous, he wrote, although "some revealed the desire to justify in the eyes of public opinion the organization of an event that is so sharply in contrast with the ultraprotectionist tendencies of the regime." He then reports the remarks of Minister Bernhard Rust, who claimed that the Third Reich had "concentrated on eliminating the nefarious influence of a decadent and sick art that had exerted itself in Germany before the arrival in power of Chancellor Hitler" but "remains perfectly accessible to the artistic beauties and to the culture of other countries," insofar – and this was the obvious, though unstated condition – as they were free of what German officials considered decadence and sickness.

The most popular work in the show, according to François-Poncet, was Roger Chapelain-Midy's *Departure* (Fig. 6), which, he said, was reproduced in all the illustrated newspapers of Berlin. *Departure* showed in the foreground a young man, satchel on his shoulder and walking stick in hand, saying farewell to wife and child, the brave threesome standing by a door that frames the view of a garden. Although the destination of the departing figure is unknown, the painting can be interpreted as pointing to the necessary division of tasks between the father, whose duty is to leave home, perhaps to go to war, and the mother, who must stay behind to take care of the family.[42] The ambassador named Vlaminck, Marie Laurencin, Othon Friesz, Vuillard, and Ker-Xavier Roussel among other favorites.

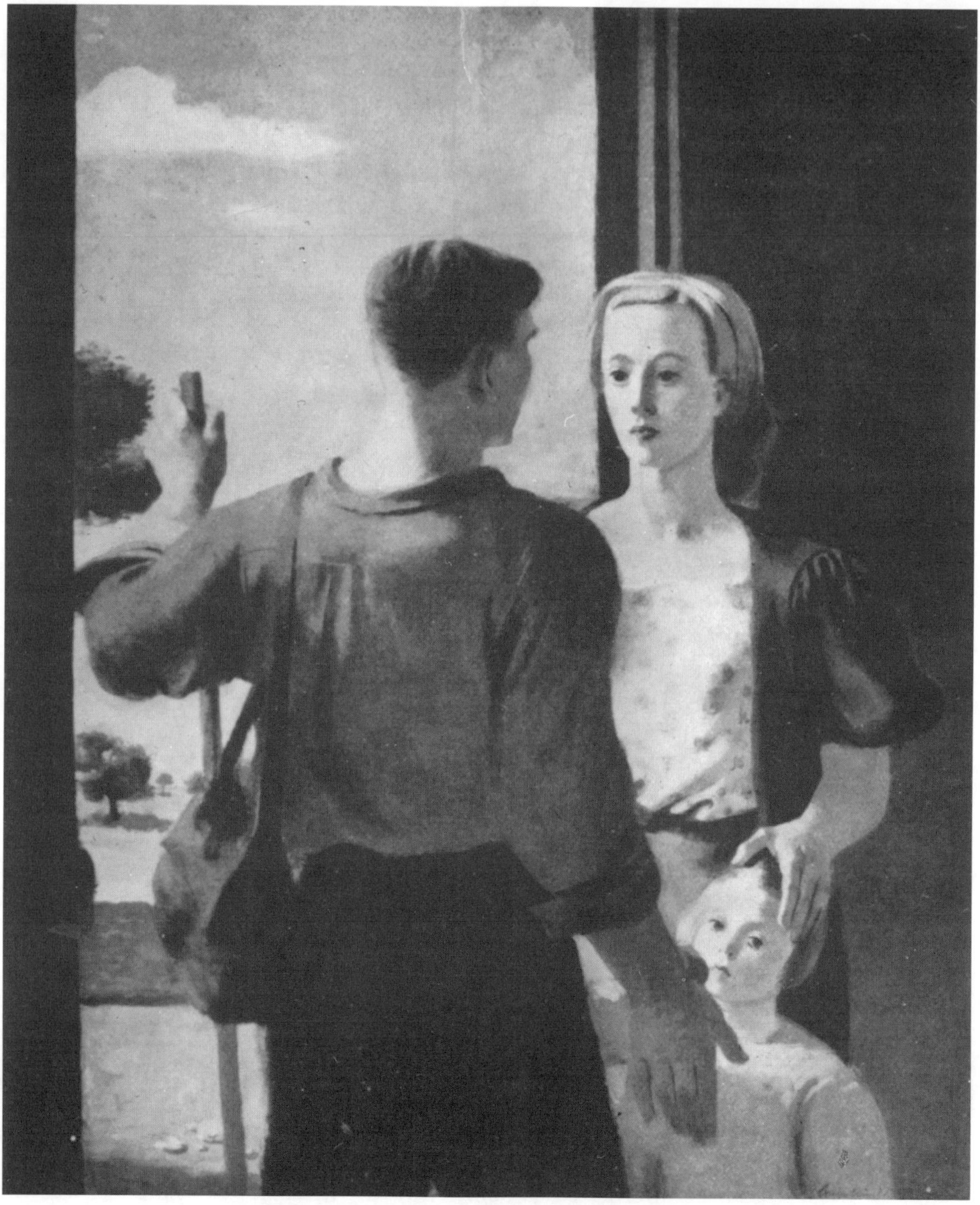

6. Roger Chapelain-Midy, *Departure.* Date, dimensions, and location unavailable (first reproduced in *Ausstellung Französischer Kunst der Gegenwart,* exh. cat. 1937; photo: Frick Art Reference Library, New York).

Aristide Maillol, the ambassador said, was qualified as one of the two or three greatest sculptors of the time.[43] As for Georges Leroux's *Group of Athletes Preparing for a Race,* it "is one of the works that M. Göring most enjoyed."[44]

One might rightly suspect the French ambassador of exaggerating the positive reception of the show and of playing down Nazi attacks on the so-called "degenerate" works in the French show. But a German art historical publication from that time confirms that the exhibition that the French had brought to Nazi Germany received an extremely courteous response. The reviewer for *Kunst,* Fritz Von Hellwag, gave a measured yet at times enthusiastic reaction to the works on view. He singled out Maurice Asselin's *Children's Vespers Bread* for "speaking directly to the German sensibility."[45] This work, showing two boys and their parents around a kitchen table in a plain, thick-walled farm interior, was indeed a sober celebration of wholesomeness, duty to the family, and a simple way of life.

But he did not hesitate to praise Matisse for his "very reserved portrait of a girl, in flat, wide, yellow and pale green brushstrokes"; Braque, "master of the still-life with a handsome harmony of his famous brown-blue hues"; Dunoyer de Segonzac, "represented by an incandescent symphony of red"; Derain, "whose marvelously balanced wooded landscape exudes a great sense of peace, and also his brilliant female portrait"; and Vlaminck, "here represented by a painting entitled 'Huts' [which] shows a sparkling, red and yellow field under a billowing blue sky." The other artists he mentioned favorably were an eclectic group ranging from Laurencin, Maurice Brianchon, Friesz, and Chapelain-Midy to Lucien Simon, Dufy, Yves Brayer, and Marguerite Louppe.[46] He concluded his review by saying that "the exhibition was a pleasurable experience . . . even if it does not make completely clear what is the artistic creativity in France in our time."[47] Illustrated in his article were the Vlaminck landscape, the Asselin and the Lucien Simon genre scenes, a Maurice Denis religious scene, and Suzanne Valadon's portrait of her son Maurice Utrillo and his grandmother.

According to information supplied by the Akademie der Künste to François-Poncet, who then sent it to Paris, in two months the exhibition was visited by 23,000 persons, 7,732 catalogues were sold, and 300 inquiries concerning purchases of the exhibited works were addressed to the secretariat. Sixteen inquiries were followed up, for which the Reich exchange office authorized the transfer of 30,000 marks (283,547 francs). Among the works sold were, according to the ambassador, a bronze statue by Maillol, two landscapes by Albert Marquet, one Utrillo, and a small marble by Louis Dejean, this last purchased by the Italian ambassador.[48] In his memoirs, François-Poncet mentioned that Hitler had purchased a statuette: ". . . Hitler's taste in this field did not go beyond the 1850s; for him, impressionism and cubism were one and the same thing, both products of the Jewish mind. Nevertheless he took the trouble to visit the exhibition and to purchase a statuette."[49]

The positive reception in Nazi Germany of an exhibition that included Matisse, Léger, Braque, Vlaminck, and other artists whose works had been removed from the museums that owned them as "degenerate art" remains somewhat mystifying. First, it should be noted that criticism was banned in Nazi Germany at that point, while injunctions on how to review an exhibition emanated from the very top of the hierarchy of the Third Reich. Since the minister for propaganda, Joseph Goebbels, had approved the exhibition of modern French art, and Göring attended the opening, such a courteous response was to be expected.[50]

On the other hand, the chancellor of the Third Reich, faced with the conflicting views of his advisers as to whether Expressionism or *völkisch* art better communicated the ideology of a new Germany to the German people, had determined that artists must identify an essentially racial Germanic tradition and make their paintings on that basis.[51] The most difficult task was to isolate this uniquely Germanic tradition. According to Berthold Hinz, comparing and contrasting images, or, in his words, "synoptic confrontation," was the devised strategy: "In the first years of the Nazis' art struggle, long before they took power in 1933, the party had pursued political polarization by polarizing – comparing and contrasting – images."[52] He cites the case of clinical photographs of human deformities juxtaposed with recent works by German Expressionists as intended to eliminate Expressionism from this new Germanic tradition and deemed to show by contrast that art representing perfect human types would belong within the new racial Germanic canon.

It is thus conceivable that the viewing of modern art symbolizing a foreign national tradition could, by comparison and contrast, highlight the essence of a pure racial Germanic tradition. This might explain why, according to François-Poncet, the Nazi press was "preoccupied . . . with making clear the general characteristics that distinguish French art from German art."[53] Acting in unison as if they had been drilled ahead of time, the reviewers for the *Bourse Gazette*, the *Lokal Anzeiger*, and the *National Zeitung* of Essen, from which the ambassador quoted, compared and contrasted French and German art, concurring that German art was "philosophical" whereas French art was about art for art's sake, about pleasure and decoration, about the natural play of light and color.[54] The philosophical – a euphemism for ideologically loaded – quality of the new German art had apparently been made clear by contrast to what the Nazi press read as the quality of art for art's sake in French art, a generalization that could only be made by virtue of the presence of paintings such as Matisse's *Branch of Lilacs* (Fig. 4) and the other Fauvist works. The Matisse still life and similar works in the exhibition that might have symbolized in other contexts French nonconformism had been turned to advantage by the Nazi press so as to make clear to German readers that art for art's sake was of French origin and did not belong within the canon of the new German art.

Although information on a curatorial and diplomatic trade-off does not appear in the correspondence concerning the exhibition, the contents of the exhibition as they are described in the catalogue suggest that there had been a price to pay for the inclusion of art by Matisse, Braque, Léger, Vlaminck, and others in an exhibition held in the heart of Nazi Germany at the very moment when works by these same artists were being removed from the museums that owned them and sold at auction or destroyed. The price was the exclusion of many other deserving artists from the exhibition. Even in the context of a rapidly shifting and narrowing down of what constituted modern French art in 1937 in Paris itself, the Berlin exhibition of French art presented a startlingly narrow and nationalist view of French art of the present.

The definition of a country's most valid artistic contribution at a given moment of its history is rarely agreed upon. In 1937 in Paris, as powerful critics endorsed the notion of French decadence in art and associated it with foreign influences on the French artistic tradition, it was less and less likely that non-French-born artists, including Jewish refugees who were contributing to the French patrimony, would be treated in the same way as French-born artists. Under these circumstances the concept of French art of the present was problematic, and what we easily condemn as a "revisionist" view of French art of the present in 1937 is only so in retrospect. Yet the Berlin show was revisionist in its own time by comparison with *Maîtres de l'Art Indédependant 1895–1937*. The two exhibitions date from the same year, were both sponsored by the Popular Front government, and had a common agenda, the celebration of modern French art.

Visually, both the Paris and the Berlin exhibitions conveyed the idea that the thirties were a time of a "return to order," a nostalgia-filled moment.[55] Both exhibitions included work by Charles Camoin, Derain, Dunoyer de Segonzac, Vlaminck, Friesz (Fig. 1),[56] Dufy, Marquet, Matisse, and Manguin among the Fauves, and Maurice Denis, Jacques-Emile Blanche, Vuillard, and Bonnard among the Neo-Impressionists and Symbolists – French masters who had made their most original artistic statements at the beginning of the century and whose production had become mainstream (and, for some, acceptable to the academy). Other works included in both the Berlin and the Paris shows were by French artists associated with Cubism: Braque and Léger, among others. The classical sculpture of Maillol and Charles Despiau (Fig. 2) also appeared in both exhibitions (see Appendix).

However, in comparison with the Petit Palais selection for the *Maîtres de l'Art Indépendant* exhibition, with its Cubist paintings by Louis Marcoussis, Pablo Picasso, Leopold Survage, its sculpture by Pablo Gargallo, Jacques Lipchitz, Ossip Zadkine, and many other modernist works next to more conservative ones by Moishe Kisling, Henri Lebasque, François Pompon, and Jane Poupelet, among others, the Berlin show did not reflect much of a push and pull between tradition and the avant-garde and was hardly a mix of talents and tastes. Reading the introduction to the catalogue of the Berlin show by Rey we learn that French tradition in the arts is rooted "in the single desire to represent nature and life in its most ordinary everyday manifestations with gentle vitality, without regard for theories and fashions."[57] Thus, works of art that referred to an interior vision and/or posed a challenge to the viewer were condemned as outside the French tradition.

Furthermore, not only was the Berlin show less eclectic than the

Paris one, it also included a large contingent of winners of the Prix de Rome, professors of the Ecole des Beaux-Arts, and Académie des Beaux-Arts nominees, all of them members of the conservative Société des Artistes Français. Among them was Jean Dupas, Marcel Baschet, Yves Brayer, Raymond Brechenmacher, André Devambez, Lucien Jonas, Henri Martin, Lucien Simon, Henry Bouchard, Jean Boucher, and Paul Landowski. The curator of the Paris exhibition, Raymond Escholier, looked on these figures of the French art world with the greatest disdain, calling them the "disciplined troops that occupy en masse the Palais des Beaux Arts [at their annual Salon des artistes Français]," and made no room for their work in the Paris show of independent art.[58] Indeed, these figures of the French art world were anything but independent. Due to their status as prestigious servants of the state and their connections with French officials, they tended to receive an unfair share of government commissions for the decoration of public buildings and to appear all too frequently in officially sponsored exhibitions.

Superficially, both the Berlin exhibition of French art and the *Maîtres de l'Art Indépendant* appeared to emerge from a common national viewpoint: both favored French-born artists. "This segregation seems today to be very nationalist," writes Bernadette Contensou. "It was at that time considered natural by everybody. Had not the State created a museum for foreign schools?"[59] Yet while the Paris show of French art was "happy to honor at the same time these artists from the School of Paris, who had come from all points of the world, Parisians before anything else," to use Escholier's own words,[60] that was not the case with the Berlin show. Picasso, Gargallo, Lipchitz, Chaim Soutine, Marc Chagall, Juan Gris, and Max Ernst had works in the Paris show, but not in the Berlin one. The Berlin exhibition conferred the title of French artist only on artists who were French-born and of Aryan type.

If rejection of the extreme avant-garde (the absence of Surrealists in Berlin and their scant presence in Paris) was a common agenda of the Paris and Berlin shows, the inclusion of artist "bureaucrats" and the exclusion of "foreign-born" and Jewish artists in the Berlin show point to a model of modern French art quite different from that embodied by the Paris one. In several respects, *Ausstellung Französischer Kunst der Gegenwart* was a censored version of *Maîtres de l'Art Indépendant 1895–1937*. It represented the triumph of xenophobia and anti-Semitism at a time when in Paris such attitudes and feelings were on the rise but could not yet be so openly put into practice. The Berlin exhibition of modern French art failed to show France in its "inclusiveness and continuity," to use Blum's chosen phrase. Whoever was responsible for the exhibition – and there seem to have been three different organizers: the French ambassador, the French curator, and the German authorities – produced a show that echoed in French terms the racial tradition being perpetrated in German art of the period.

Despite the ambassador's satisfaction with the results of the exhibition, repression of its existence began in France almost immediately. Except for an anonymous editorial in *Cahiers d'Art* of 1937 that stated – a bit too confidently – that "its" artists had refused to "collaborate" out of "solidarity for German colleagues who have been banned from the society of artists by national socialism,"[61] the French art press was silent. As for the general press, it focused on Hitler's visit to the show: "Berlin 30 June. The Führer visits the exhibition of French painting," announced *Le Temps* (July 1, 1937) in small print on its last page. The article was short and matter-of-fact:

> Chancellor Hitler visited the French exhibition of painting at the Prussian Academy of Fine Arts this morning. In the course of this visit, which lasted close to three-quarters of an hour, M. André François-Poncet, the French Ambassador, presented the paintings on view to the Chancellor. Mr. Adolf Hitler showed the most vivid interest in these works of modern French painting and sculpture.[62]

France's minister for national education during the Blum government, Jean Zay, omitted mentioning the Berlin exhibition in his memoirs (he mentions Amsterdam, Belgrade, and Cairo as cities where exhibitions of French art took place under the Popular Front government of Léon Blum).[63] Even François-Poncet, who in 1937 had taken responsibility for the show and proclaimed it a big success for France's *rayonnement culturel,* revised his role in his postwar memoirs. There, he took no credit for the Berlin exhibition of French art and tersely attributed its organization entirely to the Germans: "In June an exhibition of French painting was organized in Berlin by the Prussian Academy of Fine Arts."[64] In *La belle illusion: Culture et politique sous le signe du Front populaire*

1935–1938, the major work on cultural life in France during the years of the Popular Front, Pascal Ory names Venice, Prague, Warsaw, Bucharest, Bogotá, and Lisbon – not Berlin – as cities that received art from France.[65] More telling yet, the exhibition at the Akademie der Künste does not appear in any of the chronologies or exhibition lists of the major artists whose works were shown.

The repression of this event by the French establishment of historians of the present is hardly a surprise. French specialists do not like to deal with revelations that place their country, its artists, and its politicians in a bad light.[66] They would protect Matisse, who lent work from his studio and thus revealed an indifference to politics that reached new heights during Vichy, by claiming that his contribution to the French artistic patrimony outweighs all other considerations.[67] They would defend François-Poncet's appeasement by pointing out that appeasement was the policy of the day.[68]

In retrospect, it is difficult not to see 1937 as a low point in Franco-German relations. The rearmament of Germany, Hitler's reneging on treaties that his country had freely signed, the German reoccupation of the Rhineland in 1936, Germany's military interference in the Spanish Civil War on the side of the Fascist leader Francisco Franco in 1937 followed one another like the signposts of "an inexorable march toward war. . . ."[69] However, as the Munich accords of 1938 attest, resistance to the idea of yet another war was powerful, and appeasement policies repeatedly led to humiliating compromises on the part of democratic countries like France and Great Britain.

Jean-Baptiste Duroselle, a specialist of Franco-German relations during the 1930s, maintains that the Popular Front government did not reverse the appeasement trend set before it: "It is not in the debate over foreign policy . . . that one must look for an original path. 'Desire for peace,' 'collective security,' 'arms limitations' – in this program, nothing that makes a break with customary ideas."[70] Under these circumstances, the French ambassador's willingness to foster appeasement suited equally the mood of Blum's enemies, those who screamed, "Rather Hitler than Blum," and the mood of inveterate pacifists within Blum's Socialist party. In this context, it would have been difficult for the Berlin show of French art to go against the grain of appeasement diplomacy.

Even so, by condoning a view of modern art that was the French equivalent of a German racial tradition, the partisans of appeasement carried their policy to new extremes, for such a view helped the Nazi cause and comforted the included artists, among them Matisse, Vlaminck, Derain, Braque, and Léger, in the idea that they had nothing to fear from the Nazis. The French policy of *rayonnement culturel* had been subverted into not merely an appeasement politics but one proposing accommodation and prefiguring state collaboration.[71]

A year before, at the Olympics, the French participants had already signaled "collaborationist" sympathies by raising before Hitler what was taken as a Nazi salute. Neither the British nor the American athletes had done so.[72] British painters had apparently been approached by the Nazis for an exhibition in Berlin but, as Jane Clapp reports in *Art Censorship: A Chronology of Proscribed and Prescribed Art,* they had turned down the offer. "Germany's invitation to British painters to exhibit in Berlin, 'with specified reservations as to race and political faith' was 'promptly rejected.'"[73] As more and more events like the 1937 exhibition of French art in Berlin and images of the 1936 Olympic Games emerge from obscurity, the spread of Nazism through continental Europe comes into sharper focus, and Marshal Pétain's handshake with Hitler on October 30, 1940, at Montoire can be seen as more and more predictable.

APPENDIX

Comparative Table of Participants in the Exhibition Ausstellung Französischer Kunst der Gegenwart (Berlin) and the *Maîtres de l'Art Indépendant 1895–1937* (Paris)

Exhibited only in Berlin[74]

Robert Antral	Jacques-Emile Blanche	Robert Cami
Jean Aujame	Pierre Bompard	Carlegle (Charles-Emile Egli)
Emanuel Auricoste	Henry Bouchard	Jules Cavaillès
Gaston Balande	Jean Boucher	Auguste Chabaud
Georges Barat-Levraux	Yves Brayer	Roger Chapelain-Midy
Valdo Barbey	Raymond Brechenmacher	Pierre Eugène Clairin
Marcel Baschet	Maurice Brianchon	Gérard Cochet
Hugues de Beaumont	Auguste Brouet	Louis-Eugène Corneau
Paul Belmondo	Christian Caillard	Joaquin Costa
Gabriel Belot		

(continued)

APPENDIX *(continued)*

Exhibited only in Berlin[74]

René Cottet
Alfred Courmes
Jean Gabriel Daragnès
André Dauchez
Albert Décaris
Louis Dejean
Jacques Denier
Alexandre Descatoire
Frédéric Deshayes
André Devambez
Louis Dideron
Pierre Dubreuil
Charles Dufresne
Jean Dupas
Gabriel Fournier
André Foy
Jean Frelaut
Madame Galtier-Boissière
Odette des Garets
Denis Gelin
Pierre Girieux
Georges Gobo
Jean Gabriel Goulinat
Auguste Guenot
Georges Guyot
Louise Hervieu
Gustave Louis Jaulmes
Alfred Jeanniot
Lucien Jonas
Adrienne Jouclard
Paul Jouve
Tristan Klingsor
Jean-Emile Laboureur
Pierre Ladureau
Paul Landowski
Raymond Legueult
Louis Lejeune
Georges Le Meilleur
Philippe Le Molt
Georges Leroux
Henri Le Sidaner
Roger Limouse
Alfred Lombard
Marguerite Louppe
Berthold Mahn
Lucien Mainssieux
Henri Malançon
Jean Marchand
Henri Martin
Berthe Martinie
Jean Morin
Bernard Naudin
Louis Neillot
François-Paul Niclausse
Roland Oudot
Picart-Ledoux
André Planson
Albert Pommier
Maurice-Georges Poncelet
François Popineau
René Favier Prinet
Alphonse Quizet
Louis Riou
Sabatté
Georges Saupique
Maurice Savin
Maurice Savreux
Edmond Sigrist
Marie-Louise Siméon
Jeanne Simon
Lucien Simon
Louis-Joseph Soulas
Jean Souverbie
Jean Alphonse Stival
André Strauss
Jacques Thévenet
Henry-Georges Troussard
Henri Verge-Sarrat
Eliane P. de la Villéon
Hubert Yencesse
Jules Zingg

In Berlin and Paris

Yves Alix
Albert André
Maurice Asselin
Pierre Bompard
Jean-Louis Boussingault
Georges Braque
Charles Camoin
Edmond Céria
Maurice Denis
André Derain
Charles Despiau

(continued)

APPENDIX *(continued)*

In Berlin and Paris (continued)

Georges Desvallières
Léon Drivier
Georges Dufrenoy
Raoul Dufy
André Dunoyer de Segonzac
Georges d'Espagnat
Othon Friesz
Paul Gernez
Marcel Gimond
Edouard Goerg
Marcel Gromaire
Charles Guérin
Edmond Kayser
Marie Laurencin
Fernand Léger
André Lhote
Robert Lotiron
Maximilien Luce
Aristide Maillol
Henri Manguin
Albert Marque
Henri Matisse
Pierre Poisson
Jean Puy
Georges Rouault
Ker-Xavier Roussel
Maurice Utrillo
Suzanne Valadon
Louis Valtat
Maurice de Vlaminck
Edouard Villard
Henri de Waroquier
Robert Wlérick

Only in Paris[74]

Abbal
Emile Bernard
Joseph Bernard
Roger Bissière
Maria Blanchard
Pierre Bompard
Georges Bouche
Antoine Bourdelle
Marc Chagall
Giorgio De Chirico
Lucie Cousturier
Jean Crotti
Robert Delaunay
Raymond Duchamp-Villon
Max Ernst
Guy-Eugène Fauconnet
André Favory
Jules Flandrin
Pablo Gargallo
Albert Gleizes
Emmanuel Gondouin
Juan Gris
Auguste Herbin
Mateo Hernandez
Moishe Kisling
Roger de La Fresnaye
Amédée de La Patellière
Pierre Laprade
Henri Laurens
Henri Lebasque
Henri-Victor Le Fauconnier
Léon Lehmann
Jacques Lipchitz
Maurice Loutreuil
Jean Lurçat
Manolo (Manuel Martinez Hugue)
Louis Marcoussis
André Mare
Albert Marque
Jacqueline Marval
Jean Metzinger
Amedeo Modigliani
Luc-Albert Moreau
Chana Orloff
Amédée Ozenfant
Henri-Ernest Parayre
Jules Pascin
Charles Péquin
Francis Picabia
Pablo Picasso
François Pimienta
René Piot
François Pompon
Jane Poupelet
Auguste Renoir
Auguste Rodin
Henri Rousseau

(continued)

Only in Paris[74] *(continued)*

Claude Roy	Chaim Soutine	Antoine Villard
Paul Sérusier	Leopold Survage	Jacques Villon
Gino Severini	Félix Valloton	Ossip Zadkine
René Seyssaud	Georges Valmier	
Paul Signac	Kees Van Dongen	

2

Decadence and Renewal in the Decorative Arts Under Vichy

To THIS DAY the proper appellation of the Vichy regime remains a riddle: Was it fascist? Dirigiste? Corporatist? As a group, French historians are generally loath to call it outright fascist. Rather than seeing Pétainist ideology as becoming part of the fascist cloud that blanketed much of Europe just prior to and through World War II, they make a point of singularizing the regime. "Complexity," "distinctiveness," and "ambiguity" are the catchwords.[1] However, answers seem to vary with the criteria used, as a major colloquium on Vichy attests.

Colloquium participant Stanley Hoffmann, using as his criterion the composition of the political personnel of Vichy, observed "a progressive fascisation" of the Vichy regime.[2] Michèle Cointet-Labrousse, using the argument that the regime rejected the idea of a single party *(parti unique)*, refrained from judging Vichy a fascist regime. "It was not fascistically inspired, for what they wanted was an organic regime giving power to elites."[3] Denis Peschanski also refused to call Vichy totalitarian because even in the police-run Vichy of 1944, "the Milice was essentially the instrument of a civil war and not a tool for total control of society."[4]

First published in M. Affron and M. Antliff, eds., *Fascist Visions: Art and Ideology in France and Italy* (Princeton, N.J.: Princeton University Press, 1997).

François Bloch-Lainé, a witness of and brief participant in that period, looking at Vichy from the viewpoint of its economic organization, believes Vichy was more corporatist than dirigiste.[5] Henry Rousso sees the partisans of corporatism and those of dirigisme in opposition during Vichy, the latter triumphant since Vichy had more rather than less state interference than before. For Rousso, both dirigiste technocrats and corporatists wanted the same thing – "[to find] means to combat class warfare, to anticipate crises like those of the 1930s, and to align the industrial sector to that of the dominating country, namely the Third Reich."[6] And he noted, "nothing, except the State, impinged on the theoretical powers of heads of companies, to the loud distress of 'corporatists,' who demanded a sharing of power within the corporatist framework."[7]

Vichy's proper appellation also seems to vary with the sector being examined. In *Le Projet culturel de Vichy,* Christian Faure focuses our attention on cultural life in the French provinces, with its folkloric spectacles, vernacular architecture, popular literature, popular imagery, and primitive artifacts; on the ethnological *chantiers* initiated by Georges-Henri Rivière, head of the Paris Musée des Arts et Traditions populaires; and on Pétainist discourse to farmers and country craftsmen. He describes the Vichy period as "the golden age of folklorist theories."[8] In Faure's view, the fear of class conflict dominated Vichy ideology. Thus Vichyites sought a unifying myth capable of competing with urban workers' solidarity.

The myth of corporatism – based on natural, organic peasant and artisanal families bound together by folklore, the fulcrum of common soil, common professional interests, traditions, and race – answered that need, while leaving hierarchical separations intact:

> The myth of a unity in the farmers' and artisans' world contrasting with the parallel myth of workers' unity . . . feeds, normalizes and justifies the highly hierarchical society that the French state is trying to develop. This unity is necessary to put into place the corporatist organization, [which] substitutes the principle of class collaboration for that of class conflict.[9]

Faure finds in the Vichy cultural project a number of signs of totalitarian political interference. For example, in his concluding chapter, Faure refers to Philippe Pétain's simulacrum of a folklore renewal as a "cultural strategy that achieves a conquest *[opère une conquète]* from the base up, through associations, the village, the region." Finding racist connotations in Pétain's imposition of the peaceful myth of the earth, Faure uses words such as "indoctrination" and "innoculation" with reference to Pétain's covert messages. And he defines Pétain's *Révolution nationale* as a form of totalitarianism.[10]

However, Faure stops short of applying the word fascism to Vichy: "The *Révolution nationale*'s totalitarianism is different from the fascism of Mussolini or from Nazism because the ideologies and the personalities of their leaders differ."[11] Once again, the *Révolution nationale* is seen as a case apart because Pétain was no Hitler or Mussolini, and his ideology was distinct from theirs.

I would like to analyze a sector so far left unmined – the high end of decorative arts under Vichy. Without pretending that lifting the veil on this subject will solve the Vichy riddle, I hope that a new facet of this fascinating question will emerge from focusing on the issue of decadence in the decorative arts raised by Vichy, and on the kinds of remedies proposed to bring about a renewal. I ask whether we can gain new insights on the relationship of Vichy to fascism in this one domain by shifting our investigation from the popular arts to the high end of decorative arts. Faure in his *Projet culturel* shows the myth of renewal being played out for all its worth during Vichy; what still needs exploring is on what grounds renewal was made to appear a necessity.

The Decorative Arts on Trial During Vichy

It is not my intention to argue with the view that folklorist theories flourished during Vichy, nor to deny that the marshal's priority was to country artisans who – to quote from the 1 May 1941 Commentry speech – "had been the first to understand the great truth [corporatism], and to put it into practice."[12] But the focus on popular culture in the French provinces, which still today show vestiges of folk traditions, and the foregrounding of Georges-Henri Rivière's legendary nostalgia for artisan culture and society have left under the dust the luxury decorative arts and their ardent supporter, Guillaume Janneau, director during Vichy of the state-owned Sèvres, Beauvais, Aubusson, and Gobelins manufactures of decorative arts. What are the issues behind Vichy's interest in luxury craft that do not appear in Vichy's celebration of popular folk culture, and in what sense might they affect the conclusions of *Le Projet culturel de Vichy* and sharpen our understanding of the political nature of the Vichy regime?

Luxury applied arts had indeed a far greater economic potential to France than country craft. In the Thiers speech of 1 May 1942, the marshal made a point of addressing not only artisan-preservers of social peace – that is, country artisans – but artisan-producers of economic wealth, of factory workers: "The artisan is also the auxiliary to the industrialist. He accomplishes certain phases of the fabrication." He went on to say, "a lively and fecund craft is one of the essential elements of tomorrow's economic policies."[13]

The town of Thiers' main resource was fine cutlery, the product of hand and machine work. Manufactures of china, furniture, silver, glass, and crystalware, tapestry firms, cabinetmakers, and modern decorators *(ensembliers)* also relied on a variety of crafts professionals in their businesses. Several of these businesses were state owned. Near Paris was the Sèvres manufacture, with its various *corps de métiers* – potters, decorative artists, glazers, and other craftsmen involved in the production of porcelain. Sèvres, like the state-owned Gobelins, Aubusson, La Savonnerie, and Beauvais were founded during the Monarchy.[14] After the Revolution these manufactures remained the official providers of the offices and households of French dignitaries and embassies, and their wares were marketed worldwide. Such state- or privately-owned enterprises, somewhere between the individual country artisan and the large-scale industrialist, were very much the marshal's concern in the Thiers speech.

In several respects, luxury and folkloric decorative arts overlapped. For one thing, Vichy legislation for the creation of corporatist families involved all so-called artisanal professions. For another, the review *Métiers de France,* created by Vichy in 1941, published articles about the butcher's craft in one issue and about Sèvres ceramics in another. Its varied advertising caused further confusion, with perfume and interior decoration (June 1942), haute couture (December 1942), and even adding machines (September

1943). Finally, some of the same artists who attached their names to cheap, popular folk imagery also participated in the creation of expensive objects, including tapestries and furniture.

But in one aspect of major consequence, country crafts were looked upon in a different way from luxury crafts: while, as suggested by Faure, regional folk culture before Vichy was pictured by Vichyites as the *forgotten* art of France, "formerly relegated to the status of *'sous produit,'*"[15] luxury craft before Vichy was represented by Vichyites as having *declined* in quality.

At the 1942 conference on artists and artisans organized under the auspices of the Institut d'Etudes Corporatives, the issue of quality came up repeatedly: Guillaume Janneau spoke of "errors of taste, stylistic heresies, lack of common sense. . . ."[16] Unlike Georges-Henri Rivière, another speaker at the conference, he did not see "the folkloric cult" as a remedy, claiming that "the most acute problem was regionalism." He said, "[The country artisan] contributes to the persistence of this grave error, namely that craft remains attached to the past, constitutes one of its remnants, and shows itself inept at entering new directions."[17] This powerful figure in the Vichy government, a decorative arts critic of long-standing, a specialist of French antiques, and the author of scholarly texts on modern decorative arts, warned in his conclusion that for the *beau métier* to recover its former prestige, "it will be necessary to make it worthy of rehabilitation, something which, with few exceptions, contemporary decorative arts are far from deserving."[18]

A president of the newly founded corporatist organization of artist-decorators, Maurice Dufrène, complained about seeing quantities of works "mindboggling in their stupidity!"[19] Jacques Mayet, head of the economic section of the Service de l'artisanat, used the expression "terribly ravaging decadence of taste" for his indictment of some of the productions he had recently seen.[20]

Considering the rousing reception of art deco at the Paris 1925 international exhibition,[21] the innovative spirit of Le Corbusier, Robert Mallet-Sevens, Pierre Chareau, Charlotte Perriand, and other functionalist designers in Paris, the presence in Paris of ceramists (Jean Mayodon, Emile Decoeur), cabinetmakers, and interior decorators of great talent throughout the prewar period (Adnet, Arbus, Drouin, Printz, Groult, Jourdain, Ruhlmann, Leleu),[22] what was that critique about? Without pretending to write in a few pages the history of nearly twenty years of French decorative arts, I will try to assess in what sense and from whose perspective a decline in French decorative arts could be said to have taken place and to evaluate the contribution of Vichy to this issue.

Technical Decadence at the State Manufactures and Vichy's Response

A state-owned manufacture like Beauvais could boast artistic success at the 1925 exhibition of decorative arts, but "practically, from the point of view of clientele, it is null," wrote Luc Benoist in *Beaux Arts*.[23] Although Beauvais obtained financial autonomy from the French state in October 1926, at the same time as Sèvres, the Depression had hit by the time they had reorganized. Financial autonomy, which was supposed to make these manufactures more efficient by cutting down on the red tape with the state, did not produce the desired effect. The manufactures continued to be a burden to the Third Republic.

The manufactures' problems related to politics, waste, and what Janneau would later call "technical decadence."[24] For example, it took nine years (September 1924 to June 1933) for Beauvais manufactures to complete the commission that Raoul Dufy received from the French state to decorate a screen, make tapestry designs for the back of a sofa, four armchairs, and four chairs initially scheduled to be shown at the 1925 decorative arts exhibition.[25] This slow work pace may not be unrelated to government changes during that period. Dufy complained in 1927 about not knowing who would design the furniture for which his decorations were intended.[26] The Beauvais weavers, trained to repair priceless old tapestries, were clearly not equipped to deal with the cartoon by Dufy.[27] Although French taxpayers did not refer to such a waste of their money as decadence, this story remains an example of the spendthrift ways of Third Republic government(s) at which Vichy pointed a finger and which it was happy to use as an excuse for interference and control.

The law of 11 February 1941 (J.O. 4 April) allowed the Vichy government to take away the financial autonomy of the state manufactures, to eliminate some positions, and to appoint a single director, Guillaume Janneau, who already ran the Gobelins manufactures of fine furniture, also known as *Garde Meuble.* In addition, a government-owned shop opened on the rue de la Paix to begin selling luxury craft from all the state manufactures to the general public.

In order to accelerate the production of tapestry at Aubusson and Beauvais, Janneau proclaimed a return to traditional methods, giving the weavers greater license to simplify the cartoons provided by artists and urging painters to design cartoons with fewer than twenty colors.[28] At Sèvres, by order of Janneau, production was stopped on many ceramic pieces created there between 1870 and 1940, because they were said to be too impractical to produce. Janneau also ordered the destruction of molds and many plaster casts.[29] To increase further the production at Sèvres, Janneau ordered the manufacture to use a narrower range of porcelain pastes and to reduce the number of firing processes.[30]

Remedies for decadence at the various state manufactures appear in a new light when one realizes that during Vichy these manufactures worked for the "service artistique," the marshal's propaganda machine. Robert Lallemant, who headed the "service artistique du maréchal," was a ceramist, whose objects, many of them porcelain knicknacks, were occasionally inspired by cubism. In the early 1930s, he worked for wealthy individuals as an interior designer and created inventive modernist pieces of furniture. For unknown reasons, he abandoned his artistic vocation in the mid-1930s and became an industrialist, until tapped by the marshal's doctor to join the Vichy hierarchy.[31]

From what remains of the tapestry cartoons commissioned by Lallemant from Aubusson – illustrated in *Beaux Arts de France* – it is clear that they were intended to propagate Pétainist propaganda: the return to the soil; the celebration of work, of craft, of the family; and, of course, to present the marshal as savior. There were sixty-eight tapestry commissions by the French state, according to Georges Hilaire, the successor as General Secretary for the Fine Arts of Louis Hautecoeur.[32]

At the Sèvres porcelain manufactures, "almost all the models created . . . were related to the iconography of Philippe Pétain. . . ."[33] Some were "medallions and busts with the marshal's effigy, vases or ashtrays adorned with the *francisque* and with the marshal's sayings, to be given as official gifts to loyal followers."[34] Some were designed for the use of the marshal and for Madame Pétain. It is not known who paid for the Sèvres pieces on a "cynegetic theme" destined for Goering[35] and for the Sèvres ashtray for Hitler.[36]

The Sèvres museum has on display several white square-shaped ceramic flasks with gold imprints designed by Robert Lallemant in the 1920s, which he reused for propaganda purposes during Vichy: a profile of Pétain can be seen inscribed in a medallion in one of them, with "offert par le maréchal" written in small letters (Fig. 7). Illustrations on the theme of plowing and another one showing a potter at work (both decorated by Decaris) are found on two larger flasks of identical shape. The fourth flask has no image, only the marshal's principles inscribed in gold. The back of all of them is full of inscriptions signed "Ph. Pétain."

State manufactures were indeed sitting ducks for manipulation by Vichy. Changes in their operations could be effected by decree; they were obliged to continue their traditional function of serving the French government; their compliance with Pétainist propaganda illuminates (or caricatures) the functioning of an apolitical administration, when in lieu of serving a Republican institution, it is at the disposal of a demagogue. On another level, the situation of state manufactures during Vichy is a good example of what Stanley Hoffmann calls "state collaborationism."

Endangered Luxury Crafts and Vichy's Response

Euphoria may have surrounded the arrival in the 1920s of a new wave of designers who, behind the functionalist architect Le Corbusier, sought to adapt interior design to new lifestyles by doing away with expensive, useless ornamental objects and details, and promoting the idea of models reproducible by industry. But such ideas were hardly welcome by craftsmen whose livelihood came from the production and ornamentation of luxury craft and by modern French cabinetmakers and decorators.

There is no reason to go over Janneau's skirmishes with Le Corbusier in the 1920s on the question of "rationalism," which Janneau supported, vs. "functionalism," which he rejected, as the controversy

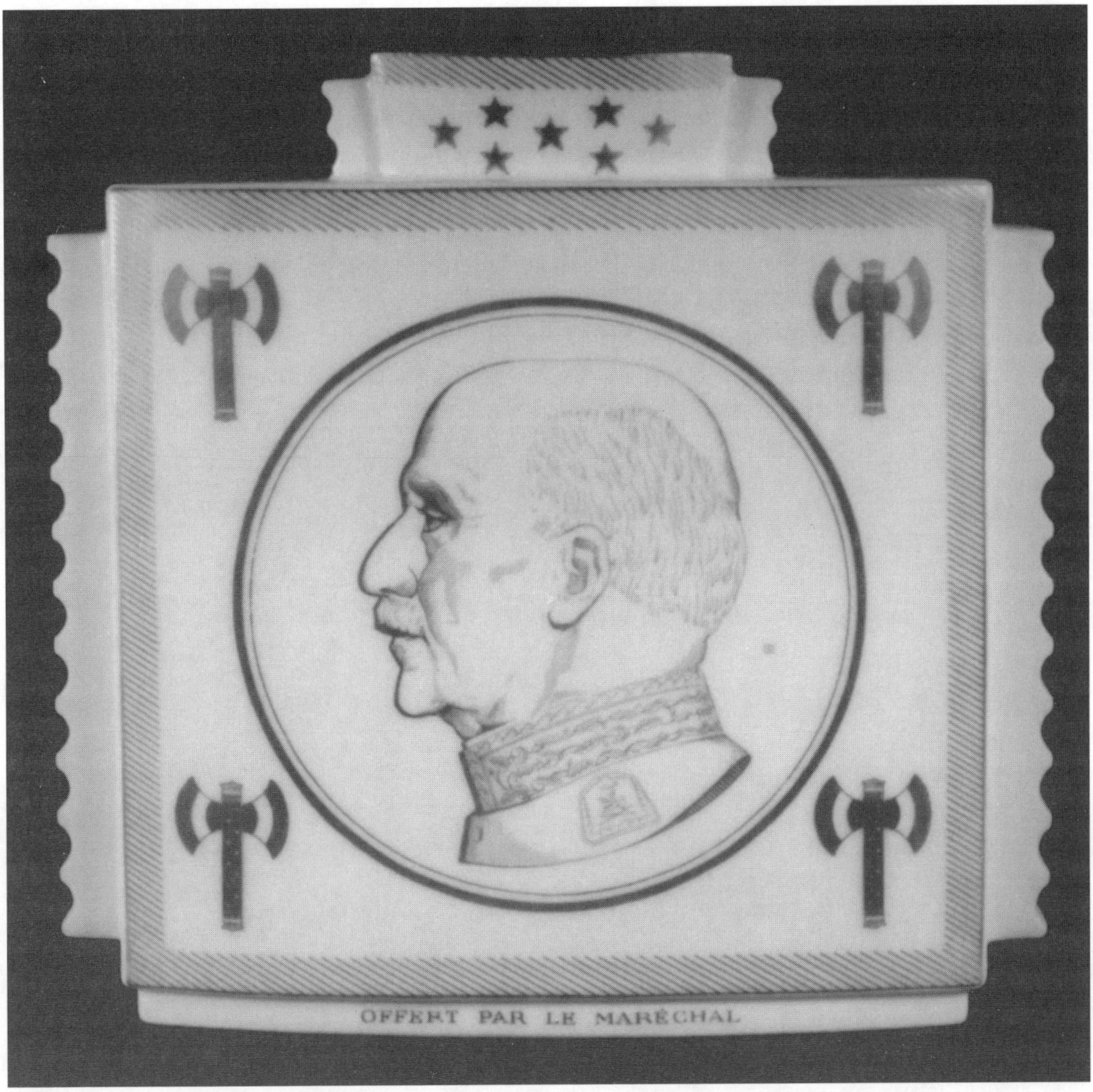

7. Sèvres vase by Robert Lallemant with Marshal Pétain's profile, 1944. Musée des porcelaines de Sèvres, Sèvres, France (photo: Michèle C. Cone).

has already been analyzed by Nancy Troy.[37] A fiercer enemy of functionalism was the art and architecture historian, Louis Hautecoeur, General Secretary for Fine Arts during Vichy, who wrote in 1928:

> [A few decorators] make chairs with metallic tubing, conceive aluminum armchairs or desks made of sheets of iron tole. They do not cover the steel with cellulaque – as does Mr. Ruhlmann in his desks. They show the metal naked. They proclaim with Mr. Le Corbusier that our age is that of steel and that decorative arts are tooling *[outillage]*. . . .
>
> No more useless knicknacks, no more fabrics on lamp shades but lamps at the end of metallic arms like in a dentist's office.[38]

Indeed, from the point of view of ceramists such as Jean Mayodon, the artistic director of Sèvres during the Occupation, an artist born at Sèvres, trained at the manufacture of Sèvres, and renowned for vases with "infinite colored variations . . . a decorative refinement requiring an extreme complexity of realization (five or six successive bakings),"[39] the anticraftsman, antiornament ethos of the new wave of functionalist designers, spelled disaster. Camille Mauclair, the traditionalist art critic whose perennial vindictiveness against modernism flourished during Vichy, pointed out in 1929 that craftsmen involved in luxury handmade decorative arts – ceramists, cabinetmakers, etc. – would become unemployed, and their métiers would become extinct if the functionalists were to succeed.[40] Without the example of the craftsmen, the French tradition of refined taste and unique craftsmanship would fade away. In the eyes of Vichy officials, that scenario had already taken place, hence the need to boost producers of luxury decorative arts before it was too late.

The state manufactures were not the only beneficiaries of Vichy's attentions. Robert Lallemant's "service artistique" called on a number of manufactures, both state and privately owned, according to the list of works presented at the 1944 Salon de l'Imagerie in Paris under the heading "Oeuvres du Service artistique du Maréchal dirigé par R. Lallemant."[41] Besides Sèvres, Aubusson, the state administration of coins and medals, and the state tobacco manufacture, the list includes the crystal manufacture of Baccarat, under "glassware for the chief of state, model created in collaboration between G. Chevalier and Robert Lallemant"; Puiforcat under "silverware, box and silver cup, ornamented by Robert Lallemant"; Canale, for a "plaquette by the sculptor Henri Dropsy, offered by the marshal to towns affected by bombings"; Guenin Lecanu, for "a metal box with the marshal's effigy done by the sculptor A. Levrillier"; Draeger Frères, for "a cigarette coffer decorated by Paul Ternat." Other firms whose objects were not yet ready for exhibition were also put to work. It is obviously difficult to find these objects today. One of them, from the Musée d'Histoire Contemporaine, is a Baccarat crystal vase. A symmetrical, V-shaped modern piece, it has the marshal's *francisque* incised in the center and the words "offered by Marshal Pétain" printed below.

It would thus seem that Vichy's assistance to threatened luxury decorative arts was not without ulterior motive. The Vichy government gave business to producers of luxury crafts who were willing to accept the conditions set out by Robert Lallemant and his "service artistique," namely to help Pétain with his image and contribute to his propaganda.

Excessive Individualism Tamed by Corporatist Organizations

Guillaume Janneau placed the blame for the decline of luxury decorative arts on excessive individualism and on the lack of cooperation between fine artists, technicians, and craftsmen. "Today, the head of an atelier, unless he himself invents his models, is nothing but the instrument of a draftsman erected to the status of author," he wrote.

> And even in the most artisanal of metiers . . . too often, the decorator intervening as master, deprives his oeuvre of this "human element" that the collaboration of the artisan might have conferred upon it. . . . Rarely has a vaster and more delicate problem of redressing presented itself to . . . the critical spirit of responsible men.[42]

Under the guise of reclassifying, workers participating in various phases of decorative applied arts were regrouped, simulating the medieval guild system. A first decree organizing "métiers d'art," the generic term for all decorative arts at that time, was signed 20 January 1941 (J.O. 5 February 1941); a second decree completing the first list was signed 3 February 1942 (J.O. 5 February 1942). A third decree of 3 April 1942 (J.O. 26 April 1942) announced the creation of the professional family of "*métiers d'art* and other diverse articles." Yet another decree of 7 July 1941 (J.O. 29 July 1941) instituted the organization of interior decorators and visual artists.

The idea behind reclassifying was to place within the same corporatist entity various categories of workers involved in decorative arts so they would benefit from each other's expertise. Decorators, for example, were placed in the corporatist organization of painters, sculptors, engravers, and medalists because these individuals were being called upon to decorate screens, sideboards, and other accessories for luxurious homes.

Valid as Janneau's argument might be that artisans and artists had suffered from their splendid isolation from one another, a situation historically associated with the idea of decadence,[43] the system put in place hardly resolved those difficulties. By blurring the hierarchy between free and applied art, between the decorative artist and the artisan, the Vichy state was trying to put every worker including "free" artists under its tutelage. Furthermore, in the new organizations, final say – such as decisions concerning the allotment [repartition] of the scarce materials necessary for the activities of the members of the decorative arts organization – was in the hands of representatives of the Vichy State. The heads of committees for each section of *métiers d'art* were chosen by a Vichy official and supervised by various levels of the new organizations: consultative commissions, bureaux, groups, and work sections (see decree of 20 January 1941, in J.O. 5 February 1941).

The Pure Frenchness Argument in Favor of Ornamentation

In 1937, with foreign decorative arts about to compete with French ones at the World's Fair, the issue of internationalism vs. Frenchness that had lingered throughout the century came vigorously to the fore once again, exacerbated by the high unemployment caused by the Great Depression. Starting in 1934 the publication *Art et arti-*

sanat representing the voice of the "groupement syndical des artisans d'art" had taken a firm stand against foreign manpower as plans for the 1937 Paris World's Fair were taking shape.[44] And in the winter of 1938–39, the review *Beaux Arts* confronted the issue of Frenchness vs. internationalism in its editorials.[45]

Since its beginnings in 1901, the organization that put together yearly exhibitions for ceramists, cabinetmakers, interior decorators, and other luxury artisans; the Société des Artistes Décorateurs (SAD), had had a reputation for its openness to the new.[46] In the beginning functionalists were welcome there, although their professed stand against the ornament, their belief in industrial processes, and their internationalist outlook close to that of the German Bauhaus and the Russian constructivists, made them suspect.[47]

Whether functionalists were expelled or seceded on their own from the SAD in 1929 is difficult to determine. What is known is that competition between the SAD and the functionalists – now organized and exhibiting under the name of UAM (Union des Artistes Modernes) – was intense. Although the latter initially hoped to serve a broader public than the SAD by mass-producing their designs and allying themselves with industry, both groups in fact addressed the same wealthy clientele because the Depression put an end to utopian intentions. Retrospectively, the division between the two groups seems more trivial than it was made to appear. On an aesthetic level, SAD decorators believed that useless ornament was not superfluous if it were part of a design, whereas UAM designers concentrated on making the smallest functional detail of the home into a work of art. One of the founding members of UAM, Jean Puiforcat – the heir to the Puiforcat flatware firm – designed elegant bath and basin faucets and stylish doorknobs in those years.

Even on the political level, the image of the UAM as firebrand progressionist by comparison to the SAD does not stand up. Pétain's artistic adviser, Robert Lallemant, was one of the lesser-known founders of the UAM. The firm of Puiforcat would work for the Vichy propaganda machine. Le Corbusier also offered his services to Vichy.[48]

As for Janneau, he had associated his name if not with functionalism – he was too much on the side of luxury decorative arts[49] – at least with rationalism. In a 1923 text on the ceramist Emile Decoeur, he wrote: "Rationalism is the heritage of French artisans. . . . Decoeur wants his decoration to express the properties of the material."[50] In a 1925 text on modernist lighting fixtures, Janneau concluded: "We are reaching a new stage toward the integral rationalism of the interior decor."[51] In 1942 when he and Louis Hautecoeur coauthored a book on modern furniture, Janneau said: "All that is not spontaneously determined by common sense, by a utilitarian spirit, in the domain of domestic decor is useless."[52] He repeated the same point of view in his 1943 *Meubles nouveaux*.[53]

Even though the ideological lines between the SAD and the UAM were never carefully drawn, the pro-ornament SAD and the anti-ornament UAM were, in 1937, farther apart than ever. The SAD's viewpoint was reinforced by the presence of craftsmen from the French provinces at the World's Fair, who also brandished their ornamental genius and manual expertise as the most prestigious signs of Frenchness, tradition, and quality. Though reason may be on the side of UAM member Robert Mallet-Stevens when he said, "It is neither fashion nor ornament that defines the nationality of a style; it is the personality of the artists and only their personality,"[54] in the conflictual climate of 1937, strong forces were pushing ornament as a symbol of Frenchness in decorative arts, and its absence as signifying foreign inspiration, hence "decadent."

All UAM members were not tagged as "foreigners" – Judeo-Marxist-decadent in Nazi parlance. During the Occupation an attempt was made to unite the SAD and the UAM under the name of Société des Artistes Décorateurs Modernes.[55] The pro-ornament forces, however, clearly had support in high places. When, during Vichy, two officials, Louis Hautecoeur and Guillaume Janneau, coauthored the text on modern furniture mentioned earlier, the point on which they were in total agreement was the question of ornament. Hautecoeur stated, "Nothing prevents the decoration of a piece of furniture with a medallion, a precious incrustation, a sculpted motif."[56] Janneau likewise concluded, "It is necessary to restore ornamentation, that is decorative sculpture and 'ciselure d'ameublement.'"[57] In addition to Hautecoeur and Janneau, Maurice Dufrène, a steady exhibitor at the SAD from 1904 through 1942, had become head of the decorators' section of the "organisation professionelle des arts graphiques et plastiques," the newly formed artists and decorators corporatist organization mentioned earlier. Among the purchases made by Vichy in 1941, one finds the names of SAD members Jules Leleu, Jean Dunand, and André Devèche;[58] in 1942 one finds Adnet, Leleu, Porteneuve.[59]

A Historicist Style Approved

The word decadent might have defined the sensibility of SAD presentations in the late 1930s. Redolent of idle wealth, pomp, and the languidity of vicarious living – set against the sense of purpose and energy conveyed by the functionalists – SAD displays from 1937 to 1939 abounded in "bedrooms fit for dreamers." Symphonies of pale pastels, with trompe l'oeil effects (actual and simulated fabrics draped on ceilings and walls in Louis Sue's "bedroom," 1939), these rooms exuded a feeling of the uncanny, no doubt because the period styles in which they were furnished reached back to antiquity yet were modern. Typical of this mood is the lounging chair of "méridienne" by André Arbus exhibited at the 1937 SAD pavilion. "It is the era of fake luxury, of theatrical mise-en-scène, of the arabesque which . . . infiltrates objects and furniture."[60]

Surprisingly, far from repudiating this mode of eclectic historicism, which has been called surrealist-influenced, some of the decorators fashionable during Vichy seem to have carried it to extremes. Reviewing the 1942 SAD, Pierre du Colombier observes, "Are we headed for a new baroque, a new rococo? It's possible." To him it feels as if "creators had escaped from the rigorousness of the times by means of an outpouring of fantasy."[61]

Wrought iron is a popular material in those years, its renaissance explained by Janneau "as the resurgence of the classical system of the grotesque" on the one hand, and the shop-sign tradition on the other.[62] Wrought iron is used like rope, curling under a marble tabletop by Marc du Plantier. For a wall fixture by Gilbert Poillerat and a small mirror by Raoul Guis, an odd mix of materials and forms are joined – as in a three-dimensional exquisite corpse – in a surfeit of time-consuming detailing and excessive handmade ornamentation. Wood, particularly oak, is subject to elaborate hand-carving. Styles continue to be hybrid as when a rectangular sideboard and elaborate figurative sculpture for the door handle coexist in the same piece.

An uncanny datelessness invades classical vases by Mayodon decorated with mythological scenes roughly sketched in, and a set of oak armchairs by Jacques Adnet with high backs ornamented with Aubusson tapestry tondos on the theme of the four seasons by Pierre Olivier.

One sometimes wonders if there was not some irony or perhaps mockery implied in such excessive and gratuitous craftsmanship on the part of cabinetmakers and their artist associates. This being said, such manifestation of the hand at work articulated several goals of the regime: the association of Frenchness, craft, and quality. The foreigner and the Jew are historic scapegoats of decadence. In the mid-1880s, avowal of decadence in decorative arts had already been a leitmotif of xenophobes. Then, "[Louis] de Fourcaud called on the government to support the Central Union's developing program to revitalize the crafts through nationalism. . . . 'Restore our French genius,' he urged, 'help our French art works to triumph.'"[63] Closer to our time, Marcel Duchamp, although a French artist, had first sensitized society to the possibility of art without craftsmanship, and another French artist, Fernand Léger, had predicted the phasing out of the métier of artist and praised the modern machine-made object. Yet "decadence" was repeatedly ascribed to foreign influences by, among others, the man who became General Secretary for Fine Arts under Pétain, Louis Hautecoeur.[64]

Once again, as pointed out by Nancy Troy, "French decorators found that the only way to be modern yet remain French was to invoke the styles and to the extent possible, the modes of production that they believed had made their decorative arts so successful in the past."[65]

To Conclude:

The question of origin is imbedded in the disagreement observed at the outset of this paper on the proper appellation of the Vichy regime. Zeev Sternhell sees the origin of Vichy ideology in the theories of fascism that emerged in France (as well as Germany) at the end of the nineteenth century. For him, a French fascist tradition exists, which resembles German *volkism*. For the French historian René Rémond and his followers, Vichy has roots that go farther into the past. It is tied to the French monarchic tradition, and its ideology had to do with reversing the changes achieved by the French revolution.

Given that the decorative arts were among the jewels of the French monarchy, the behavior of Vichy with respect to them is far from irrelevant to the Rémond/Sternhell debate. Let us then compare the tapestry subsidized by Vichy entitled *National Renovation* by Paul Charlemagne (Fig. 8) showing Pétain surrounded by workmen with one of Louis XIV surrounded by artisans. In the great tapestry from a design by Charles Lebrun entitled *Louis XIV Visiting the Gobelins* (Fig. 9), the Sun King stands discreetly behind and to the far left of the medley of artisans showing off their wares. It is they who "reflect the power and splendor of the sovereign and the state."[66] By contrast, in Charlemagne's work, Pétain in uniform and on horseback occupies center stage and the workmen are diminutive figures at his feet. Whereas Lebrun shows the Sun King as promoter of the decorative arts and friend of its artisans, it is the image of a military man promoting himself that is conveyed by Charlemagne, the marshal's "courtisan."

A similar conclusion could be drawn from comparing the use of ornament during the monarchy and during Vichy. Throughout the classical age, which, according to Jacques Soulillou, all fascist regimes pretend to revive, ornament was never thought of in terms of "supplement," of "*parergon*."[67] But whereas under the monarchy a new style of ornament would herald a change of leader, a certain datelessness characterizes the decorative arts during Vichy; previous ornamental styles are recycled. The inscription "Philippe Pétain" adorns objects in a variety of styles. More significant than the style of decorative arts is the "cult of personality" latent in their content.

The discourse on decadence during Vichy, though consistent with that condemning loss of craftsmanship in modernist painting and sculpture, had less to do with recovering the virtues of quality and taste associated with the French monarchy than with transforming the decorative arts into cult objects. The decorative arts

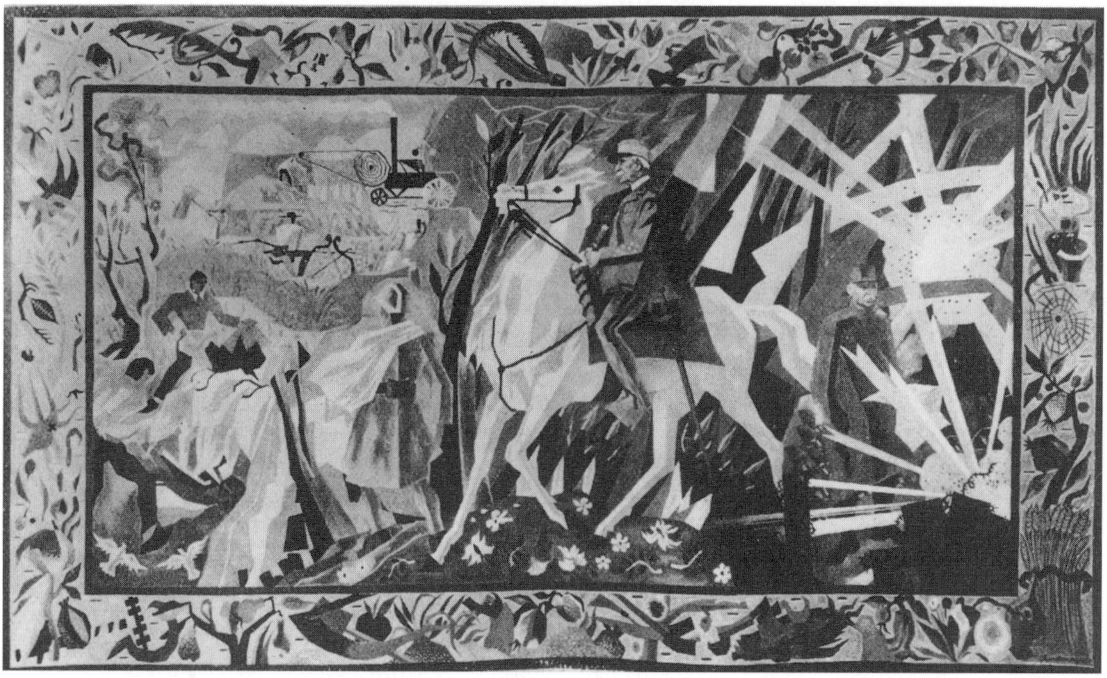

8. Paul Charlemagne, *National Renovation,* 1942. Size and location unavailable (photo: Jacques Faujour)

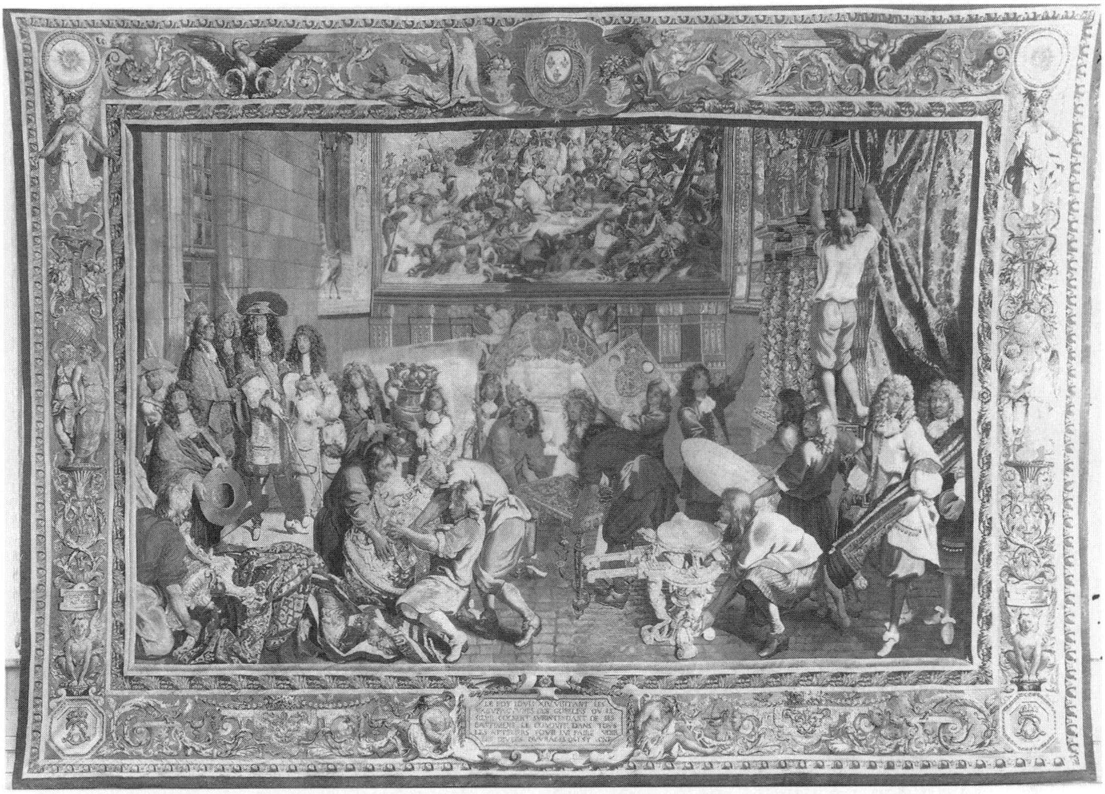

9. Charles Lebrun, *Louis XIV Visiting the Gobelins,* 1673–80. Tapestry from the series "L'histoire du Roi." Size unavailable. Mobilier National Collection (photo: Mobilier National, Paris).

under Vichy, rather than announcing the era of a new monarch with a new decorative style, continued to be torn between modernity and tradition. The main beneficiary of an alleged recovery was Pétain himself.

The importance of the myth of cultural decadence for fascist ideology is hardly new, and it has been noted by a number of scholars. Eugen Weber has observed that allegations of decline in quality and standards of literary and artistic products can broaden "into the belief that decline in these realms mirror[s] deeper and more significant corruption, an incoherent literature, art or politics being the mere reflections of incoherent times."[68] The relationship of decadence to ideology is formulated somewhat differently by Zeev Sternhell, who considers that "the problem of decadence is one of the major preoccupations of fascism," because at issue is "not only the fate of the nation but also that of civilization."[69] Roger Griffin's contribution to the fascist debate is to shift attention from the rational tenor of fascism – namely its dogma, to its irrational workings – the alarming myths on which it plays in order to justify itself in the eyes of society.[70]

In the period under scrutiny, the Great Depression had certainly threatened all luxury industries, and the luxury craftsman was an endangered species to the extent that his production remained inefficient, costly, and dispensable in times of economic crisis, and that he could not withstand the international competition of more standardized products. Instead of helping artisans adapt to a changing world, Vichy waved the flag of decadence against real or imagined competition – the machine, the foreigner, the Jew, meanwhile taking control of French manufactures, and of professional organizations.

In sum, the call for renewal in the decorative arts on the part of the Vichy regime cannot be separated from a more general attempt to justify the regime's break from democratic forms of government. The efficiency resulting from a corporatist approach to the decorative arts was said to be a cure for the technical incompetence and the excessive individualism that plagued decorative arts production under the Third Republic. In similar fashion, the Vichy regime contrasted its embrace of an ornamental style, grounded in the French tradition, with the functionalism supposedly promoted by foreign artists or those non-French or foreign entrepreneurs whose support of mass production methods had undermined French craft. The fact that technical incompetence, individualism, and functionalism were equally condemned in the name of decadence serves to remind us that mythic ideology permeated all aspects of Vichy arts policy. No solution for the plight of decorative arts was found, other than the invocation of decadence in the name of a para-fascist national revolution.

3

Lucien Rebatet

Anti-Semitic Art Criticism During Vichy

> There looms, within abjection, one of those violent, dark revolts of being, directed against a threat that seems to emanate from an exorbitant outside or inside, ejected beyond the scope of the possible, the tolerable, the thinkable.
>
> Julia Kristeva, *Powers of Horror*

WHAT MIGHT BE this thunderbolt, "exorbitant . . . ejected beyond the scope of the possible, the tolerable, the thinkable?" Who is this enormous presence that, Kristeva says, "beseeches, worries, and fascinates desire, which, nevertheless, does not let itself be seduced?" What sprinting demon, "like an inescapable boomerang, a vortex of summons and repulsion places the one haunted by it literally beside himself?"[1] This fantasy creature (it, she, he?), without contours, spreading abjection, terror and envy, lust and disgust, is . . . the Jew in the head of the French anti-Semite (as well as the Jew "inside" the anti-Semite): "Anti-Semitism, for which there thus exists an object as phantasmatic and ambivalent as the Jew is the sociological thrill, flush with history, that believers and nonbelievers alike seek in order to experience abjection."[2]

First published in L. Nochlin and T. Garb, eds., *The Jew in the Text* (London and New York: Thames and Hudson, 1995).

At no time in recent history did the propensity to paint the Jew in the colors of abjection reach a greater level of sophistication than during the Nazi era. Germans aroused by their Führer, but also Nazi sympathizers in countries occupied by Germany, partook of that activity. In France during the Occupation years, the Institut d'Etudes des Questions Juives (Institute for the Study of Jewish Questions, IEQJ) was the main creator and distributor of thoroughly repugnant and destructive images of Jewish identity. Its art section, according to document CXCIII–162 from the Centre de Documentation Juive contemporaine (CDJC) in Paris, was handed over to the notorious anti-Semite Lucien Rebatet, who is also listed in the press service (CDJC document XCVI–80).

The influence of the IEQJ's anti-Jewish propaganda exerted itself directly through anti-Semitic pamphlets such as *Journal, Bulletin,* and *Cahier jaune;* through the travesty of scientific exhibitions it organized, in particular that called "Le Juif et la France," and through other forms of brainwashing under the guise of learned lectures and technical conferences. And it exerted itself indirectly through its infiltration of the media. Sold on the Nazi point of view, the weekly *Je suis partout* did not need infiltration. Filling the art columns of that nasty sheet, under his own name or the pseudonym of "l'Encadreur," was the man put in charge of artistic matters at the IEQJ, Lucien Rebatet (1903–73).[3]

On the surface, the content of Rebatet's art columns demonstrated a taste for harmony and refinement that stood for pure Frenchness: "One realizes that almost all these French artists, even the least clever ones, are harmonists by instinct," he wrote after visiting the Salon des Tuileries in 1941. "They are the only race in the world who, after the medieval miniaturists, know how to juxtapose the most vivid blue and green by marrying them, who can vary ad infinitum and continually renew this play on values, from the most discreet and evanescent grays and pinks to the most sumptuous orgies of chrome and vermilion."[4]

To his readers, Rebatet presented himself as a formalist art critic. Reviewing Lionello Venturi's book *Peintres modernes,* he wrote in 1942: "M. Lionello Venturi has made great strides to disengage himself from clichés *[les poncifs],* and from the useless verbiage of contemporary criticism. He has returned to honest formal *[plastique]* analysis as it was practised during the last century, when Eugène Fromentin offered a model of it that is still celebrated. . . . In the end it [plastic analysis] is indispensable for providing reference points *[repères]*, comparisons, and for discovering the pictorial substance that lies truly within an *oeuvre.* It is far more difficult than a logical improvisation on the picturesque . . . For it demands that one know how to read modeling, values, planes, and volumes, the composition of a painting, of a drawing, or of a print."[5]

How then did Rebatet reconcile artistic refinement with vulgar outbursts against the Jewish "virus"? How did he combine his role of anti-Semitic propagandist with that of a formalistic critic of modern art? In order to make sense of the connection, I shall start by unveiling the critical image around which anti-Semitic propaganda at the IEQJ operated. As its major undertaking "Le Juif et la France" reveals, it was the image and myth of the vampire that became a central motif of anti-Semitic messages during the Occupation period.

Why did anti-Semites appropriate the elusive image of the vampire for their propaganda? What were the deep human fears and desires on which the vampire myth played in France for the generation of Lucien Rebatet? These are the issues I shall first address. Only then will I be able to show that Rebatet's voice on modernity was not inconsistent with his role as a mouthpiece for anti-Semitic propaganda. The image of the male Jew as living corpse – vampire – runs subliminally through Rebatet's prose, stirring fear of the virus he carries, and fear of the death of art that his virus causes. Rebatet's notion of the "Jewish virus," of "aryanization" as a form of artistic purification, will be discussed. In lieu of a conclusion, the essay will ask whether the use of the vampire in anti-Semitic propaganda, besides unveiling symptoms of psychopathic traits, was not also a foil for the desire of anti-Semites for a Fascist victory.

Le Juif et la France: The Demonizing of the Jew

The unique function of the IEQJ was the fight against Jews. An anti-Jewish brigade, and a special section in charge of arrests, searches, seizures, and surveillance (in liaison with the Gestapo) made up one branch of its organization. The other branch was divided into "services," among them the Service de la Propagande. That service or section "was in charge of propaganda in all domains, through the press, the radio, the cinema, the theatre, posters, publications, and organization of courses and conferences; it kept an eye on the tendencies of the press, of the cinema, of the radio, and of the theatre (supporting or combating them), on public opinion, and on the effects of anti-German and anti-collaborationist propaganda, and it took charge of counterpropaganda measures, including productions, or suggestions for the German services."[6]

The most visible propagandist undertaking of the IEQJ was the exhibition "Le Juif et la France," inaugurated at the Palais Berlitz in Paris in September 1941 (Fig. 10). It is that vulgar compendium of misinformation presented as oversized panels with diagrams, photos, texts, caricatures, and as gigantic pieces of sculpture, that demonstrates in sufficient detail the shameless motivations of anti-Semites at that particular moment of French history – to crush the Jews of France.

One way to accomplish this goal was to raise collective consciousness on the "excessive" presence of Jews in the social and cultural national body, by teaching the public how to recognize Jews from non-Jews. C. Laville, who headed the "Service de Recherches Scientifiques" at the IEQJ thus explained the meaning of the diagrams at the exhibition: "As each of us can learn from looking at the illustrated panel exhibited at the Palais Berlitz, Jews result from a triple conjunction between whites, mongols (yellow) and negroes, so that their traits owe something to each of the three great primordial races . . . frequently in opposition to one another." Admittedly, the author went on, Aryans are also of mixed origin. In Jews, however, the originating traits have not become merged: "One Jew is negroid through his eyes and lips, mongol through his hair and nose, while another Jew is mongol through his slanted eyes and heavy lips, negroid through his kinky hair."[7]

One might deduce from this analysis that the Jewish physique is a collage rather than a synthesis of human typologies, and that although existing in various disguises, and hence "ambiguous," the Jewish physique always has some "African" feature – negroid eyes and lips, kinky hair. One might go further and propose that this view of the Jewish physique is not without a connection to early

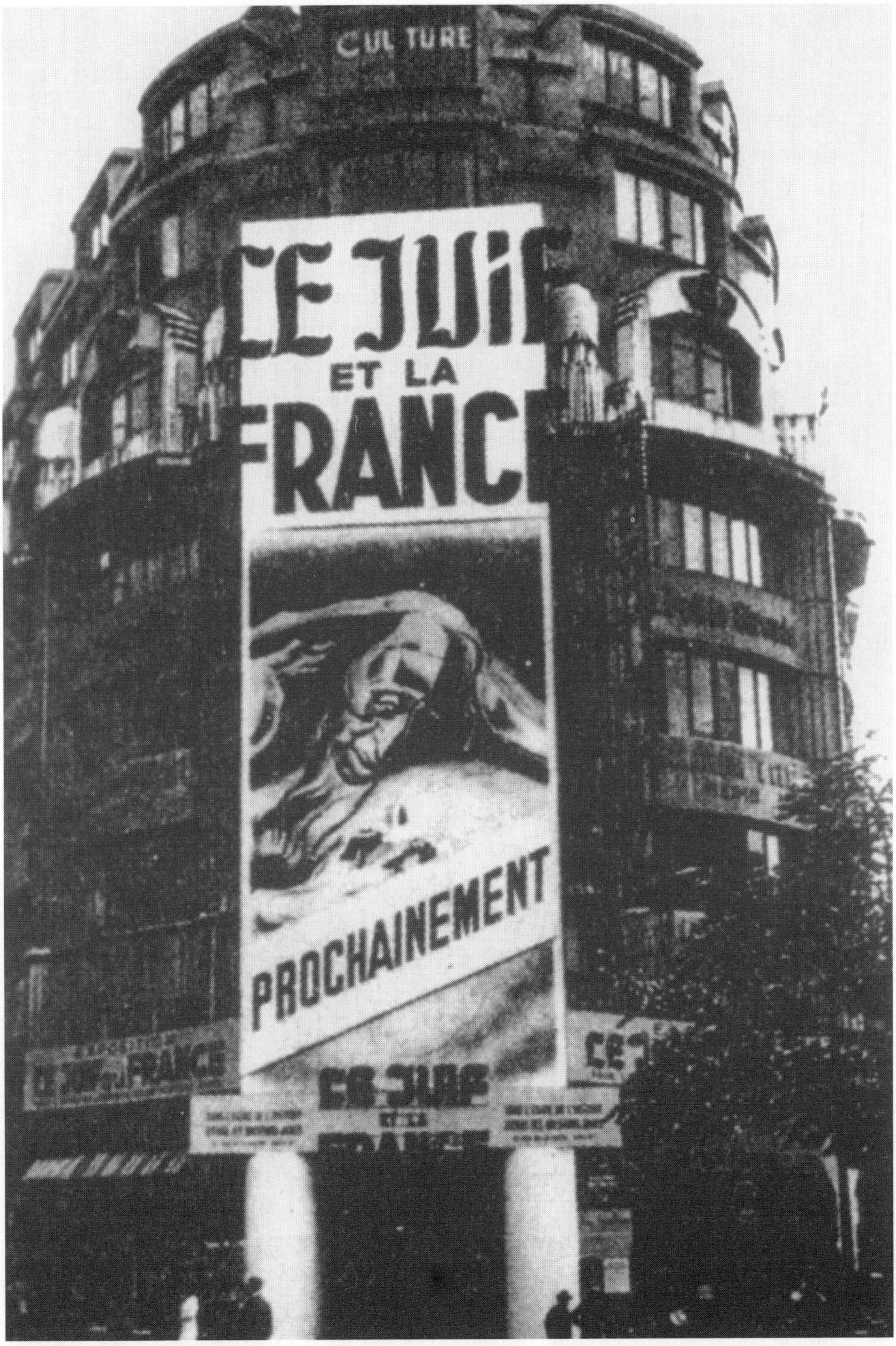

10. The exhibition "Le Juif et la France," Paris, 1941: entrance with poster (photo: CDJC, Paris).

Cubist representations, which were equally abhorred. In the giant three-dimensional head of a generic Jew featured in the exhibition, all the "Jewish" features are seamlessly joined, suggesting an Expressionist caricature rather than the disjointed planes of Cubist figurative sculpture (Fig. 11).

On the one hand, the composite typology of the Jew revealed by "Le Juif et la France" connoted a physical monstrosity when compared to Aryan types, but, on the other, the variety of Jewish types was such that imaginary Jews could be seen lurking everywhere, vampire-like, thereby stirring paranoia in the collective psyche. In *Bagatelles pour un massacre* (1937), Louis-Ferdinand Céline, the famous anti-Semite, had put it this way: "The Jews, you know, they're all camouflaged, disguised, chameleon-like, they change names like they cross frontiers, now they pass themselves off for Bretons, Auvergnants, Corsicans, now for Turandotes, Durandards, Cassoulets . . . anything at all . . . that throws people off, that sounds deceptive."[8]

The goal of assimilation was widely shared by Jews in France, even after the Dreyfus Affair: "their political theory and their political strategy was that of assimilation . . . the Dreyfus Affair proved to be not a turning-point in the history of the Jews in France, but rather a momentous landmark in their steady march toward the goal of assimilation."[9] Even though during the 1930s, refugee Jews from central Europe and Nazi Germany, more conspicuous than the Jews of France, appeared to arrive in hordes, the total number of Jews living in France in 1939, 300,000, remained less than 1 percent of the French population.

Not only did the exhibition "Le Juif et la France" seek to arouse fear of the "excessive" number of Jews in France but it also raised a fear of their nefarious influence: the guide to the show, a brochure with a long article entitled "Pourquoi une exposition juive?" by J. Marquès Rivière, who liaised between the IEQJ and the Occupation authorities, sought to demonstrate in words what the show did via captioned photographs, drawings, and sculpture, namely that something particularly abject in the Jewish character had undermined society and culture from the beginnings of history to the present. The sayings of famous thinkers from the past were called to testify:

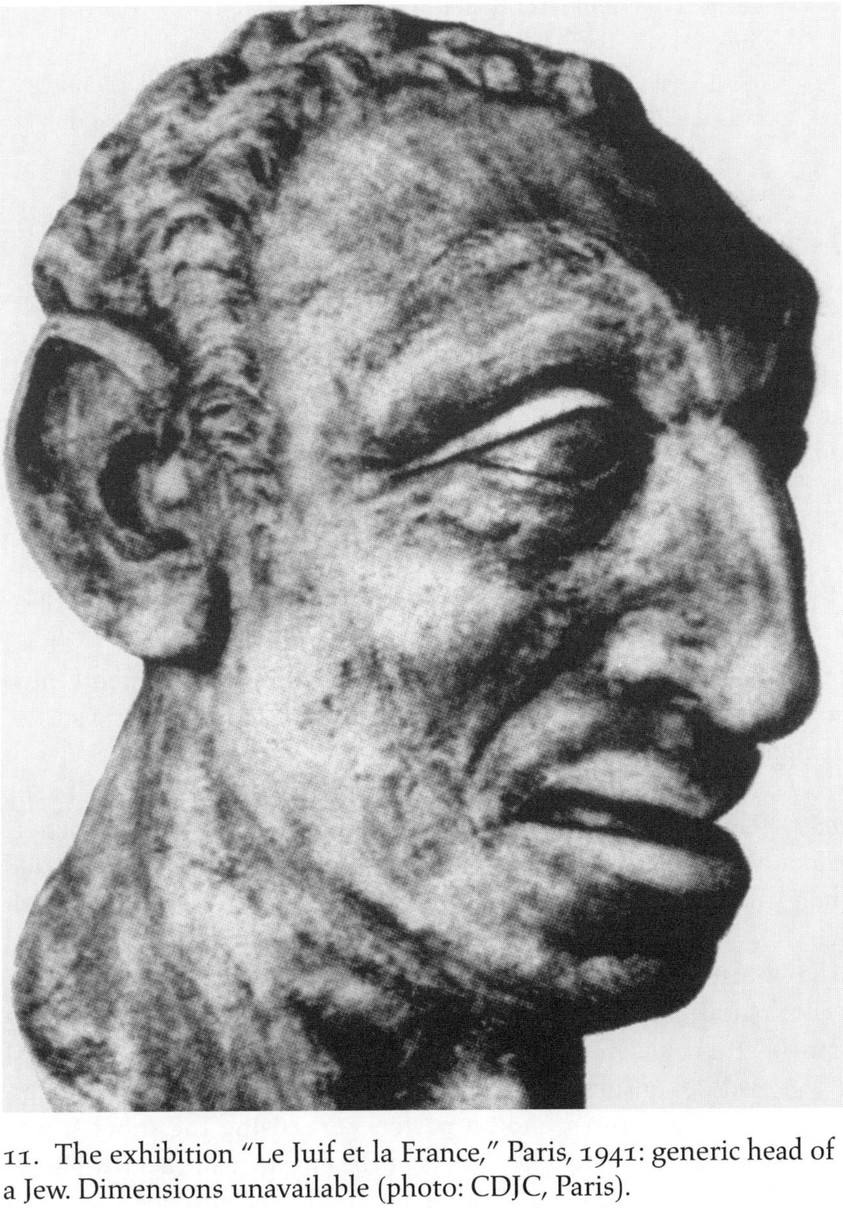

11. The exhibition "Le Juif et la France," Paris, 1941: generic head of a Jew. Dimensions unavailable (photo: CDJC, Paris).

RENAN: "The semitic race is recognizable almost solely through its negative traits: it has neither mythology, nor epos *[épopée]*, nor science, nor philosophy, nor fiction, nor plastic arts, nor civil life . . ."

LUTHER: "They are just so many venomous, perverse, cruel, satanic beasts which from 1400 on . . . have been and continue to be the ruin of governments."

VOLTAIRE: "You will merely find in Jews an ignorant, lazy, barbarous people who for a long time have combined the most undignified stinginess with the most profound hatred for all the people who tolerate them and enrich them."

The author added his own list of anti-Jewish traits. He called Jews greedy and conspiratorial: "The Jews control secret societies, which form provisional governments and shift to the benefit of Jews *[la juiverie]* all the political and social upsets *[bouleversements]*"; domineering and destructive: "The Jews were masters of French democracy: She could only die from it;" thriving on the work of others: "From their earliest history, the Jews present themselves as useless businessmen, living off the sweat and the work of others . . ."[10] In all of these characterizations, the Jew threatens now governments, now society, now individuals' wealth, work, life, and soul, by some sort of demonic conspiratorial power.

La France se libérant des juifs (France Liberating Itself from the Jews) (Fig. 12), the thirty-foot-high sculpture of a tall, attractive, and athletic young female (France) subduing a repulsive, greedy old man (the Jew) with her knees, and pushing another one down with her free hand, found in the rotunda of the exhibition, suggested what must be done. France must crush the Jews so that a new genealogical line of pure Aryan types like the baby in France's upheld arm could start.

A two-dimensional version of the greedy old man appeared on the cover of brochures, and on posters advertising the show. It was also the image that greeted visitors at the entrance of the exhibition. The *Illustration* reviewer, Robert de Beauplan, described it as "a great allegorical composition representing a kind of vampire with long beard, thick lips, and crooked nose, whose fingers, like the claws of a bird of prey, clutch the terrestrial globe."[11]

It does not take a great deal of familiarity with contemporary

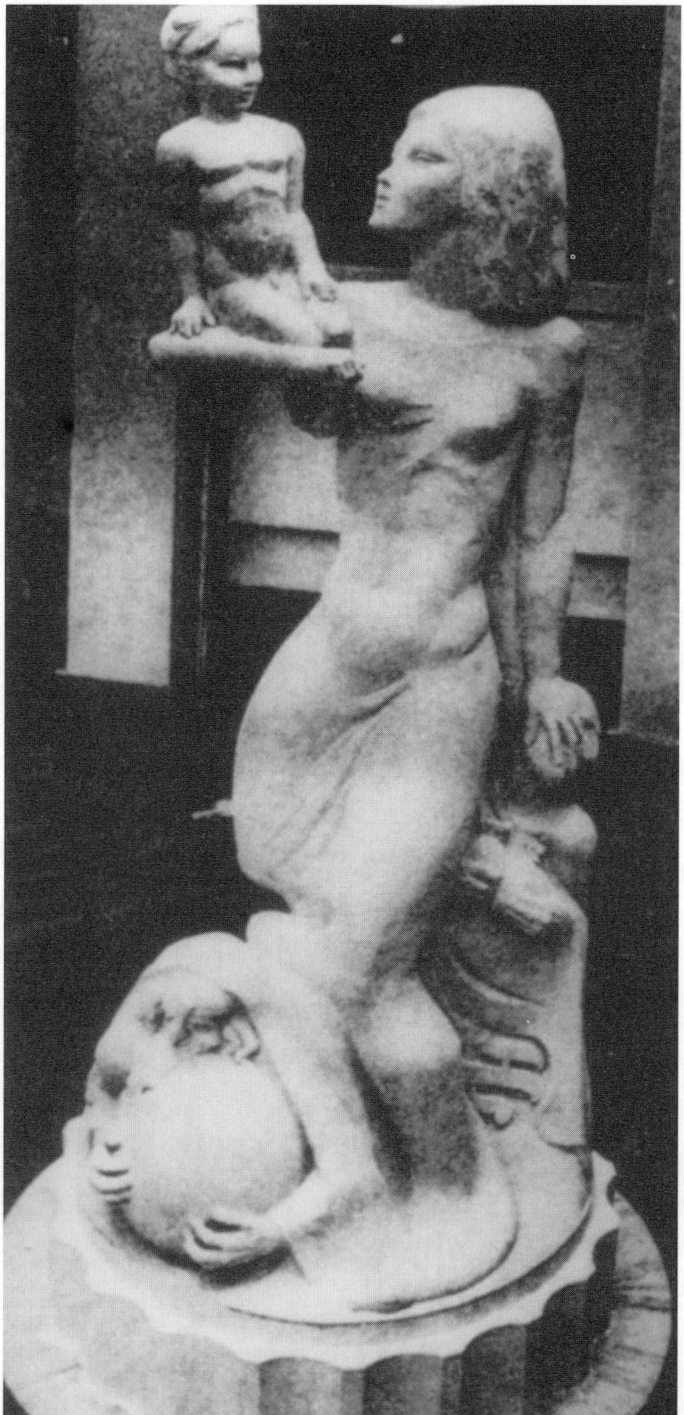

12. The exhibition, "Le Juif et la France," Paris, 1941. Perron, *France Liberating Itself from the Jews.* Height 30 ft. (photo: CDJC, Paris).

visual culture to sense that the image being described had as much to do with the Walt Disney witch (made famous in the 1938 movie *Snow White,* ecstatically reviewed by Rebatet)[12] as with bloodsucking bats, female ghouls, or the legendary Dracula in Bram Stoker's novel. None of the "vampires" in films that a French critic of those years might have encountered – the actor Conrad Veidt in *The Cabinet of Dr. Caligari,* Max Schreck in *Nosferatu,* the stern old lady in Carl Dreyer's *Vampyr* – wore a wispy beard and a Jewish kaftan.[13] Yet de Beauplan found in "vampire" the image around which the other Jewbaiters had been circling. For as the participation of Jews in the political and cultural life of France increased so did the demonization of the Jew.

The deceptively fascinating male or female vampire of nineteenth-century literature (and twentieth-century film) could feed the myth of a conspiring Jew out to get political power through charm and seduction.[14] Anti-Semites could also use the image of a bloodsucking vampire against Jews whom they accused of living off the wealth and the sweat of others. (In Rebatet's *Les Tribus du cinéma* [1941], Jews are accused of having monopolized that medium to the detriment of French *metteurs en scène.*) In the eyes of anti-Semites, the Jew thus shared with the mythical vampire the status of "an object of hatred and desire, of threat and aggressivity, of envy and abomination."[15] Small wonder that without necessarily being named – the fat capitalist Jew depicted in cartoons by Ralph Soupault wears the elegant top hat and tails of the lethal seducer[16] – the vampire makes an appearance in "Pourquoi une exposition juive?" and other propaganda texts around "Le Juif et la France."

It is curious that "Le Juif et la France" does not seem, from the plan of the show, to have devoted much of its space to a critique of modern art. The section *art juif* is small compared with the bay devoted to the cinema. We do know that the presence of a work by Salvador Dali prompted the General Consul of Spain to send a letter to the IEQJ asking that it be removed since Dali was not a Jew, and that it be replaced by "painters of the same school but of French nationality and Jewish origin."[17] Perhaps the organizers thought that the contrast of style visible in the statue *La France se libérant des juifs* expressed the views of the IEQJ judiciously enough: the Expressionist distortions of the "Jew" denoted *L'art juif* in the process of disappearing; the idealized neoclassical effigy of the goddess France symbolized "art at the end of the vampire age. . . ." In any event, the IEQJ had at *Je suis partout* an art connoisseur with a lashing tongue perfect for the task at hand.

Lucien Rebatet on the Jewish Virus

Endowed with a bilious tongue and acerbic verve on the subject of Jews, Rebatet was a minor-league Céline. Like that author of *Voyage au bout de la nuit* (1932), *Bagatelles pour un massacre, L'Ecole des cadavres* (1938), and other famous works, Rebatet, using organic metaphors and slang, went out of his way to make Jews responsible for everything that had gone wrong in France.[18] That Céline of the art world detested Salon art as much as what he called the Jewish virus. In 1941 he announced in his first and most polemical piece, "Entre le juif et le pompier" ("Between the Jew and the Pompier"): "If the teaching at the Ecole des Beaux Arts had not been in such decrepitude . . . surely the Jewish virus could not have gnawed into us with such ease."[19] In this way he sketched for us his imaginary Jew, a virus-carrying vampire whose bite poisons and destroys. Modern art, he felt, had been attacked by such a virus, which had drained it of its vitality, and left it "etiolated," like the victims of active vampires, "pale, languishing, without appetite."[20] To recover its energy, art must be "aryanized."

Rebatet explains in "Entre le juif":

> It [modern art] is a tree whose trunk is still vigorous, but whose branches are etiolated. Its disease appears that much more evident for its having borne magnificent fruit in the course of the XIXth century, and in the first years of this one. . . .
>
> It is necessary to cut off the purulent branches. It is necessary to *aryanize* the fine arts. It is an essential task, that which must precede all others. For it is Jews who through their excessive number *[pullulement]* like parasite insects, threaten the beautiful plant. . . .
>
> Jews, painters or sculptors propagating the most pernicious example, Jewish dealers with their hideous speculations, critics praising *[glosant]* with unstoppable enthusiasm the mores and works from this vast ghetto, their presence must be forbidden. And they must be told why they are condemned, and how their

> influence has been devastating *[funeste]* for us, and that even if some of them have talent, that talent is completely foreign to the spirit of our country, and only serves to contaminate our artists.

The notion that the tree that nurtured the beautiful fruits of European culture might have become sickly (or decadent) was a perception shared by a great many intellectuals prior to the world wars. "What generation since Renan and Taine," asks Zeev Sternhell in *Ni Droite ni gauche,* "did not have the feeling of living the end of an epoch? . . . Who did more than the generation of 1890 to shake up the faith in Progress and in reason? . . . How can one make the war responsible for an ideological phenomenon to which Bergson and Sorel, Barrès and Le Bon, Michels and Pareto contributed several years before 1914?"[21] However, by discounting natural causes for the allegedly "sad" state of the "tree," and naming instead contamination, intentional poisoning by parasites, Rebatet, like other anti-Semitic Fascists, shifted the grounds of discussions to the guilty other, the Jew.

Furthermore, Rebatet's argument that Jewish artists had "infiltrated" the Paris art world and received more attention than their due, thanks to a well-organized network of partisan critics and dealers, was hardly new either. In 1929, the future Director of Fine Arts under Pétain, the art and architecture historian Louis Hautecoeur, had published a book, *Considérations sur Part d'aujourd'hui,* in which he had spoken of the dangers of the peaceful invasion of foreign artists and complained about their sense of publicity, "so that this foreign colony plays a role in our midst that their production does not always justify."[22] However, only by building on the subconscious fear of a killer-invader (vampirism) of French art could Rebatet utter his solution – doing to Jews what they allegedly did to others, "bleeding them dry" through exclusion from society as individuals, and as alleged practitioners of a certain form of art.

Rebatet on the Aryanization of Art

Although Rebatet entitled his article "Entre le Juif et le pompier," his image of a specifically Jewish art was as evanescent as descriptions of vampires by their viewers. Only the sentence "it is necessary to prune the purulent branches" hints at what it might be. For the image of pruning presupposes the idea of excess and of disequilibrium, while the image of organic decay and death is often associated with the Expressionism of Soutine and his followers (see Fig. 23). The view that Expressionism "mostly practised by Jews and other foreigners" had been a major trend of French art in the interwar years was shared by eminent art historians of modern art. René Hyghe, Bernard Dorival, and again Hautecoeur had made that point.[23] But only Rebatet had a definitive solution for reversing the trend: spread the word that the influence of Expressionism was "funeste," fatal, a harbinger of the death of art. De-vampirize, aryanize art, he said, and the threat of death would go away, leaving art in the state of timeless purity evoked by Baudelaire's famous lines: *"Là, tout n'est qu'ordre et beauté,/Luxe, calme et volupté."*

Aryanization in Rebatet's rhetoric did not exclusively imply the abject fantasy of "ethnic cleansing." Aryanization had an artistic counterpart – a purifying thrust. Had Rebatet believed that painting ought to be judged through "discovering the pictorial substance that lies truly within an oeuvre" – to quote his own words in his review of Venturi's *Peintres modernes,* he would have welcomed the search for structural essence in painting and sculpture attempted by the international modernisms of the 1920s. For Rebatet, however, artistic purification did not imply a forward glance but a turn of the clock back to an earlier time, a time prior to the invasion of France by the "Jewish virus." That at least is what emerges from his review of the Salon des Tuileries of 1941.

This exhibition, Rebatet told his viewers, was showing signs in the right direction:

> Jews, "métèques" from the orient and from central Europe, have fled at last. They exhibit in Cannes or Toulouse while waiting to depart forever. Disencumbered of their presence, the new Salon has now an air of probity and of elegance, I would say of good company, if it were not interpretable in a bourgeois sense, which is contrary to my thoughts.

However, Rebatet lamented, the new Salon was far from realizing the fantasy of a totally aryanized vision. The Jewish virus was far from dead: "In front of . . . the expressionism of André Marchand (among others) . . . we still find many signs of all the disorders, all the facilities, and all the stupid paradoxes that have brought us to low. . . ." The Expressionist influence was still present, and to his great regret, art had not yet "returned" to what it was before the Jewish virus had struck: "What is still lacking is a return to a denser painting, which knows how to define a shape, while keeping this freshness of sensation of which Corot and the Impressionists gave us the secret."[24]

What was so desirable about this "return" to Corot and the Impressionists? In purely artistic terms, both Corot and the Impressionists had, in his view, purified painting from the stranglehold of the academy without contamination by "foreign" influences. In extra-artistic terms, Corot and the Impressionists stood for a vision of the world and for a time when someone named Dreyfus could never have acceded to the rank of captain in the French army.

Coupled with the construction of a myth based on the demonization of the Jew was the construction of a new one, based on the fantasy of a purely "Aryan" society, and Aryan culture. In order to make the new myth attractive, not only did its creator have to promise eternal life and timeless pleasure, but the old one had to be painted in the most abject terms. By transforming the Jew into the equivalent of a virus-spreading vampire, it became possible to proclaim that the Jew must be killed before he destroyed French culture and society.

To read the art criticism of *Je suis partout* is to realize that Rebatet had far more in common with the vampire of the myth than did the Jews in France whom he was accusing of killing French culture. For, if Jews from central Europe, chased by the threat of Nazism, had descended "vampire-like" on a country already suffering from the effect of the Great Depression, bringing their talents and their traditions to bear on something called French culture, Rebatet welcomed them like the impaler Vlad of the vampire legend.

The Vampire in Anti-Semitic Propaganda

It is tempting to analyze Rebatet's yearning to expel the Jew from the art life of France in psychosexual terms, using Kristeva as a lead. Kristeva is convinced that the anti-Semitic craving of Céline has to do with his fantasy image of the male Jew's sexuality. "The fantasy of a Jewish threat, weighing against the Aryan world . . . in a period when, to the contrary, persecutions against the Jews were beginning, cannot be explained in any other way; but emanates directly out of that vision of the Jew as . . . issuing from the All in which he joys, and especially from the immediate sexualization of that *jouissance.*"[25]

Céline, she feels, is envious of the Jew's penis; secretly dreaming of being sodomized by him, hates to the point of abjection the thought of submitting to his desire. At the heart of this interpretation is the view that the projection of abjection onto another is inseparable from self-hatred, that is to say, dread of the abject repressed within the self. "To each ego its object, to each superego its abject."[26]

Substitute Rebatet's name for Céline and dread of vampires for fear of sodomists, and the anti-Semite emerges as a psychiatric monster, finding sexual pleasure at the sight of blood and of human body parts, living with the temptation of rape, entertaining the dream of "consuming" human flesh, and, exceptionally, acting on his or her perverse desire, as did Jack the Ripper, Gilles Garnier, Pierre Stumf, Clara Geissler, the originator of the vampire myth, Vlad the Impaler, and . . . Adolt Hitler. "In usual [psychiatric] language, the term vampirism designates . . . the worst of sadism – homicidal monomania, and all forms of necromania," writes Jean Goens, the French authority on real and mythical monsters.[27]

It is also tempting to read the anti-Semites' yearning for the total exclusion of Jews as a cover for the desire of Aryans to regain positions and territory held by Jews. Rebatet himself occupied a position at *Je suis partout* abandoned by François Fosca, a Jew, who returned to his native Switzerland after the Nazi Occupation of Paris. This interpretation harking back to the first vampire legend of Vlad the Impaler, turned into a bloodsucking monster by the usurpers of his throne, has no doubt a great deal of truth, but this form of desire is not specific enough to characterize the anti-Semite of the period 1940–45.

At a time when power was on the side of Fascism, the yearning to expel the Jew, it seems to me, shows evidence of a desire other than sexual perversion (although probably related to it); of more than a desire to recover lost territory (although again not inconsistent with that): it had to do with a passionate desire to help fashion the Fascist victory. For a Fascist like Rebatet, who did not hesitate to say in 1942 in *Les Décombres* (his memoirs) "I have never had an ounce of democratic blood in me," the destruction of Jews was necessary because Jews (and equally, abhorred Americans) were a major force standing in the way of triumphant Fascism, at a moment of crisis for democracy.[28] A cartoon entitled *Liberty . . . at last shines on the world!* (Fig. 13), which appeared in the collaborationist newspaper *La Gerbe* on May 25, 1944, shortly before the Normandy landings, makes that point quite clearly: *Liberty,* depicted as a sinister vampire-like giant (America) brandishing a menorah, is shown striding through the air, destroying everything in its path and threatening to "rape" what still stands of a "Fascist" Europe. Once again, threats from an imaginary vampire were being used to help the usurper keep his throne.[29]

The vampire myth always seems to revive in times of paroxystic tension in the social and political realms. Goens proposes in *Loups-garous* that the historical Vlad Tepes of Moldavia (formerly Wallachia), a remote region of central Europe, was "like Richard III, the posthumous victim of political propaganda, that made him a monster in order to justify the presence of illegitimate rivals."[30] Vlad Dracul, in order to protect his region from the Turks, imposed the dreadful punishment of impalement on his enemies, who in turn accused him of reveling in blood, hence his posthumous reputation as Dracul, the vampire, after his death in 1476. (Is there not irony in the fact that Vlad's war took place in central Europe and involved Christians against Moslems?)

The vampire myth was revived, according to Goens, in eighteenth-century France, a period when non-believers and Enlightenment philosophers were seriously questioning Roman Catholic dogma and naive superstition. The priest Dom Augustin Calmet wrote an extremely popular treatise proving the existence of supranatural presences including vampires, *Traité sur les apparitions des anges, des démons et des esprits et sur les revenants et vampires de Hongrie, de Bohême, de Moravie et de Silésie* (1746–51). It was a compendium of testimonies by travelers to central Europe who told of villagers visited by their dead at night, of bloodsucking incidents, and of bizarre deaths.

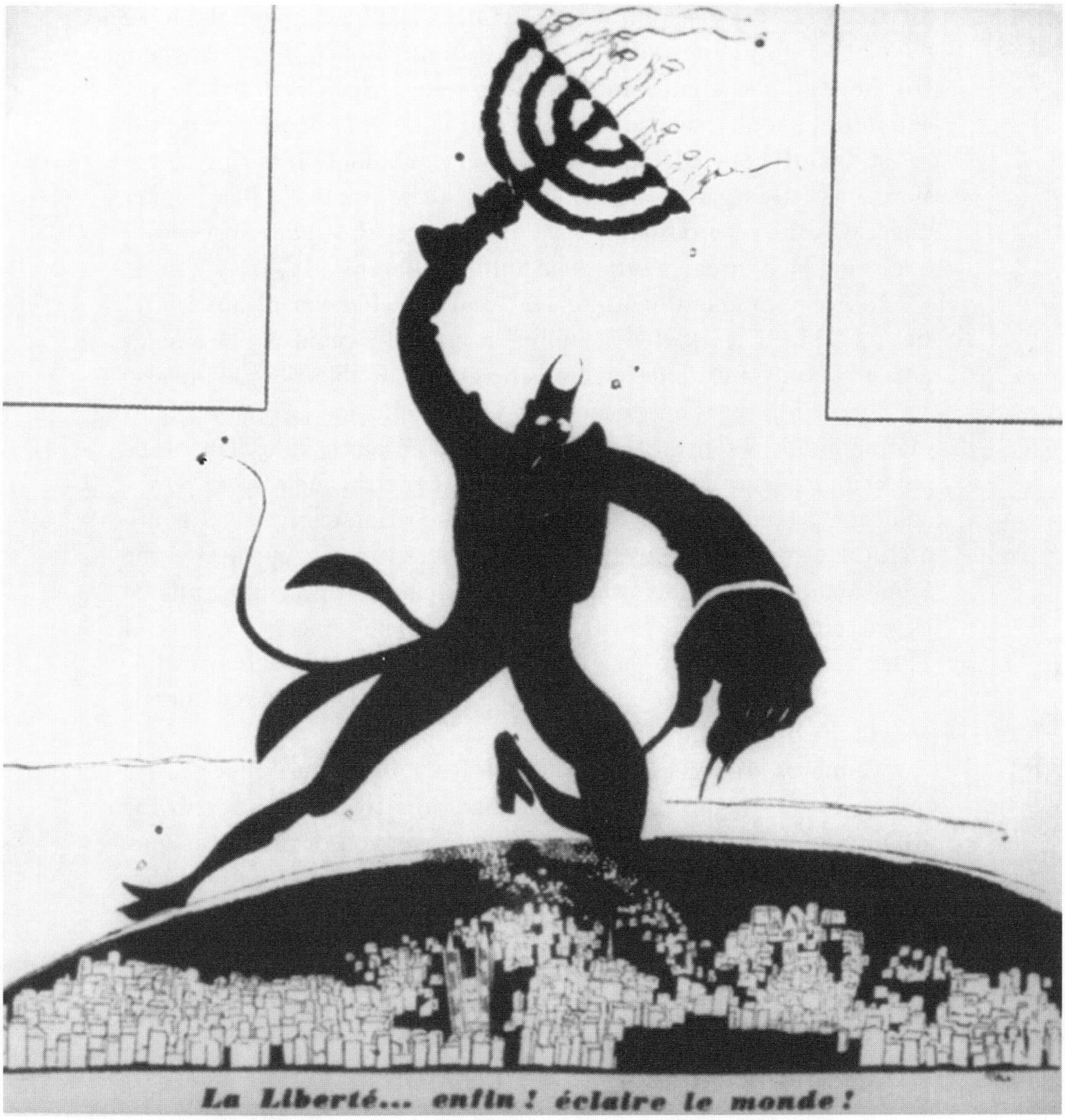

13. Mara, *Liberty . . . at last shines on the world!* (published in *La Gerbe,* May 25, 1944).

In 1897, at the height of the Victorian age in England, the most popular of gothic novels, *Dracula* by Bram Stoker, was published. For Goens, "it is significant that Victorian society, haunted by sex and death, should have engendered on the one hand Jack the Ripper . . . and on the other Dracula, the literary sublimation of this obsession, and a transparent metaphor of Jack the Ripper."[31] The Stoker novel was the inspiration of several vampire films, the most recent one being Neil Jordan's *Interview with the Vampire* (1994).

In every moment of its revival, and by whatever means it carries its "abject" work, the "vampire" is double-faced. For, like a magnet, it concentrates onto itself all the givens of abjection, while also acting as a foil for the defense of the status quo and against contamination by ideas contrary to those of the dominant group. The original vampire legend helped the usurper of the throne stay in power and set a precedent for the successful persecution of rivals, religious, political, economic, or cultural. The Calmet "vampire" protected the French church from the sweep of rationalism that was disseminated by the philosophers of the Enlightenment. The Dracula vampire of Bram Stoker put an obstacle in the way of women's sexual revolution. As for the vampiric virus of the age of AIDS, it stands in the way of the gay revolution.

Vampires are thus associated with fear of a "virus" that poses a threat to life – as in the tradition that runs from antiquity to the AIDS virus – but also with fear of the subversion of the status quo, "social fear." It is that enduring feature of the vampire myth that can explain its usefulness to anti-Semitic Fascists, among them critics of modernist culture during the Occupation years in Vichy France.

The Break of 1943

4

"Abstract" Art as a Veil

Tricolor Painting in Vichy France

On January 30, 1943, two and a half years after the occupation of Paris by the Nazis and a few weeks after the Allies had landed in North Africa (November 8, 1942), an article entitled "La Peinture bleu blanc rouge" (tricolor painting) signed by the painter Jean Bazaine[1] appeared in *Comoedia,* the leading cultural weekly during the Occupation.[2] Like all officially sanctioned publications at that time, this literary and artistic review (whose roster of contributors included Colette, Jean Cocteau, Jean Giraudoux, and even Jean-Paul Sartre) conformed to the regime of censorship then in effect.[3] In his essay Bazaine wrote that a nation does not choose its flag by change, that the colors of its flag coincide with the deepest instincts of its people, including its artists;[4] he also expressed his belief that "through the subtle rigour of a few pure tones, a young and fresh reality was about to be realized in painting, so obsessive that it would impose itself as a daily reality."[5]

First published in the *Art Bulletin,* Vol. 54, no. 2, June 1992.

Bazaine did not name the artists who might fulfill his prophecy. They were, besides himself, Francisco Borès, Maurice Estève, André Fougeron, Léon Gischia, Charles Lapicque, Jean Le Moal, Alfred Manessier, Edouard Pignon, Gabriel Robin, Gustave Singier, and Jacques Villon, twelve painters who were about to exhibit together at the Galerie de France (February 6–March 4, 1943) under the title "Douze Peintres d'aujourd'hui." Nor did Bazaine attempt to link them through their style, although he did point out, by connecting them to Impressionism and Fauvism, that for the third time in modern art history, a coloristic fervor was manifesting itself in French painting. In the catalogue essay for the exhibition, the critic Gaston Diehl contrasted the label "abstract" that had been flung at the artists with his own reading of their novelty, the spiritual as well as artistic cleansing that their art represented. To Diehl, the painters' spontaneity, sincerity, humility – traits often associated with the medieval craftsman inspired by the Catholic faith – denoted their "primitivizing" outlook.

That a new national impetus toward avant-gardism in painting was able to assert itself in occupied Paris is not concealed in histories of modern art that came out of France right after the Second World War. For a long time, the path to innovation had been blocked, such histories explained, and artists had no idea in what direction to go. Painters and sculptors could not look back to academicism, nor did they know how to forge ahead, without repeating what had already been done by the older generation. Curiously, the 1940 disaster on the battlefield had marked a before and an after in art. "After the armistice of 1940, a single option remained for the French, it seems: to gather all of their energies, and to move forward. . . . And that is what they did, from 1940 on. . . . Once again, painting participated in the life of the French conscience. . . . Painting moved forward," one reads in *Les Etapes de la peinture française contemporaine* by Bernard Dorival.[6] "And who, among those who pride themselves on loving the arts, would have suspected that at the very moment, in the middle of catastrophe, an important evolution in painting was underway?" Pierre Francastel asks in *Nouveau dessin, nouvelle peinture.* "The latent crisis explodes and, from 1941 onward, in the midst of the Occupation, French painting responds to the invader by rallying all its forces of audacity," René Huyghe asserts in *Les Contempo-*

rains.[8] Pointing to the development of the aforementioned painters, these art historians concurred that this "forward move," this "important evolution," this new "audacity," had to do with a synthesis of Cubist form and Fauve color, with the abandonment – to varying degrees – of representation, and with an occasional glance at the Romanesque and the Gothic.

Contestable as the achievements of this new vanguard may be – abstract art was hardly a novelty in the 1940s, and few of the artists involved in this vanguard gave up representation altogether – the shock effect of "tricolor" painting in the context of other art seen during the Occupation period in Paris cannot be denied. At a time when most galleries were exhibiting timid proto-Impressionism and academic realism, tricolor painting probably did convey to its audience a sense of new energy and change.

This paper will examine the validity of the claim made by René Huyghe, among others, that "the art of experimentalism and boldness thus naturally found itself allied to the Resistance."[9] I will test the underlying assumption of an automatic link between formal experiment and resistance to mainstream culture and politics, and I will also question the reverse side of this assumption. For, as I hope to demonstrate, Resistance-inspired images of this period were not concerned with "experimentalism and boldness," but relied on codes of recognizability.

First, I will argue that the pictorial "move forward" does not date from 1940–41, as proposed by Dorival and Huyghe, but from later in the Occupation period. It will be seen that its origin was predated to give credence to the myth that French artists were opposed to Vichy and to the Nazis from the beginning. Calling it "the myth of resistancialism," Henry Rousso describes this construct as "a process that sought: first, the marginalization of what the Vichy regime was, and the systematic minimalization of its hold on French society . . . ; second, the creation of an *objet de mémoire*, the 'Resistance,' far greater than the algebraic sum of the acting minority who were resisters . . . ; third, the assimilation of this 'Resistance' into the entire nation, notably a characteristic of Gaullist resistancialism."[10] In the art world, thanks to the myth of resistancialism, art history had been written as if opportunistic turnabouts had not taken place; and the title of resister had gone to those who had made a pictorial breakthrough, irrespective of their politics. Further, it will be shown that the artists' motive in "moving forward" is compromised by the way this art was used by Vichy and by the Nazis.

In recent years, the issue of artistic reception, which can imply guilt by association with the wrong contexts, has received renewed attention. The possibility, for example, that American Abstract Expressionist paintings were used as weapons of international maneuvering by the American government during the Cold War has often been put forward."[11]

The use of reputedly anti-establishment abstract artworks as decorative elements and their presence in politically incorrect contexts has also called into question the ability of abstract art to "resist" economic appropriation by the "bourgeois" class. On the subject of a photo by the *Vogue* photographer Cecil Beaton, showing Pollock paintings as a backdrop for high-style models posing in expensive clothes, the critic T. J. Clark argues the need to respect Pollock's utopian intentions – pointing the way from easel to mural – and his "meditations on medium,"[12] but he acknowledges his unease with respect to the photograph in *Vogue*.

Political and economic discussions relating to the artistic reception of abstract painting have so far skirted the issue of the propaganda use that can be made of "free" experimental abstract art, when it is seen and discussed in a country whose citizens are deprived of the most elementary freedoms and subject to arbitrary arrests, deportations, torture, and death, as was the case in Vichy France. While Clark writes that "an art that does without the figure lays itself open to being used as a ground on which . . . *another* figuration can take place,"[13] I would propose that French tricolor abstract or semi-abstract painting was used as a metaphoric veil *behind* which unimaginably tragic scenarios could and in fact did take place.

Given this was the case, how could the Resistance make itself heard through art? In France during the period 1940–44, the most unambiguously Resistance art – art made by participants in the artists' Resistance network and sold for the Resistance cause – was not formally vanguard. Indeed, in the urgency of conveying an unequivocal message, Resistance art relied on a variety of mimetic modes, from old-fashioned allegory to expressionist distortions to classical portraiture with a satirical intent.

That Vichy and the German occupiers received nonconformist productions favorably should not lead to the conclusion that conservative taste and conservative politics are not repeatedly linked. The Vichy case simply demonstrates that politically correct art need not refer to a formally vanguard model any more than a politically correct stance necessarily goes with a formally advanced art practice.

Hitler's hatred for avant-gardism made martyrs of many nonconformist artists in all the countries of Europe under Nazi occupation. But the positive reception of certain nonconformist productions in France shows that avant-garde artists were not all martyrs. However, neither were they ideological "collaborationists," individuals who actually wished for the victory of Germany and who shared Hitler's anti-Semitism and anti-Communism. Rather, their behavior at the beginning of the Occupation tends to conform to what the historian Stanley Hoffmann has called "la collaboration d'Etat," a form of collaboration that grew up in France after the Armistice of June 1940, when a French state was installed under Pétain, allegedly protecting the interests of France, but at the price of obedience to the demands of the German victor.

Dorival and Huyghe concur that the new artistic trend began with an exhibition entitled "Painters in the French Tradition," which opened at Galerie Braun, rue Louis-Le-Grand, in Paris, on May 10, 1941; that an association for culture called Jeune France sponsored it; and that the painter Jean Bazaine, head of the visual arts section of Jeune France, and André Lejard, an editor of art books, were responsible for the selections.[14]

Thanks to an article by Jean Bazaine in the *Nouvelle Revue française* dated August 1941, the names of the participants are known – a medley of newcomers to the Paris art scene: Jean Bazaine, Alfred Manessier, Gustave Singier, Jean Le Moal, François Desnoyer, Charles Walch, Edouard Pignon, Maurice Estève, Charles Lapicque, Suzanne Roger, André Beaudin, Francisco Borès, Lucien Coutaud, Jean Bertholle, Berçot, Jean Lasne, Lucien Lautrec, Raymond Legueult.[15] "Shortly before the opening," according to Bazaine, the show was visited by two resplendent German officers. They looked briefly around, and went out without saying a word."[16] What they saw remains an enigma to this day, as the exhibition left few traces.

Sarah Wilson, the first art historian in recent years to show an interest in the art of the Occupation period, surmises that the Braun exhibition, "while it mostly comprised landscapes and still lifes painted before the war – 'sacramental pears conservatively ringed in violet or red' – was distinguished by the religious strain running through some of the young painters"[17] (Fig. 14). Wilson attributes this religious strain to the "esoteric tendencies" of a Lyons-based movement called Témoignage,[18] which had included the painters Manessier, Bertholle, and Le Moal, and to the involvement of Jean Bazaine in the "personalist" review *Esprit*.[19] The memoirs of Gino Severini further reveal that in the early 1930s a number of artists, including Chagall, Beaudin, Gilles de la Tourette, Tériade, Edmond Humeau, Ivan Denis, Pablo Gargallo, Pierre Courthion, Suzanne Roger, and himself, briefly entertained the idea that they could form an artistic group based on the uplifting views of *Esprit*, and they apparently were encouraged in that direction by Emmanuel Mounier, the editor-in-chief of that review. A first and second manifesto were prepared. The second one, drafted by Severini, concluded:

> We are against: eclecticism, confusion of genres, "mannerisms," "stylisms," aestheticism, academicism, and all spiritual cowardice.
>
> We are for: authenticity, purity, all forms of beauty that are rich in spiritual content, frankness, honesty, absolute sincerity, toward ourselves as much as toward art and all of its problems, even the social, political, or economic ones that might arise.
>
> For we are not indifferent to these problems (we no longer believe in the ivory tower of art), but we insist that, our common bases being eternal truths, and the work that we are proposing to do aiming mostly at absolute values, we intend to keep our spiritual freedom outside and above the realm of the contingent.[20]

A willingness to confront social, economic, and political problems, accompanied by an absolutist view of art as "outside and above" the contingent, promised controversy. According to Severini, the artists could not agree on this wording of the manifesto to be published, and the group disbanded.

Not surprisingly, the formal features of the religious strain

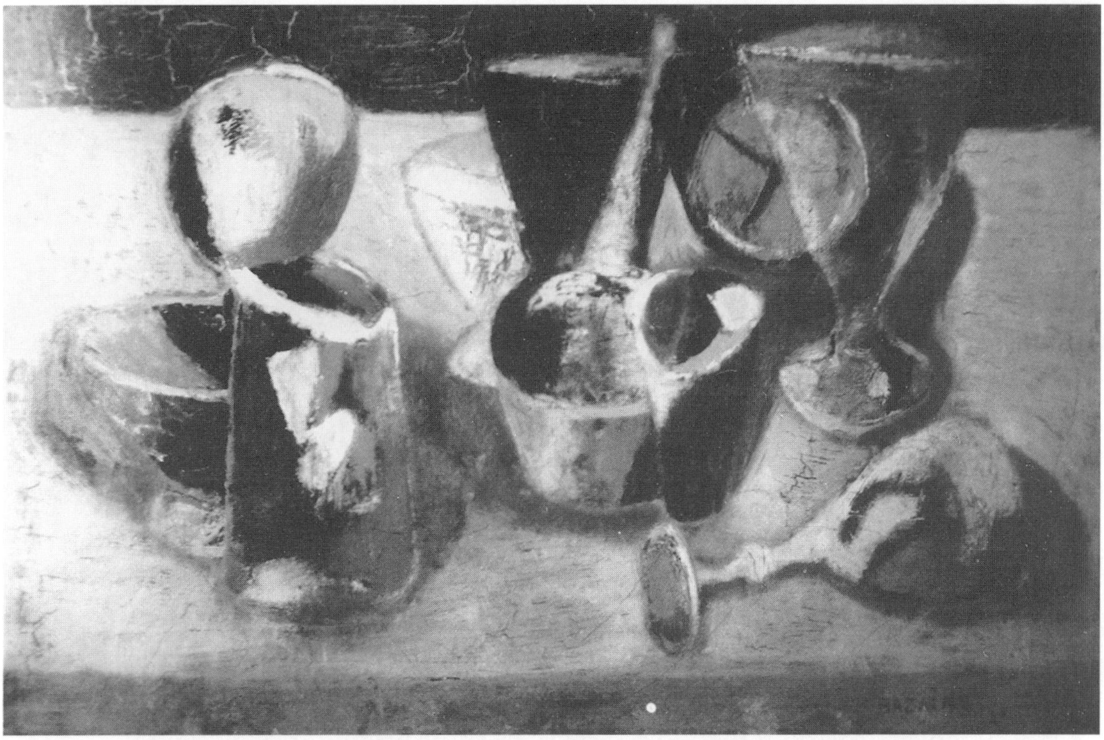

14. Jean Bazaine, *Glassware,* 1937. Dimensions unavailable. Grenoble, Musée de Grenoble (photo: Jacques Faujour, Paris).

remain vague. And if Manessier, Le Moal, Bertholle, Bazaine, and probably Suzanne Roger, five out of the twenty-some artists in the Braun exhibition, evinced some sense of the spiritual in their work, what of the others?

In his August 1941 article in the *Nouvelle Revue française,* Bazaine pointed out that not one of the artists in his show had earned the Prix de Rome,[21] a key remark meant to distinguish his group from the artists who, during that same period in 1941, had exhibited their paintings and sculpture at the ultraconservative Salon de la Société des Artistes Français, a beehive of academicians and former Prix de Rome winners, presided over by a blatant collaborator, the sculptor Henri Bouchard, whose admiration for the cultural aspect of the Nazi regime was well known. Unlike Bazaine, Bouchard was in favor of the creation in France of an artists' corporation that would emulate Nazi-invented "art chambers," designed to benefit the ideological allies of the regime and to exclude political, racial, and aesthetic undesirables.[22] The absence of Prix de Rome winners did not, however, imply formal audacity on the part of Bazaine's group. Including any art form to the left of the far right on the spectrum of recent artistic possibilities, it must have been an eclectic assembly. Bazaine himself admits today, "I took what I could find."[23]

But even if a burst of avant-gardism had taken place in French painting as early as May 1941, it would hardly have been Resistance-inspired, given the sponsorship by Jeune France of the May 1941 Braun show. Jeune France, a cultural association organized in January 1941 by the music expert Pierre Schaeffer, was subsidized by the French Ministry of Education and Youth, and it counted four Vichy officials on its board.[24] Although Jeune France was abruptly disbanded by a Vichy edict dated March 20, 1942 for allegedly misspending its funds and "moving in a direction inimical to the government's goals,"[25] the guiding lights of the association belonged to an intellectual milieu, the "neither left nor right" milieu of the review *Esprit,* with which some at Vichy sympathized. Emmanuel Mounier, the editor of *Esprit* and a board member, was an influential person in Jeune France, as was the painter Jean Bazaine, who headed the visual arts section of Jeune France in the occupied zone.

I have already noted the tenor of the aesthetic program of *Esprit,* its emphasis on purity, authenticity, spiritual courage, and abandonment of the "ivory tower of art." But in the 1930s Mounier had already spoken harshly in the pages of *Esprit* against both capitalism and Communism, and had lamented the state of decadence of Third Republic politics, and he would continue to do so in the same publication after the Pétain regime was installed. As the occupiers became more and more demanding, and the Vichy regime acceded to these demands, Mounier, realizing that his allegiance to Vichy entailed serious moral compromises, turned against the regime and joined a Resistance network. But, commenting on a February 1941 article by Mounier in *Esprit* entitled "On the Intelligentsia in Times of Crisis," Zeev Sternhell remarks, "It is difficult to see in this text a call [in favor] of the Resistance."[26] That Bazaine had not questioned the racial censorship then in effect further diminishes the claim to early resistance among the artists that has been presented by Dorival and Huyghe.[27] Indeed, it would appear that the pictorial breakthrough noted by these art historians came about slowly and in several stages, the final episode taking place after the successes of the Allies had given heart to the true or recently converted partisans of democracy and freedom in art.[28]

The official response to the May 1941 exhibition revealed to French artists that the occupiers were not going to impose their own set of values; in 1942, a show of early Fauve paintings took place at the Galerie de France, and even the Cubist work of Jacques Villon was passing censorship. Some of the artists from the Braun show cited at the beginning of this text began to heighten their colors and to tamper with spatial illusionism in their otherwise easy-to-read figurative images, although no evidence suggests that there was a rush to paint in red, white, and blue at that point. (In the case of Charles Lapicque, red and blue harmonies predate the war.) Medieval French churches, as well as a recently opened museum in Paris full of replicas of Romanesque frescoes and sculpture, the Musée des Monuments Français on the Place du Trocadéro, provided the Braun exhibitors with a primitivitizing iconography at a moment of spiritual and formal disarray.

In 1942, conventional motifs, such as still life or a figure in an interior, continued to abound within the group about to be named "tricolor" by Bazaine. In a painting by Maurice Estève, *Woman with Shopping Bag* (1942; Fig. 15), figure and ground are brought together in a continuum of brittle shapes, and yellow light pervades the work. So full of resigned dignity is the simplified image of the young woman reading, seated by a jumble of kitchen supplies within sight of an empty shopping basket, that a title such as *The Madonna of the Shopping Basket* readily suggests itself. In 1941 and 1942, Edouard Pignon painted a number of maternity scenes in bright, flatly applied colors (though not those of the French flag), similarly bathed in golden light.

In the most formally daring of these interior paintings of 1942, the color harmonies found in the kitchen or simple dining room are repeated in the landscape seen through a window. In Bazaine's *Still Life in Front of a Window* of that year, which features a chair in the foreground, a chaotic array of objects dispersed on a table-top, and a Cubist landscape framed by a window, the entire surface is unified as a patchwork of acid red, blue, and green lozenge-like shapes. Jean Bazaine, in a postwar interview with Viveca Bosson, thus described his formal breakthrough that year: "It is in 1942, with objects in front of the window, that a violent coloristic transposition is beginning to upset and re-create the space of the picture, forms and colors from the outside landscape invading the room, penetrating objects."[29] Having thus "re-created the space of the picture," Bazaine still had to reach the point where he could do away with nature as a referent. In *Mass for an Armed Man* (Fig. 16), signed and dated July 1944 (shortly after the Normandy landings but before the liberation of Paris), a figure in armor can be detected enmeshed in the grid-like surface. Manessier, Singier, Le Moal were other tricolor painters who followed a parallel course at about the same moment.

Not only does the abstract and semi-abstract art of the period by these artists fail to show a clear message of resistance in its genesis, but the context in which it evolved, the story of the paintings' "public life," is equally revealing on this score. Indeed, far from emerging in a clandestine manner, the paintings of 1942–44 by Estève, Bazaine, Pignon, Manessier, and also Gischia, Lapicque, and others, were openly displayed not only in private galleries but also in official contexts throughout the Occupation period. The works were

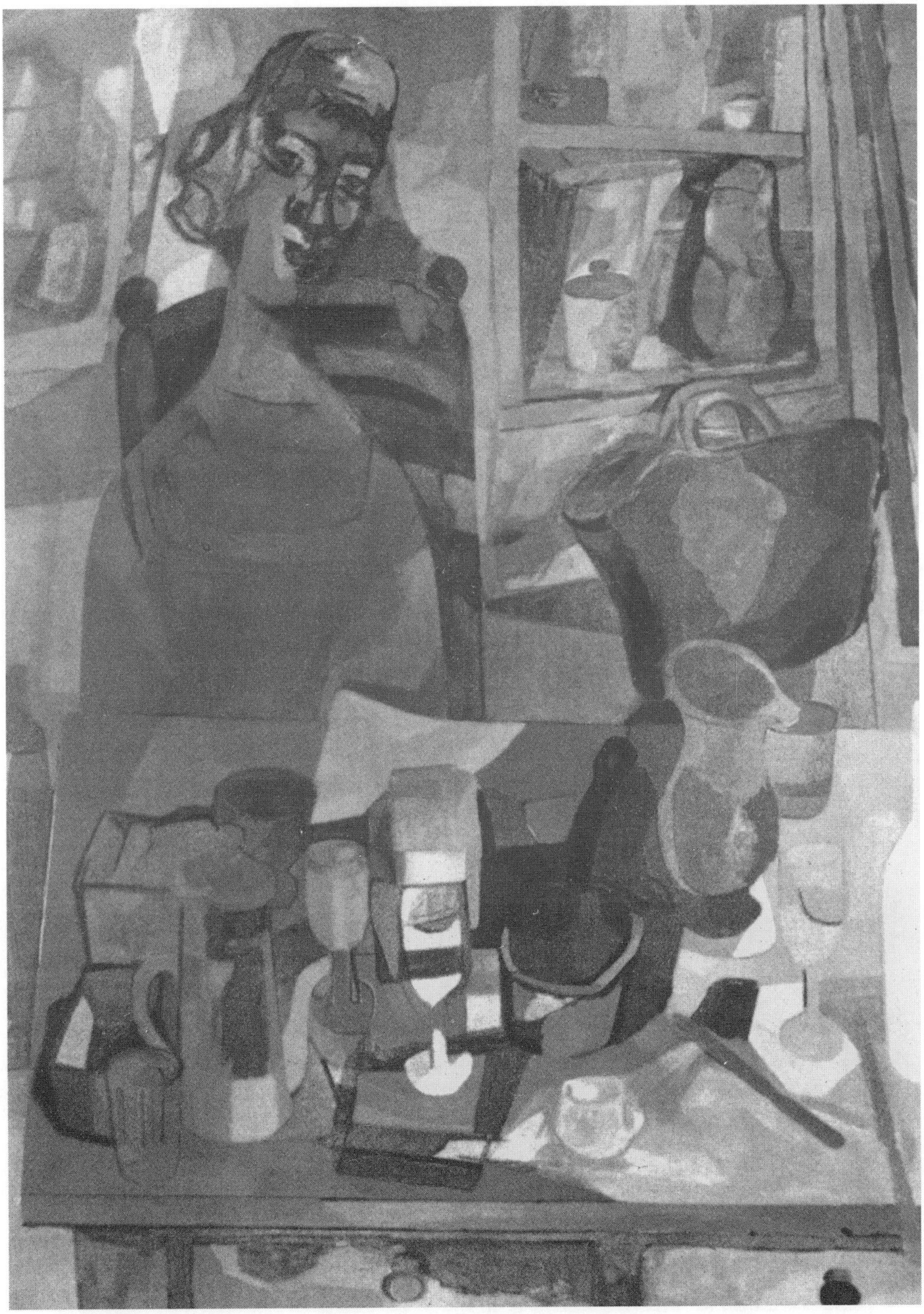

15. Maurice Estève, *Woman with Shopping Bag*, 1942. Dimensions unavailable. Private collection, France (photo: Michèle C. Cone).

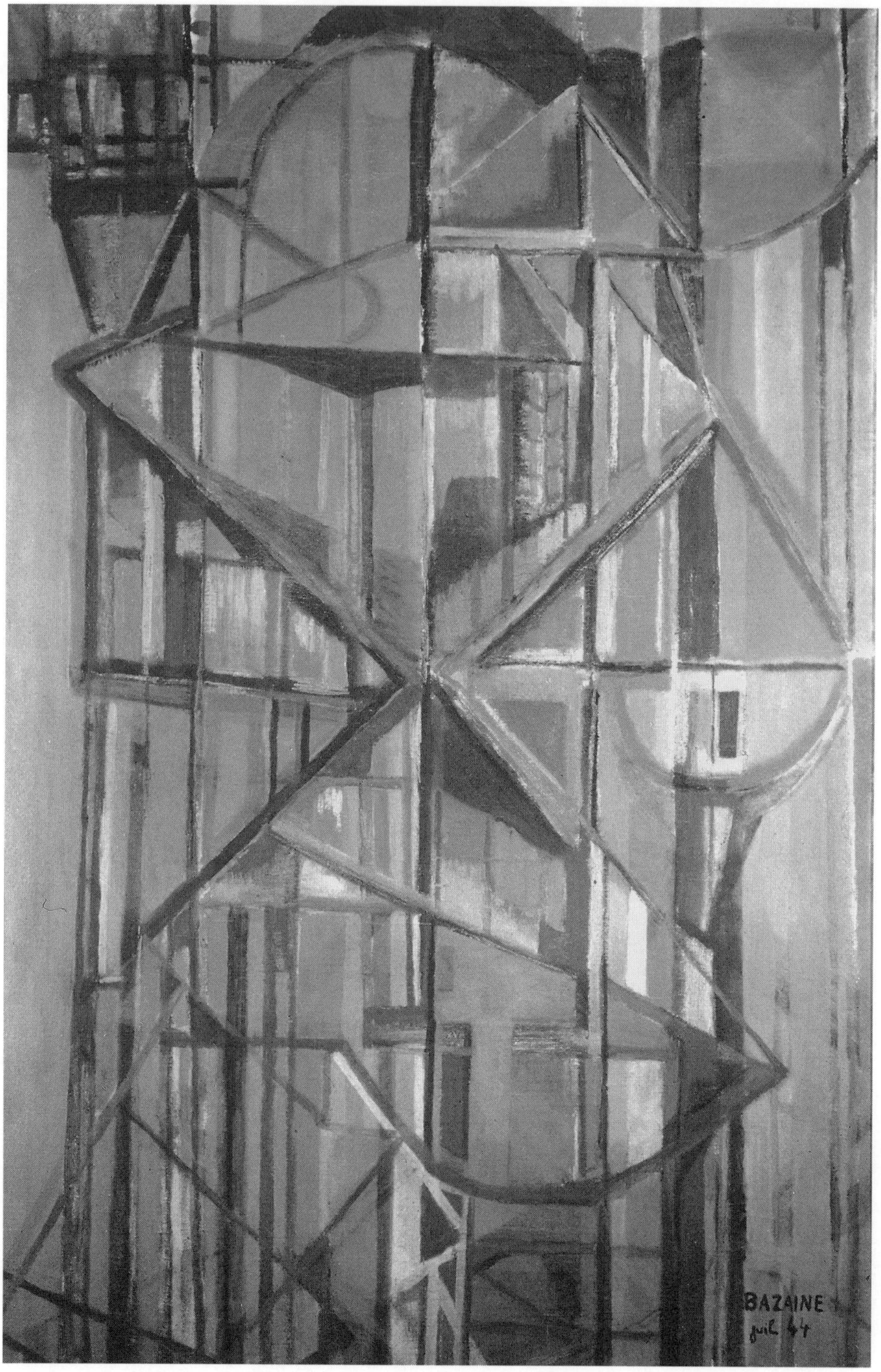

16. Jean Bazaine, *Mass for an Armed Man,* 1944. Dimensions unavailable. Paris, Collection Mr. and Mrs. Adrien Maeght (photo: Galerie Maeght, Paris).

routinely discussed in the official press, where they received the expected mixture of condemnation and accolades.

Galerie Jeanne Bûcher, Galerie Friedland, and Galerie de France included works by these artists in group exhibitions during the Occupation years.[30] Galerie Louis Carré gave them solo shows, and the yearly Salon d'Automne included them. Some of their paintings were put on view when the Musée National d'Art Moderne (run by the French government) was hurriedly opened in the summer of 1942 in its new location at the Palais de Tokyo.[31] Some of their paintings also traveled to Switzerland and to Spain in 1942–43 under the official auspices of the Action Française Artistique à l'Etranger.[32]

What undoubtedly gave the painters their greatest support as "resisters" was the way their art was attacked in some of the official publications of those years. The Fascist anti-Semite Lucien Rebatet referred to a show of five tricolor painters at Galerie de France in the fall of 1943 as "the most remarkable collection of mistakes, a laborious rehashing of Cézanne, Picasso, Rouault, Lhote, a bunch of aborted deadheads, full of arbitrariness and impotence," and announced that France was mistakenly returning to "its judaic sweets *(ses friandises juives)*.[33] Jean Marc Campagne, known for his catalogue essay on Arno Breker, the official sculptor of the Third Reich, wrote in his regular column in *Les Nouveaux Temps* in early 1943: "The farce of abstraction has lasted long enough. If, in certain milieux, there is an interest in prolonging it, let it not be qualified as a Renaissance with a capital letter."[34]

Whatever aura the art of the tricolor painters may be said to have gained from being maligned by these two critics is tarnished by the positive reception they received in other official publications of those years: not only *Comoedia* (Jean Bazaine), but *Aujourd'hui* (Gaston Diehl),[35] *Le Rouge et le bleu* (Roger Lesbats, alias Frank Elgar),[36] *Confluences* (Bernard Dorival),[37] and – most surprising of all – in a German-language newspaper for German troops in France with a regular cultural page in French, the *Pariser Zeitung.*

In an article entitled "Visage Français, considérations sur le Salon d'Automne," dated October 24, 1943, Paul Strecker, a German painter but also a critic, analyzed tricolor painting impartially and rather favorably. Instead of condemning it outright as Judeo-Marxist and decadent for its remoteness from National Socialist artistic criteria, he noticed the formalism of the art, its "innate Frenchness," its vaguely Catholic connotations; and he observed with satisfaction the total absence of Surrealist influence:

> French art having become national by necessity . . . has mobilized its autochthonous forces. Foreign influences have been hurriedly set aside. . . .
>
> After Surrealism, the last artistic movement, mostly promoted by foreigners, was set aside due to the departure of its practitioners, . . . it was possible to discover more flourishing plants. Fauvism, abandoned too soon by its founders, appeared to be a favorable terrain on which to build. . . .
>
> Painters are going back to purely formal problems. There is no pathos in their subjects. . . . They build their pictures tridimensionally by means of violently colored stains, somewhat reminiscent of the vivid colors of old stained glass.[38]

Could it be that the images in question were sufficiently distinct from the stock images of National Socialism to give the artists the appearance of political courage yet not subversive enough to alarm the German censor? According to Albert Speer's memoirs, Hitler, upon hearing that there was decadent painting at the Salon d'Automne, exclaimed, "Are we to be concerned with the intellectual soundness of the French people? Let them degenerate if they want to, all the better for us!"[39]

The Nazis' tolerance for French "degenerate" painting also reveals their masterly use of art as propaganda. "Advanced" painting in the French tradition was a "diversion" in the double meaning of the word: it kept the usual public for art entertained, and it acted as a metaphorical veil, simulating normalcy. It gave the illusion that both Vichy and the Nazis respected vanguard culture, and it served as a false symbol of artistic freedom, distracting attention from innumerable and unforgivable instances of total disrespect for human rights on the part of Vichy and the Nazi occupier.

As is all too well known, the persecution of Jews included Jewish artists and their production. Paintings by Soutine, Modigliani, and other Jewish artists risked being slashed by censor-visitors during exhibitions, and the dealers who dared to show them put themselves at risk. Among the victims of the Holocaust were the sculptor

Moishe Kogan, vice president of the Salon d'Automne before the war, Otto Freundlich, caught by the Gestapo in his hideaway, an abandoned old tower near the Spanish border, and many others of lesser renown.[40] A directive from Vichy resulted in the exclusion of Jews from all Salons and instituted a procedure at the Salon d'Automne whereby exhibitors were required to sign a register certifying that they were French and not Jewish. The Vichy government forbade the exhibition of artists who had left France and thus lost their French nationality;[41] and the Franco government in Spain put pressure on Vichy to prevent Picasso from exhibiting.[42]

Art officials, art critics, and art historians were dismissed from their positions on political and racial grounds (the *Statut des Juifs);* Georges Huisman, the head of the fine arts department at the Ministry of Education, was dismissed because of his religion.[43] On the basis of his leftist politics, Jean Cassou was let go just after being named head curator at the Musée National d'Art Moderne in Paris.[44] Henri Focillon was expelled from the Collège de France because he was a Freemason.[45] Those who could write or teach were expected to censor themselves. By uniting under the banner of their shared Aryan Frenchness, Catholic traditions, and roots in French modernisms and French primitivism, the tricolor painters censored themselves as well.

That there was anti-Nazi sentiment hiding in art made at that time and authentic resistance in the artists' milieu is also undeniable. Fautrier produced a series of paintings dedicated to the memory of civilian victims of Nazi reprisals, his *Hostage* paintings; they were not, however, publicly exhibited until after the liberation of Paris. It is my contention[46] that Picasso's wartime production – although cautiously thought through, and mostly seen by the artist's visitors at that time – expressed the sentiments and fears of those whose lives hung by a thread. Although he did not have it in his power to save the life of Max Jacob,[47] Picasso made generous gifts to stateless artist compatriots forced to live in complete hiding.[48] He illustrated poems by friends in the Resistance, as did the painters Fautrier, Gromaire, Pignon, and Fougeron, among others.

Romanin, an etcher, watercolorist, and cartoonist before the war, was none other than Jean Moulin, better known for his political career and his leading role in the Resistance movement. Among the tricolor painters, Pignon and Fougeron, both of them Communist artists, were active in a Resistance network called Le Front National des Arts,[49] under whose auspices an album of lithographs – devastatingly anti-Nazi and anti-Vichy – was published in 1944.

Of the twelve lithographs included in the album, not one is done in a formally advanced style. Some depict Nazi atrocities expressionistically, others allegorically: in *A mort la bête* by Fougeron, a hand strangles the neck of an open-mouthed Fuhrer spewing out bones, skulls, and crosses onto a pile of corpses. Several images caricatured Vichy officials. A portrait of Pétain by Pierre Ladureau is entitled *Judas.* Designed like an enlarged postage stamp, and marked as worth thirty deniers (the sum Judas received for betraying Christ), its border adorned with swastikas and the marshal's emblem (the "francisque"), it depicts the head of Pétain, drawn in a rigorous classical style, typical of Nazi-approved draftsmanship, looking directly at the viewer. Pétain wears not the French marshal's képi but the military headgear of a German SS officer. On his collar appear both the Nazi and the Vichy emblems. All these elements converge toward the message that Pétain had betrayed France and was collaborating with the Germans. This album, printed in an edition of three hundred, was clandestinely distributed, so its impact was necessarily limited.

Indeed, one of the most arduous challenges for an artist in an extremely repressive society is to make art that not only encourages resistance but also reaches many viewers. The artist must avoid the ire of the censor but also avoid diluting the message to the point where it becomes "double-edged" – as Derrida has claimed for Paul de Man's wartime writings, and as might also be said of French tricolor painters, since at that time both Marshal Pétain and General de Gaulle were acting in the name of the French tricolor flag. A successful work would pass the censor despite his suspicion that the painting might be subversive, and be exhibited with its pro-Resistance message intact. *Homage to Jacques Callot* (1942) by Francis Gruber (1912–1948), a friend of the poet Antonin Artaud in the 1930s, and an active member of the Resistance network of artists during the Occupation years, comes closest to answering all these conditions (Fig. 17). The work was exhibited in 1942 in a group show at Galerie Friedland. Each network was intended as an homage

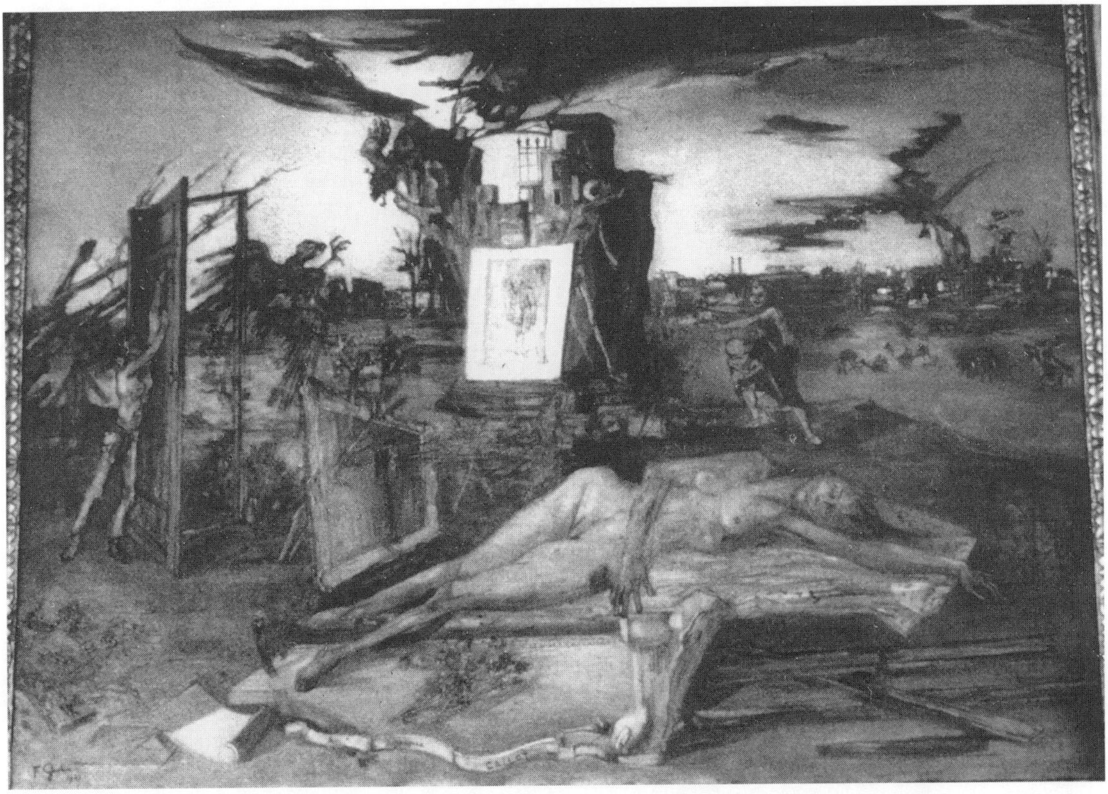

17. Francis Gruber, *Homage to Jacques Callot,* 1942. Dimensions unavailable. Menton, Collection Jacques Bazaine (photo: Michèle C. Cone).

to an admired ancestor.[50] Gruber's painting shows a young woman lying nude and defeated in a landscape of devastation, a tricolor bouquet in her right hand. Fearful that she might be read as a symbol of France after the Armistice by the viewing public, and that it might lead them to want to punish those who had defeated her, the German censor ordered the bouquet painted over. In the painting today, the memory of the bouquet is evoked by tiny droplets of red, white, and blue paint in the area where it used to be. But that is not all. Jacques Callot, to whose work Gruber was paying homage, came from Lorraine and is said to have refused an offer to paint the defeat of Nancy for the king of France, Louix XIII, claiming that his allegiance was to Charles, duke of Lorraine.[51] Gruber's painting is neither vanguard nor successful as a work of art, but its secondary message through its citation of Callot, to abandon King Philip (Pétain) and follow Charles, duke of Lorraine (Charles de Gaulle was from Lorraine), was unequivocally pro-Resistance.

This paper certainly cannot resolve the issue of modernist practice vs. Resistance posture. It suggests that one should take seriously the "guilt by association" argument invoked earlier, even if, as T. J. Clark asks: "Is not any art of real complexity fated to be used, recruited, and misread?"[52] To judge by the images that passed censorship, formal avant-gardism is not necessarily symptomatic of a free society, and it may simply serve to simulate freedom. On the other hand, there may be instances when, in order to express without ambiguity the views of a resistance consciousness, old-fashioned allegory and even straightforward classicism are entirely appropriate modes. Thus, as Linda Nochlin pointed out in her review of the 1981 exhibition *Les Réalismes* at the Centre Pompidou, there is "immense difficulty . . . in attaching a specific political position to a style per se, especially such a wide-ranging and ill-defined style as the realisms represented here."[53] Mimetic modes have acquired negative connotations because they are associated with fiercely authoritarian regimes, such as Communism and Nazism. But to dismiss manifestations of a return to the figurative in art since 1915 on ideological grounds, by assuming that there is a "simple causal connection, a mechanical reaction, by which growing political oppression necessarily and irreversibly generates traditional representation,"[54] is to overlook the fact that no single style "'expresses' the world view of a given period."[55] A semblance of freedom can be signified by the veil of abstraction as easily as lies can be told by means of representations.[56]

The situation in France that has been analyzed in this paper is hardly a unique case in the annals of artistic culture arising from the ashes of a fallen regime. In this century, drastic changes in political regimes have often brought with them the enthusiasm of formerly ignored or maligned vanguard artistic groupings. What distinguishes the French case from the others, however, is that the government that substituted itself for the Third Republic had no real autonomy and depended for its survival on its willingness to collaborate with Nazi Germany, and to encourage the French people to do likewise. Frequently, the ability to make a living and – in the case of artists – to exhibit one's work (be it conformist or vanguard) required the tacit endorsement of Nazi racial policies. One example is the signing by well-known artists, among them Jacques Villon and Charles Despiau, of the Salon d'Automne register, the stated goal of which was the exclusion of Jewish artists.

No doubt many artists shared the reaction of the French *lycée* teacher Simone de Beauvoir, who, in order to continue her teaching, signed a form certifying that she was French and not Jewish: "I found it repugnant to sign, but no one refused, for most of my colleagues as well as for me, there was no alternative."[57] The outright pro-Nazi "ideological collaborationism"[58] that taints the writings of literary figures such as Céline, Lucien Rebatet, Pierre Drieu La Rochelle, and Robert Brasillac, may not have had its exact visual counterpart during the Occupation years, but with the Pétain regime, France and some French artists embarked on a treacherous course nevertheless.

5

Jean Paulhan and His Artist Friends

DURING THE OCCUPATION, Georges Braque, Jean Fautrier, Jean Dubuffet, and Chaim Soutine had in common the patronage of Jean Paulhan (1884–1968), one of the few prewar figures of the Parisian intellectual community to remain influential during the war and for several years afterwards.[1] Paulhan either wrote about these artists, proselytized on their behalf, or bought their work. Unlike the *Bleu Blanc Rouge* painters, who thought they were creating a non-decadent avant-garde, and the *Between-the-Jew-and-the-Pompier* contingent of the romantic realists supported by the anti-Semitic critic Lucien Rebatet,[2] the artists that Paulhan admired assumed their "decadent" vanguardism despite the prevailing antidecadence rhetoric in the official art press.

Although the subject of death and decay was unwelcome in a country allegedly going through national renovation under Marshal Pétain, it frequently appeared in the work of Paulhan's favorites. And, at a moment when an expressive *matière* denoted decay, decadence, obscenity, and Jewishness in art, it continued to be used by the artists who interested Paulhan. However, with respect to *matière* – the autonomous language of paint and of other materials of painting – Paulhan felt that his artists also parted from Picasso. "*[Matière]* is

First published in the catalogue of the exhibition *Picasso and the War Years 1937–1945* at the Palace of the Legion of Honor in San Francisco and the Guggenheim Museum in New York (London and New York: Thames and Hudson, 1998).

in Rembrandt (not in Bosch): it is in Soutine or Rouault . . . It is Fautrier ([but] not in Picasso who makes admirable colored drawings. . . .)" Paulhan wrote to Fautrier in 1943.[3] Put in more flattering words, whereas in Picasso's wartime skulls, death often has the look, form, and feel of dry bones, death images tend to be spectral in Braque and Dubuffet, and viscous in Fautrier and Soutine.[4]

In the context of the rampage against decadence by Vichyites and collaborationist critics, and of the reverence in which Picasso was held by enemies of Vichy and of the Third Reich, Paulhan's opinions revealed a singularly independent turn of mind. But then, Paulhan was used to assuming difficult positions. In his role as editor of the prestigious *Nouvelle revue française* (NRF), which he took over in 1925, he often had to critique the writings of famous authors who thought they were beyond reproach. He managed to remain a friend of the painter André Lhote while assailing his art. On the intellectual plane, Paulhan fit in with groups that hated each other: he was close to the surrealists in the early twenties and to Georges Bataille and his colleagues of the Collège de Sociologie in the late thirties. During the Occupation, he contributed to Resistance publications while also playing artistic mentor to Nazi officials stationed in Paris.

Caught in the unoccupied zone near Carcassonne after the invasion and partition of France, Paulhan – who had been associated with leftist causes – had difficulty obtaining a pass to return to occupied Paris. The negotiations with the Vichy government that made it possible for him to return home, like those which enabled so-called degenerate artists also caught in the unoccupied zone to return safely to Paris after the Armistice, remain something of a mystery. A French official at the prefecture, André-Louis Dubois, has taken credit for "protecting" Picasso during the Occupation.[5] In the case of vanguard artists who were French nationals and not Jewish, the issue of degeneracy turned out to be more serious in the eyes of Vichyites and French critics than of the Nazis. Early on, Pierre Drieu la Rochelle, a French mouthpiece for the Nazis and Paulhan's successor at the NRF, had exceptionally exonerated Braque from the onus of decadence in the cultural weekly *Comoedia*.[6] "Your Braque piece in *Comoedia* is excellent," was how Paulhan expressed gratitude to the man who made it possible for Braque to work in peace.[7]

Braque and the old-time NRF editor had met in 1935, long after Paulhan bought his first Braque, a 1912 collage. The friendship intensified after the Armistice when Paulhan decided to write his thoughts on Braque for publication, and started to spend many hours at the artist's studio watching him work and hearing him talk. The first version of what was to become *Braque le patron* came out in *Comoedia* 31 October 1942.[8] "Am I still a friend of Picasso? I wrote on Braque," Paulhan answered the poet Jean Grenier, who had queried him on that subject.[9]

Meanwhile, the book with text by Paulhan and lithographs by Braque was taking shape at the atelier of Fernand Mourlot: "I will always remember seeing Braque during the Occupation arrive at the atelier rue Chabrol on a prehistoric bicycle; he was magnificent, an impressive stature, with a remarkable head, pale eyes and white hair," recalled Mourlot in his memoirs.[10] Paulhan came too, to look things over and to correct Braque's grammar, for in the initial project the artist's thoughts were to be included verbatim at the end of the Paulhan text.[11]

Although Braque was hardly a discovery in 1940, Paulhan befriended the famed cubist at a critical time in the artist's development – the start of a new phase of sometimes monumentally sized paintings depicting abruptly cut-off views of painterly, somewhat abstract interiors with still lifes – a hairbrush, washbowl, and water jug on a table in *The Wash Stand* (1942–44; the Phillips Collection, Washington, D.C.); a grill, a fish, a platter, a large fork and sieve on a kitchen table in *Kitchen Table with Grill* (1943–44; private collection, Switzerland); a coal scuttle, stove, palette, waste basket, and heavy table in the workplace of an artist in *The Stove* (Fig. 18), and sometimes the black silhouettes of female or male sitters such as *Patience* (1942; private collection, Geneva). Paulhan in fact became the owner of one of the tall, narrow kitchen paintings and received as a gift one of Braque's still lifes with black fish. He also acquired a sketch of an interior with two female figures.[12] In February 1942, Paulhan wrote to his friend the novelist Marcel Jouhandeau: "Yesterday [I went to] Braque. His latest canvases are marvelous. What serenity, what presence, I remain enchanted."[13]

Referred to as examples of Braque's "late works" by the organizers of the 1997 exhibition at the Royal Academy in London, paintings by this artist dating from after 1938 probably influenced the works of the *Bleu Blanc Rouge* painters, whose first group exhibition took place in early 1943. Similarities with the work of Braque are seen in the penchant of Edouard Pignon and Maurice Estève in particular for somewhat abstract interiors with a plain still-life motif arranged on a table, the pervasively silent mood, the occasional view out of a window, with a female presence inside the room, and everything compressed within a shallow pictorial space (Fig.15). But the 1943 paintings of these *Bleu Blanc Rouge* painters are more conventional in subject matter and in form.

They include no bathroom paraphernalia, no camouflaged "forms which have no literal meaning whatsoever."[14] There is none of the "metamorphic" confusion that Braque said was fundamental to what he sought to express and that Paulhan admired in art and poetry.[15] Furthermore, the *Bleu Blanc Rouge* painters' use of mostly primary colors gives their paintings cheerful connotations totally at odds with Braque's more muted palette. Indeed, as pointed out by John Golding, "whereas the earlier paintings [of Braque] were characterized by an air of serenity and a quiet, restrained splendour, [his] wartime pictures tend to be austere, at times even tragic in their implications."[16]

In conveying confinement, the cold of unheated interiors in the winter, the heightened importance of food, and also in a recourse to a palette dominated by grays, black, dark blues, and browns, paintings by Braque are closer to Picasso's output during the same years than to the *Bleu Blanc Rouge* painters. But in the treatment of the death image, Braque and Picasso part ways. Like Picasso, Braque painted a number of skulls during the Occupation years, but he later denied their symbolic connotations, insisting to John Richardson that what fascinated him in painting a skull next to a rosary was "the tactile quality of the rosary and the formal problems of mass and composition posed by the skull."[17]

There is indeed a striking difference in the skull images by Braque and by Picasso. For one thing, Braque did not make skull sculptures, but only paintings where a skull form is present. For another, Braque's painted skulls are far less assertive than Picasso's; they glance to the side rather than confront the viewer directly, and they have a ghostly, evanescent quality, not the dry and bony texture of skeletons (Figs. 19, 20). And most telling, when seen in profile, a palette image can transmute into both a skull and an amoeba

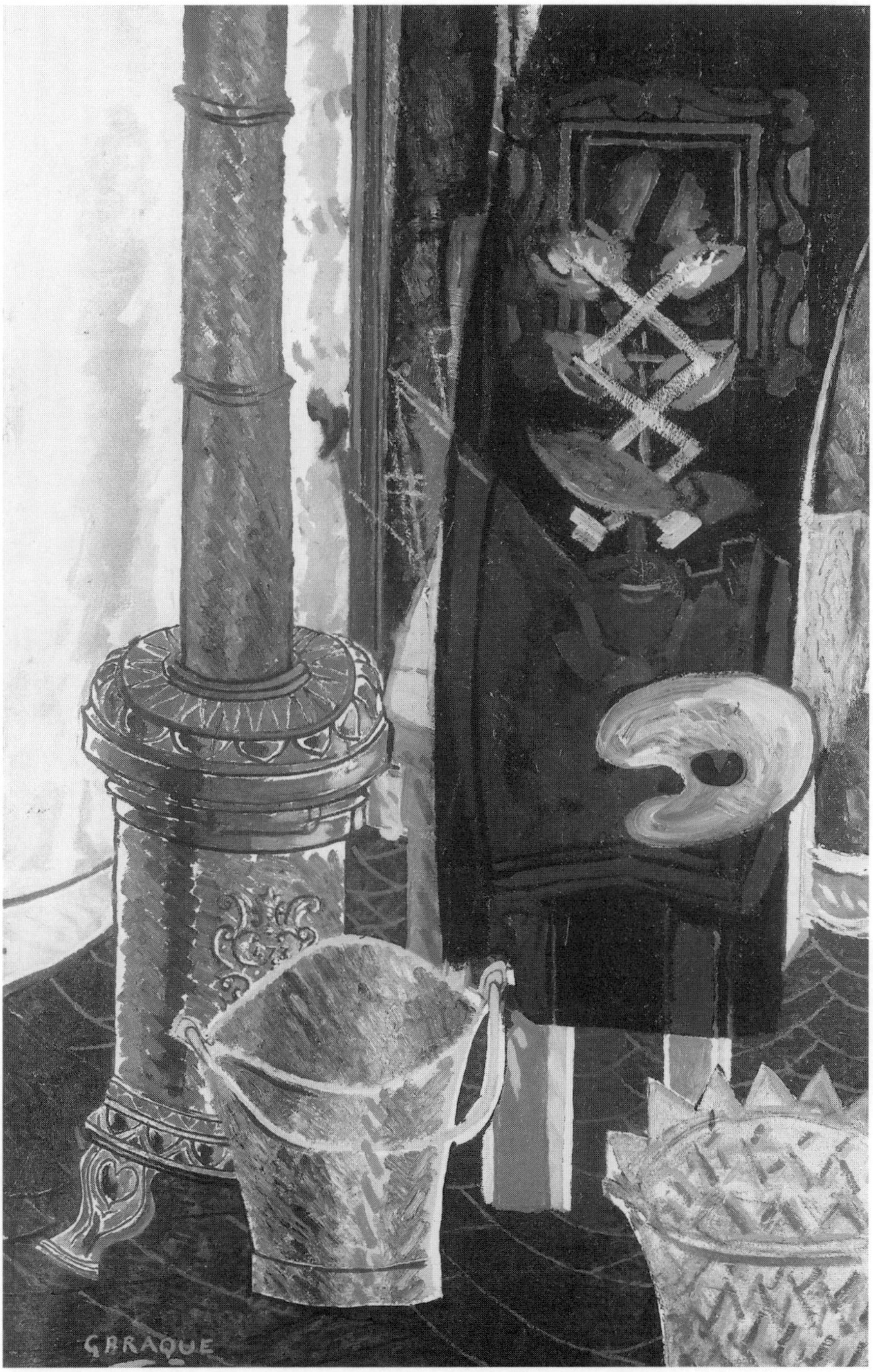

18. Georges Braque, *The Stove,* 1942. Oil and sand on canvas, 57⅜ × 34¾ in. (145.7 × 86.4 cm). Yale University Art Gallery, New Haven, Connecticut. Gift of Paul Rosenberg and Company in memory of Paul Rosenberg (photo: courtesy of the museum).

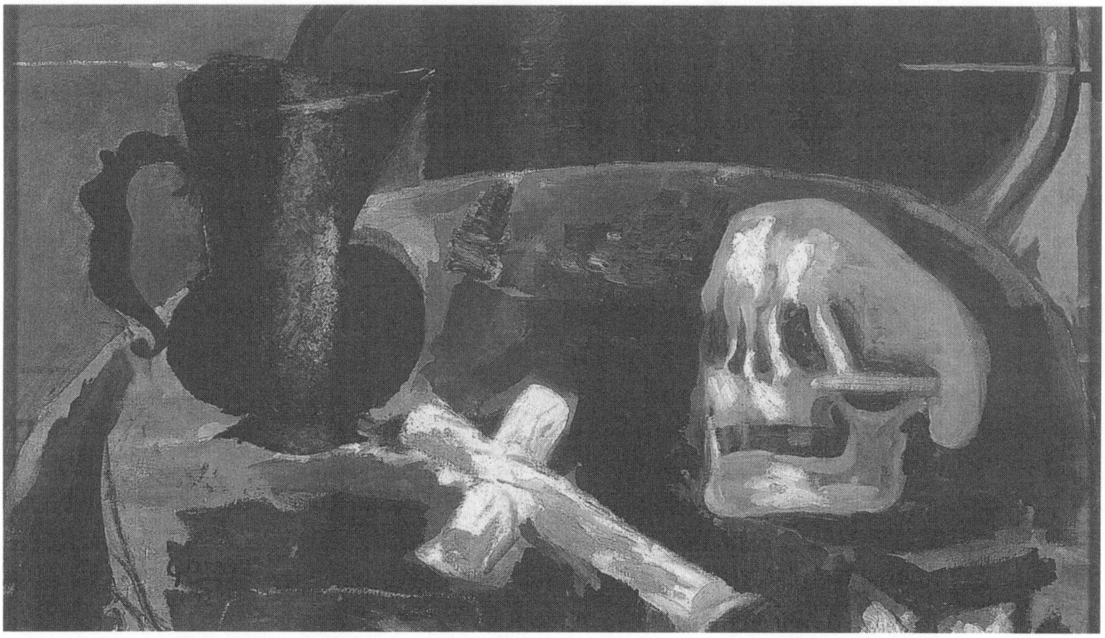

19. Georges Braque, *Pitcher and Skull,* 1943. Oil on canvas, 18⅛ × 28¾ in. (46 × 73 cm). Saarland Museum, Saarbrücken, Germany (photo: courtesy of the museum).

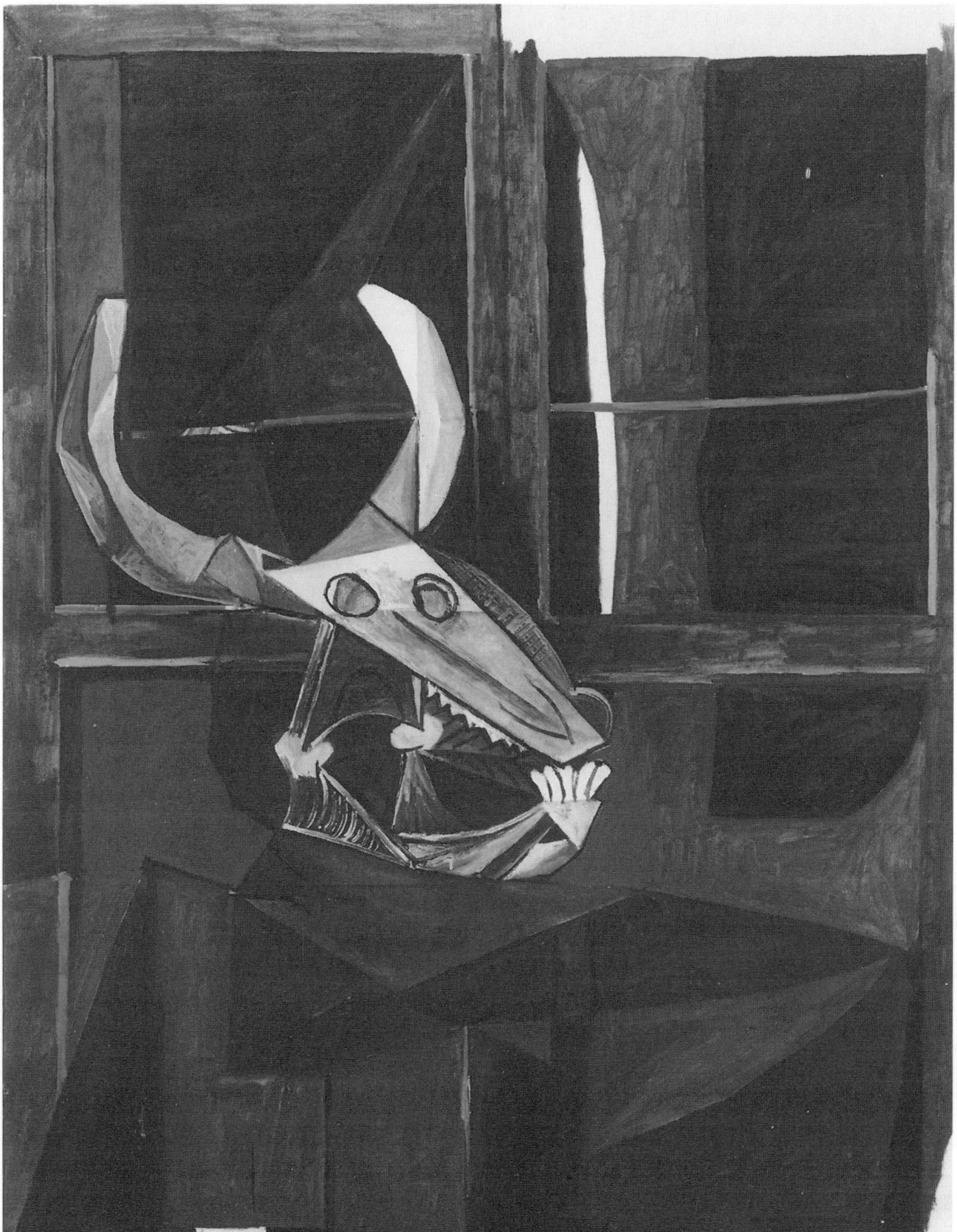

20. Pablo Picasso, *Head of a Bull on a Table,* 5 April 1942. Oil on canvas, 51½ × 38⅛ in. (130 × 97 cm). Kunstammlung Nordrhein-Westfalen, Düsseldorf, Germany (photo: courtesy of the museum).

(*The Stove; Large Interior with Palette* [1942; the Menil Collection, Houston]; *Still Life with Palette* [1943; The Saint Louis Art Museum]). Thus, rather than expressing fear of the finality of death or insisting on a dichotomy between death and life, these works suggest that there might be a continuum between the end and the beginning of life.

Paulhan, who favored Braque's *matière* over Picasso's and who liked Braque far more than he did Picasso (Paulhan and Braque apparently shared an interest in Tibetan Buddhism), wrote of his preference from the point of view of a Frenchman who believes in national characteristics. He appreciated Braque's lack of brashness and attributed to him a typically French understanding of the materials of his craft: "Picasso makes so much noise that one loves Braque first for his discretion, then for his silence, and finally because one imagines that he knows so much more than the other . . . ," he wrote Jouhandeau in 1932, three years before meeting Braque in person.[18] He reiterated his preference to Jouhandeau in 1939: "The Braques are remarkable . . . It greatly surpasses Picasso . . . I think that what I like in him [Braque] . . . is the patience, the fine touch of the French artisan . . . One is never more keenly aware of the Cocteau side of Picasso than in front of a Braque."[19]

In 1943, the Galerie de France offered an aperçu of Braque's early works, soon after which twenty-two recent paintings and nine pieces of sculpture were featured at the 1943 Salon d'Automne. While the *Je suis partout* critic, Lucien Rebatet, sneered at "the resurgence of an old world that clings to the debris of its past, both anarchical and academic,"[20] positive reports on visits to the artist's studio filled the pages of the more moderate cultural weekly *Comoedia*. From Marguerite Bouvier we learn that Braque was a fanatic of the Greek author Hesiod. From the painter Jean Bazaine (one of the *Bleu Blanc Rouge* painters) we hear that Braque liked comparing himself to a gardener among his trees: "I prune, I clip, I command."[21] Braque emerged from the war untainted, although he confided to the printmaker Mourlot that he might have gone on the propaganda trip organized for French artists by the Nazis "had they liked his paintings."[22]

Overall, the Paris to which Braque and many other artists returned after the Armistice had a very strange atmosphere. No exhibition could open without first being visited by a Nazi censor. In galleries and in museums, art by Jewish artists was kept definitely out of sight. The surrealists were rarely on display, either. New names signed the columns of an aryanized art press, and at the *Nouvelle revue française,* Paulhan had to deal with the pro-Nazi appointee, Drieu la Rochelle. The gallery scene was also transformed. Paul Rosenberg, whose gallery had represented Braque, had left for the United States. Galleries owned by Jews were aryanized – handed over to collaborationist owners, or fictitiously sold so that the true owners could remain silent partners. Galerie Louise Leiris owned by Daniel-Henry Kahnweiler was in that category, as was the Galerie René Drouin owned by Leo Castelli.[23]

It was at Galerie Drouin that Jean Fautrier was launched in October–November 1943. "I convinced René Drouin to give Fautrier a major exhibition," Paulhan wrote to a friend on 29 September 1943. "He [Drouin] has, on place Vendôme, the most beautiful gallery in all of Paris."[24] Paulhan took many friends on studio visits to Fautrier's atelier at 216, boulevard Raspail, including resisters and collaborators, pro- and anti-Semites, and even the Nazi official, Gerhard Heller, who would remember Paulhan as "my mentor in modern art."[25] Paulhan wrote the catalogue essay for the 1943 Drouin exhibition, the first version of a longer text entitled *Fautrier l'enragé.*[26] He also published an article on the artist in *Comoedia* (13 November 1943).

To this day, Fautrier (1898–1964) is best known for his Hostage series of paintings started in 1943 and exhibited in 1945, which unveiled a new process – the building up of a tactile relief on which the artist could then draw or paint, a new vision[27] and a resonant subject matter – the routine Nazi roundup and killing of hostages in retaliation for the assassination of one of their men. (For a while, fearing arrest, Fautrier lived in hiding at Châtenay-Malabry outside Paris, within earshot of woods where the Nazis came to finish off their victims by gunshot.)

This view of Fautrier's career – revised by a retrospective exhibition at the Musée d'Art Moderne de la Ville de Paris in 1989 – obliterates some twenty years of his painting production prior to 1943 and omits the important exhibitions of his art at Galerie Visconti in 1924, at Georges Bernheim in 1928, and at the NRF gallery in 1934. The wartime Drouin retrospective showed both old and new work by an artist then in transition.

Among the early paintings on view were two still lifes of a decomposing boar, and *Rabbit Skins* (Fig. 21),[28] a luminous painting showing five dead hares dangling in graceful abandon from the end of a string in a dark, cavelike space. A delicate, sometimes furry texture and soft contours predominate, not only in black-on-black still lifes of dead animals from the mid-twenties, but also in mostly black paintings like *Black Flowers* (1926; Limmer Gallery, Freiburg), *Still Life with Pear* (1928; private collection, Germany), and *Nude* (1926; Limmer Gallery, Freiburg). Like Soutine, whom it is tempting to compare to the Fautrier of *Rabbit Skins*, the French-born artist had stayed away from the whole episode of cubism. Indeed, his late twenties and early thirties demoiselles (*Young Women* [1929; Marie-José Lefort Collection, London]), had more to do with "precultural representation"[29] than with the cubist distortions of Picasso's *Demoiselles d'Avignon*.

Present in the Drouin selection was the painting that began Paulhan's Fautrier binge, *Open Corpse*, a human body in front view, open as for an autopsy, its guts a zigzagging line within a dark oval. "This cadaver that has just been broken open for an autopsy, resembles some marching condottiere,"[30] Paulhan remarked, discovering in an ambiguous overlay of two states of being the sense of metamorphosis that he also valued in Braque's late works. Paulhan, who had seen death closely during World War I and become fascinated with morbid images, hung *Open Corpse* in the dining room of the home on rue des Arènes that he shared with his wife, and to which he brought his writer friends.

The list of works for the Galerie Drouin show indicated a hiatus in Fautrier's production between 1932 and 1938 (when the artist left Paris and became a nightclub owner and instructor in a ski resort), and a reprise in 1938 of fruit and flower paintings, still black with blurred contours, such as *Fruit in a Bowl and Flowers* (1939; Michael Werner Gallery, Cologne). In 1940–41, Fautrier was going to give up oil and canvas, as he began to layer absorbent paper mixed with paste in lieu of a simple prepared canvas base.[31] In *The Rabbit* (1941; Limmer Gallery, Freiburg) and *The Fish* (1943; private collection, Paris) – two works that have been traced back to the Galerie Drouin 1943 ret-

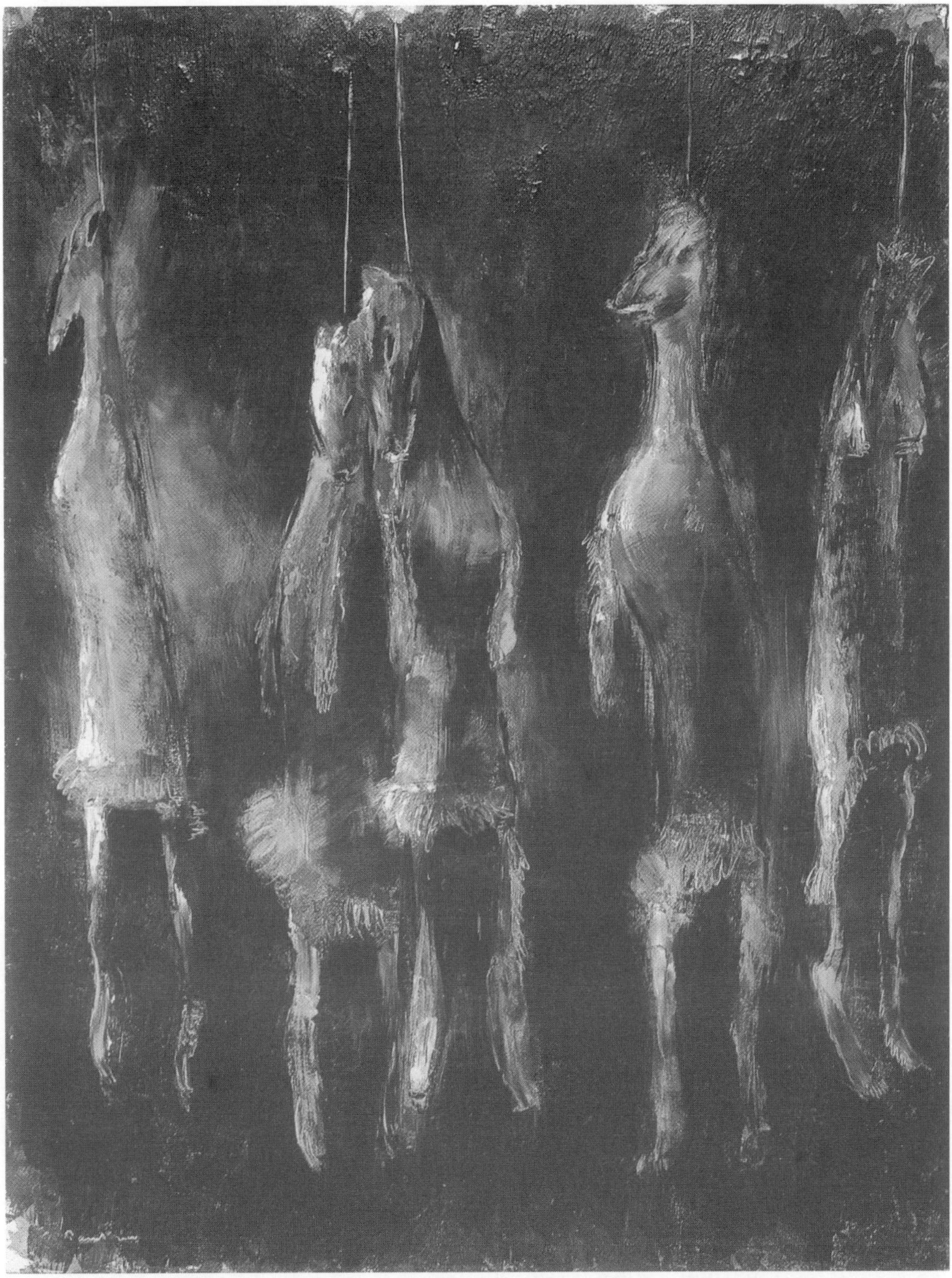

21. Jean Fautrier, *Rabbit Skins*, 1927. Oil on canvas, 51½ × 38⅛ in. (131 × 97 cm). Marie-José Lefort Collection, London (photo: courtesy of FAMSF Publications, M. H. de Young Memorial Museum, San Francisco).

rospective[32] – contrasts of light and dark are disconnected from the outlined skeleton of the depicted objects. Graffiti-like, gestural short markings identify the subject matter. The catalogue list also included several landscapes from 1943 as well as two paintings of heads dated 1943. In addition, it showed five pieces of sculpture (including four heads from 1942–43), a number of unidentified drawings from 1942–43, and three sets of book illustrations.

It would thus appear that a number of works in the style of the Hostage paintings might have been seen in the 1943 exhibition, though – no doubt for safety reasons – none bore a title that risked offending the Nazi censors. More intriguing than the subject matter at that point was the change in surface quality from flat to impastoed, as if a fragment of Soutine's raised and heavily textured surfaces were being analyzed in close-up view (Fig. 22).

Fautrier not only exhibited art that was flagrantly "decadent" by the standards of his enemies, he illustrated the poems of Resistance friends, and helped a Jewish artist survive. A letter from Paulhan – who had taken an interest in a Jewish painter named Benn [Rabinowicz] – reveals that in 1943 Fautrier spent 3,000 francs for a work by Benn.[33] Soon after this letter Paulhan thanked Fautrier for a precious gift. "I don't think that our friends in [internment?] camps could have received anything better or more nourishing."[34]

Not surprisingly, Fautrier's exhibition aroused the passion of Lucien Rebatet, the pro-Nazi critic of *Je suis partout:* "If you want an aperçu of *dementia praecox,* go see [Fautrier's] mauve or yellow landscapes, his pink apples . . . These kilos of paint . . . What debauchery, for God's sake! What a waste of canvas which could have been more usefully employed for making sheets or baby diapers."[35] Rebatet favored watercolor, the medium most antithetical to Fautrier's raised impastoed surface, and, among contemporary watercolorists, praised romantic realists Roland Oudot and Maurice Brianchon, whose Between-the-Jew-and-the-Pompier aesthetics combined escapist themes, refined taste, harmony and moderation, and a Bonnardian lightness of touch.

At a time when thick painterly *matière* was abhorred by all major French critics as un-French, degenerate, and, in the words of Jean-Marc Campagne, the critic at *Les Nouveaux Temps,* typical of Jewish art,[36] Fautrier's use of it daringly flaunted the acceptable. In

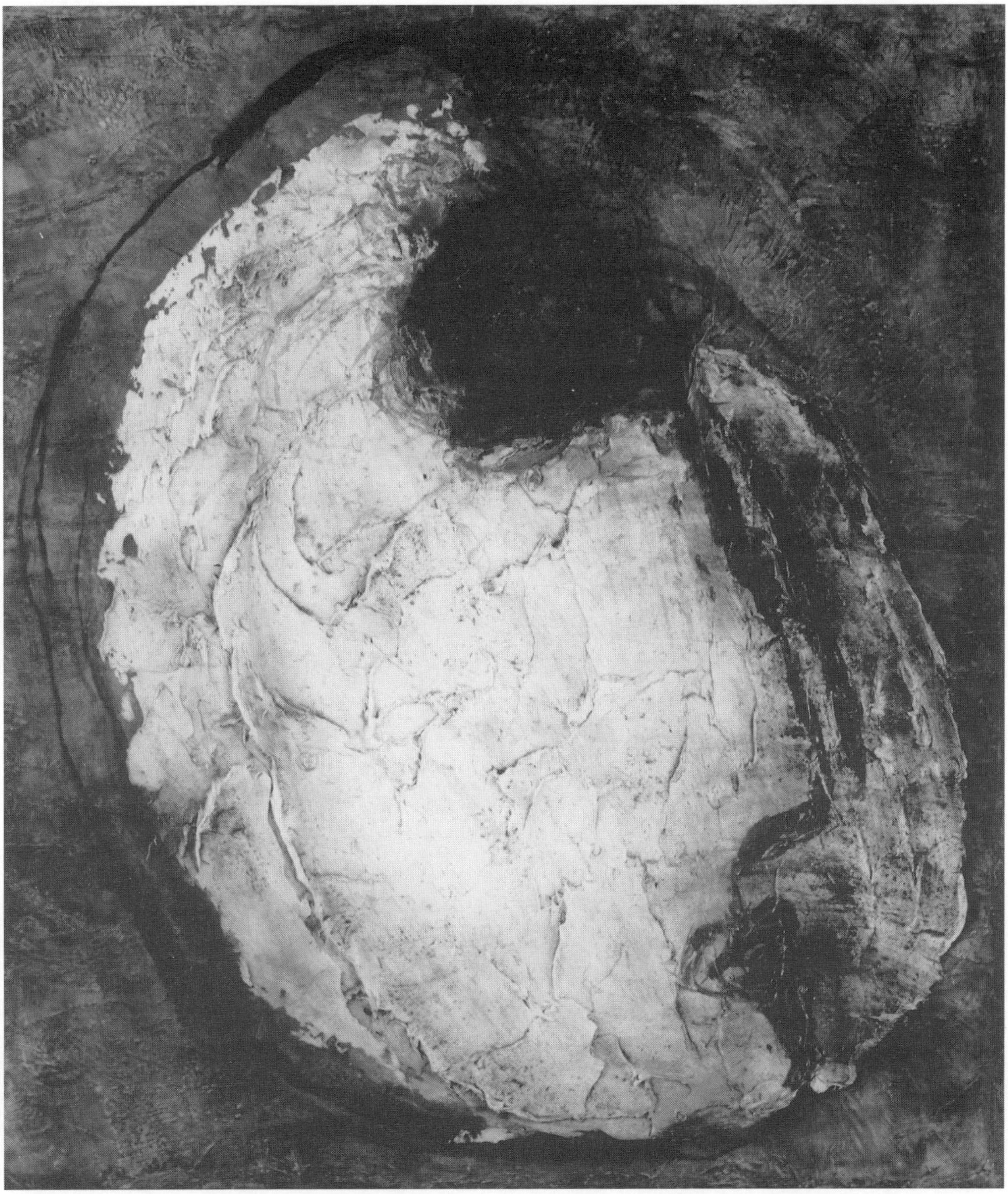

22. Jean Fautrier, *Hostage Head,* 1944. Oil and pigments on paper laid down on canvas, 25⅛ × 21¼ in. (64 × 54 cm) (photo: courtesy of Galerie Daniel Malingue, Paris).

inventing an original way to address artistic and racial issues, Fautrier was exceptional among French artists. And, in pushing the issue of *matière* beyond Soutine's viscous surfaces, he was making visible the link between Soutine and postwar anti-form.[37]

Although Fautrier and Soutine were near contemporaries (Soutine was born in 1893 and Fautrier in 1898), may have lived at La Ruche during the same years, and while the dealer Paul Guillaume bought paintings by the two of them,[38] no evidence exists that they knew each other. A portrait by Fautrier of Soutine's first dealer, Leopold Zborowski, is the sole evidence of a possible personal link.[39] Furthermore, everything in their backgrounds and personalities would have separated them. Soutine's father was a poor Jewish clothes mender in a small Lithuanian village from which young Chaim had run away in order to pursue his goal of becoming an artist. Fautrier had a wealthy French mother who uprooted her son to London at age ten, letting him study at the best London art schools. One was short and pudgy, the other a natural athlete.

In a well-known photograph, Fautrier displays the ascetic face of Marcel Duchamp, distorted by an Antonin Artaud grimace. Sensual lips on a chubby face characterize Soutine's physiognomy in a 1938 photo portrait. "Handsome, elegant, nervous, he startled, intimidated, fascinated, was either adored or hated, yet felt forever alone on his mountains," is how one female admirer remembered Fautrier.[40] For her part, Soutine's companion in the late thirties, Gerda Groth, better known as Mlle Garde,[41] found Soutine singularly lacking in seduction. He was also, she discovered, incapable of creating a particular atmosphere around him. "He settled in a lodging without changing a thing, as if he were provisionally camping there."[42]

Yet far apart as they might be, they shared a strange ambivalence – attraction and repulsion – toward decaying flesh and viscous matter that was totally foreign to Picasso's fear of death syndrome and images of dry, bony skulls. Something in their past experience – memory of the shtetl for one, trench life in World War I for the other –seemed to have familiarized them with gory sights to such an extent that they could contemplate death from a perversely formal viewpoint. Indeed, Fautrier's most powerful works – both his early representations of the dead hare, dead boar, and human corpse, and his World War II Hostage images – bring to mind Elie Faure writing of Soutine's *Carcass of Beef* of 1928: "It is in dead flesh that he finds his most erotic pleasures."[43]

Paulhan was himself very much aware of a Fautrier–Soutine connection. Explaining his initial reticence toward Fautrier to the critic Marcel Arland, he wrote to him in 1941: "I never slighted Fautrier. At the same time, I found him estimable, brilliant – and yet he did not interest me very much. I said to myself: he is obviously gifted and what else? Neither the ardor of Soutine, nor the faith of Rouault."[44] The Soutine reference remained in the foreground even after Paulhan overcame his doubts about Fautrier. In a letter of 28 June 1943 written to Marcel Jouhandeau, he said, "I would like some day to take you to Fautrier. I don't think that, other than [André] Masson (and maybe Soutine), there is a greater painter today."[45] And to his friend Henri Pourrat, in a letter of 24 August 1943, he noted, "He [Fautrier] is with Soutine the greatest of painters among the young: a thousand feet above [Roland] Oudot, [Maurice] Brianchon and the others."[46]

In fact, Paulhan coveted owning a Soutine long before he went on his Fautrier binge, and it is likely that Paulhan turned to Fautrier's strangely morbid paintings in part because of their affinity with Soutine's sensibility. "I have often dreamt about [owning] a Soutine," he wrote to the paraplegic poet Joë Bousquet, a conduit to the surrealists and to Jewish artists during the war, asking him to find one or two works by Soutine "at 15 no more than 20,000 francs."[47] We do not know if Paulhan's wishes were fulfilled at that time, and if so, what painting or paintings Paulhan bought. What we do know is that with the exception of *Maternity* (1942; Madeleine Castaing Collection, Paris), showing a seated mother holding the limp body of a child on her lap, "in his last phase, the years of Vichy France, Soutine's focusing image was not death, dying or the depiction of life," as Maurice Tuchman has pointed out in his recent contribution to the Soutine catalogue raisonné.[48]

The last paintings, although steeped in the French countryside and in the observation of French country people, evoke the artist's nostalgia for another place and time, as if the roots he had so diligently repressed had surged back to the surface. Mlle Garde was a witness to this change: "One day, watching me cry, Soutine asked me the reason. I told him I was nostalgic for my parents, and I added, 'How can you not think about yours without sadness?' He immediately wrote a letter to Lithuania and awaited an answer every day."[49]

It might well be the world of Soutine's youth that he depicts in *Maternity,* in the portrait of a little girl in a pensive pose leaning on a balustrade entitled *Young Girl at Fence,* in *Thérèse by the River* (ca. 1942; private collection, Paris), in *Grandmother and Child* (ca. 1943; private collection), showing a white-haired older woman dressed in black who smiles at the child holding her hand – paintings with the quality of Proustian memory. They look as if Soutine had posed French models but painted them as characters from the shtetl. Even *Return from School after the Storm* (Fig. 23), with its dark blue-green trees rising in an empty plain and children shuffling along a dirt path, speaks of walks through windblown Russian steppes rather than the French countryside.

The nostalgia present in Soutine's last paintings – the distant memory of friendly faces and familiar sights – is hardly surprising. The small village in occupied France where he stayed in hiding during the war could easily merge in his mind and in his art with the village in distant Lithuania where he was born and raised. Furthermore, the persecution of Jews in his country of adoption, occupied France, could well remind him of his early encounter with racial persecution in his native village in Lithuania.

Indeed, no sooner was the Armistice signed by Marshal Pétain in June 1940 than the first anti-Jewish measures were instituted. More and more ignominious obstructions were put in place in the occupied zone, affecting the daily life of Jews, both foreign and French ones. On an early morning in July 1942, the Vélodrome d'Hiver roundup took place. Thousands of Jews were awakened by the French police, told to take a few personal things, and put on buses headed for the Vél d'Hiv sports stadium. After a few nights and days spent at the open stadium, most of them were transferred to the Drancy internment camp outside Paris, the antechamber of Auschwitz.[50] As of June 1942, Jews were forced to wear the yellow star to make them more easily identifiable for arrest.[51] Routine

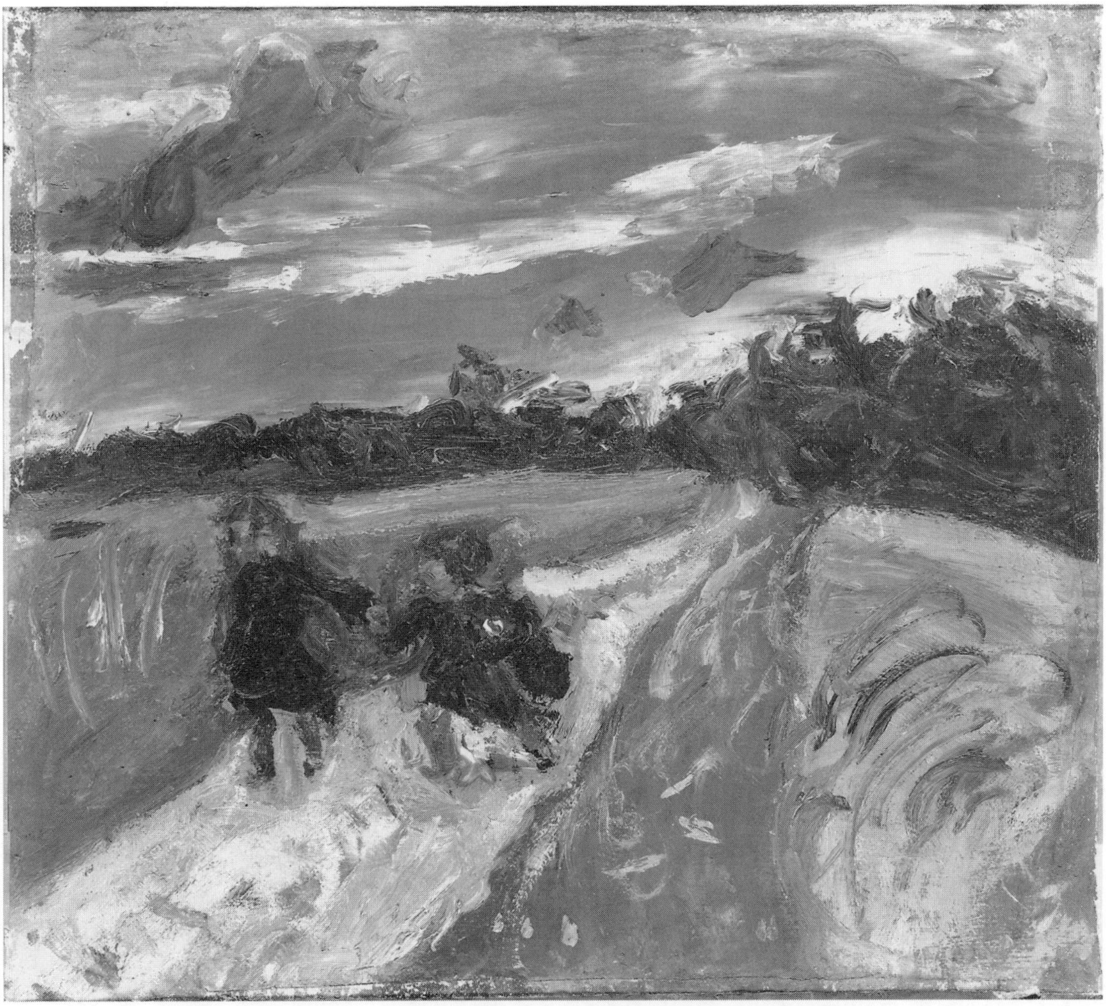

23. Chaim Soutine, *Return from School after the Storm,* ca. 1939. Oil on canvas, 17 × 19 ½ in. (43.2 × 49.5 cm). The Phillips Collection, Washington, D.C. (photo: courtesy of the museum).

roundups took place, in the course of which men were asked to lower their trousers for signs of circumcision, then taken away.

Aged forty-six in 1939, Soutine was at the peak of his career, the years of starvation in Montparnasse behind him. He lived comfortably in the Villa Seurat (some claiming that he was sympathetic to the right-wing Action française), his medical and emotional problems were attended to by his devoted companion, Mlle Garde, and his ego nurtured by Madelaine Castaing, his major collector at that point. Suddenly his foreignness and then his Jewishness boomeranged back at him, transforming his everyday life into a permanent nightmare. In September 1939, when the war broke out, he was at Civry near Avallon with Mlle Garde, visiting an art dealer. As Soutine was a Russian and Garde a German national, they were told by French officials –the then-French government feared the presence of traitors among foreigners – that they could not return to Paris, and must remain at Civry in *résidence surveillée.* They escaped and went back to Soutine's atelier in Paris.

In May 1940, when German nationals were isolated from the rest of the population, again as potential traitors – Mlle Garde was sent to Gurs, the ignominious internment camp in the Pyrenees that, under the Vichy government, became a way station for Auschwitz. (Among the lucky ones, she was not deported, but never saw Soutine again.) In a panic after her disappearance, Soutine turned to Madeleine Castaing. From the June Armistice signed by Marshal Pétain's anti-Semitic government until his transport to the Junot hospital in Paris in August 1943, Soutine stayed in hiding around the village of Champigny – in the care of a new companion, Marie-Berthe Aurenche (Max Ernst's former mistress).

When hardly anyone dared to mention his name, much less buy his work, the Castaings continued to collect it to the very end of his life.[52] On 9 August 1943, he died during an operation for his stomach ulcers. Mlle Garde, by then living in hiding in Paris, reported, "Two days later, I followed the funeral to Montparnasse Cemetery. There were very few people, for most of Soutine's friends, and the painters of Montparnasse, had to remain in hiding. However, Jean Cocteau, Picasso, and Michonz followed the funeral procession."[53]

Paulhan never established a personal relationship with Soutine the way he did with Braque, Fautrier, and Jean Dubuffet, explaining to Bousquet that "I could have met him but there was a time when I found it more proper not to see the painters that the NRF talked about. It was a bit stupid."[54] Paulhan's meeting with Dubuffet occurred in the last months of the Occupation, when the outcome of the war in favor of the Allies seemed assured. "I have discovered another brilliant painter whose name is Dubuffet; in a minuscule atelier on the rue Lhomond he paints puppets, and metro scenes. Otherwise, wine merchant (wholesale) and friend of [Georges] Limbour," he wrote to Jouhandeau in March 1944.[55]

Born in 1901, and slightly younger than Fautrier and Soutine, Dubuffet belonged with their generation. Like Fautrier, Dubuffet had given up painting during the thirties for a more lucrative activity. He resumed his vocation in 1942, "resolved to devote two or three years (with enough money to live on for that length of time) to making paintings for my own use and without worrying about whether or not they were susceptible to being approved by anybody."[56]

As with Fautrier, more attention has been paid to Dubuffet's postwar art in relation to *l'art informel* than to the work that came before. Overlooked in particular are the May–June 1944 "messages" scribbled in an awkward hand on messy newspaper print, which simulated the anonymous graffiti used by lovers, the deranged, and resisters to communicate. Sentences like "The key is under the shutter," "I think of you," "Thank you very much my health is excellent," "Georges arrives tomorrow morning," "Emile has left," are also reminiscent of messages scribbled in prison or heard over the BBC radio during the war.

Typical of the Vichy years are also colorful oil paintings and gouaches based on children's art, made at a time when the art of children was much celebrated and even shown in museums. But whereas the children's drawings on view at the Paris Musée Galliéra paid homage to Marshal Pétain, Dubuffet's works concentrated on scenes of the wartime everyday, filled with expressive, toylike figures. In these works, sad-looking people stand in a crowded subway car, go about their business on foot on a city street, play jazz, bicycle on an open road, and milk cows. All these "puppets from the city and the country" (the title of the series) – Hoffmanesque automatons – operated in the odd terrain of plastic naïveté overlaid with mature emotion. Dubuffet noted that

> I liked the kind of painting that children make, and aimed at nothing more than to make equivalent ones, for my sole pleasure. I believed that paintings deprived of technique like those made by children, effortlessly and quickly, can be as effective, even more effective than paintings produced in the cultural circuit, and that they can also be carriers of unexpected bonuses offering novel overtures to thought.[57]

One such painting, *View of Paris: Everyone at the Windows,* depicted an old building façade with little white stick figures standing on the window sills, the arched windows suggesting an alignment of tombstones. Made the day after the poet Max Jacob's memorial, it was given to Paulhan. (Both Dubuffet and Paulhan had been friends of the dead poet.) According to the artist, it was inspired by "the wall of ghosts that surged in [my] mind during the ceremony"[58] that he and Paulhan had attended.

René Drouin, at the urging of Paulhan, included Dubuffet in two group exhibits at his gallery – The Nude in May 1944 (with *Seated Woman in Front of Blinds* [May 1943; C. Renault Collection, Paris]) and Twenty-One Landscapes in July 1944 (with *Grassy and Earthy Landscape* [February 1944; private collection, Zurich]). The critic Georges Limbour, a longtime friend, expressed his admiration on the soon-to-become-defunct *Comoedia* on 8 July 1944. The critic Gaston Diehl, who had championed the *Bleu Blanc Rouge* painters and might have responded positively to the cheerful look if not the less than cheerful content of Dubuffet's works, called his art "a dangerous joke" ("une facétie dangereuse") in the about-to-disappear newspaper *Aujourd'hui* on 17 July 1944. This comment was not going to deter Drouin from giving Dubuffet a one-man show at his gallery in October 1944, for which Paulhan wrote the catalogue introduction in the form of a letter to the artist.

One might well ask what criteria allowed Paulhan, the famed editor and discoverer of literary talent, to switch so easily from new authors to new artists. As the critic André Berne-Joffroy conceded, "One cannot forget that his strange lucidity – so suddenly displayed in the realm of painting soon after 1940 – was sustained by the very same qualities he had cultivated with *extraordinary* care in literature . . . on the basis, it is true, of exceptional talent."[59] Indeed, his beginnings as an art "critic" coincided with the publication in 1941 of *Les Fleurs de Tarbes,* a summation of his views after fifteen years as arbiter of contemporary literature and poetry in Paris.

In this pessimistic and disorienting text – offered as a series of glimpses rather than a demonstration – creativity is shown to be at a near impasse. Everything has been said "and in the end every word becomes suspect if it has been used before."[60] What is left to explore is the very *matière* of language, its texture dissociated from sentences, from words, and even from letters.[61] Paulhan's commitment to *matière* in painting would seem to have derived from the priority that he assigned to *matière* in literature. But no sooner had he laid down his demand for *littérature de la matière* (that would be obviously incomprehensible) than he declared the cliché, the banal, the *lieu commun* – which he intuitively disliked – to be a necessity of literature if language were to recover both its adhesion to the world and its communicability.

The idea of the commonplace also partook of his judgments on art, as when he said of Braque in *Braque le patron* that

> What I meant to say also is that Braque's painting is banal. No doubt fantastic but ordinary. Fantastic – when one thinks about it – as it is to have one nose and two eyes, and the nose precisely between the two eyes.[62]

As John Culbert pointed out with regard to Paulhan's writings, "one of the dominant traits of Paulhan's work is the refusal to settle differences."[63] In order to interest Paulhan the critic, a work – whether of literature or of art – must waver on the cusp of the accessibly seductive and the repulsively difficult, always risking failure like a high-wire act. It was thus hardly surprising to read Paulhan saying of Fautrier's wartime painting that it was very close to insult and to filth.[64]

But Paulhan did not suddenly become an authority on new art. He himself had mentors. One of them was Henri Michaux, the Belgian surrealist poet/painter and contributor to NRF who had "long tried to interest Paulhan in a new possible orientation in painting."[65] Michaux had traveled to the Far East and become fascinated by

Tibetan Buddhism. The Buddhist view of dying as a process of metamorphosis between two states of being, which Paulhan may have discovered himself when he lived in Madagascar from 1908 to 1910, probably influenced his fearless affinity for morbid images as much as death's routine presence at the front lines during World War I had when he fought with the Zouaves. But more important was Michaux's discovery in China of a new approach to making art: "[I]n Chinese painting, images are there and yet they're absent. Like delicate phantoms that haven't been summoned by desire."[66] In Michaux's description, we recognize traits that applied to the art that Paulhan admired.

This being said, at a time when the romantic realists Oudot and Brianchon were being celebrated in the pages of the Fascist sheet *Je suis partout,* and the *Bleu Blanc Rouge* painters Jean Bazaine, Edouard Pignon, André Fougeron, Maurice Estève, and Alfred Manessier were claiming attention as the new French vanguard, Paulhan's support of Fautrier, Dubuffet, and Soutine showed unusual courage. Small wonder Rebatet called him "an Aryan ashamed of his foreskin and of his baptism" in the pages of *Je suis partout.*[67] And yet, considering his support of Braque and circumventing of Picasso, who was as engaged against fascism as he was, Paulhan's choices seem to have been more personal than ideologically motivated.

6

The Picasso Album

A Landmark of Artistic Resistance

In 1943 "... hope changed camp, the fighting spirit changed.... The enemy may have beeen turning increasingly implacable, the Resistance hardened and returned blow for blow," the Resistance poet Pierre Seghers writes in *La Résistance et ses poètes.*[1] From the point of view of anti-Nazis, "hope began to change camp" in November 1942, when the allies landed in North Africa. Then in February 1943, Russian troops defeated the German army at Stalingrad and, in July 1943, the Mussolini regime fell.

Confronted with these setbacks, the enemy did turn increasingly implacable. In retaliation for the allies' landing in North Africa, and after the fall of Mussolini, the Nazis extended their witchhunt of Jews to the formerly free zone of France and to areas previously controlled by the Italians, sending more men, women, and children to their deaths. In February 1943, because of new laws that threatened an increasing number of Frenchmen with forced labor in Germany, young men fled to the woods and joined a Resistance network, but many were caught, tortured, and deported to concentration camps that year. In July 1943, the Gestapo chief Barbie caught the top brass of the French Resistance movement, and tortured the Resistance leader, Jean Moulin, to death. Under these

First published in French in an issue of *La Herne* dedicated to Robert Desnos. Translated by the author.

circumstances, It did take "courage" – as in Paul Eluard's exhortative poem of 1943, "Courage": "Paris a froid Paris a faim Paris ne mange plus de marrons dans la rue" – to keep up the fight.

This text is about an example of courage, the landmark publication by Editions du Chène in December 1943 of an album reproducing sixteen paintings by Picasso, with a preface by the Resistance poet Robert Desnos. In 1943, Robert Desnos carries out dangerous missions for the Resistance group Agir. The publisher, Maurice Girodias, simply by being half-Jewish, risks arrest, deportation, and death. As for Picasso, in 1943, the Gestapo intensify their visits to him, hoping to find incriminating traces of his gifts to Spanish loyalists. Being the paradigmatic degenerate artist at that time, he is not allowed to display his work publicly in any Paris gallery. His misguided appropriations of nontraditional forms and cultures are said to be responsible for the decadence of French painting. Thus, publishing a book on Picasso with a text praising the artist was a taunting gesture against the Nazis. In a telephone interview, the publisher (who has since died) modestly explained: "We took small risks. What I was doing was a not very dangerous form of provocation."[2]

Maurice Girodias was young and inexperienced when his father, the publisher of pornographic novels at Obelisk press, Jackie Kahane, died in 1940. After the Occupation of Paris, Maurice Kahane managed to change his last name to that of his mother, Girodias, and became himself a publisher, this time of art books. Why publish art books? There was no censorship of art books, he said. They [the censors] were lenient. Heller (Gerhardt Heller), who headed the censorship office in Paris, was friendly to writers. There was an odd, evanescent side to their milieu, and a desire to charm, at least at the beginning. Girodias spoke to me with enthusiasm of the talent of art-publishing technicians in the forties, and of the human quality that reigned in his publishing house, notwithstanding the generalized madness of the times.

The fact that *Cahiers d'art* and *Arts et Métiers graphiques* had stopped publication gave Girodias a unique opportunity. He named his publishing house Editions du Chène. His right-hand man was André Lejard, formerly director of publications at *Arts et Métiers graphiques,* whom he had met through a mutual friend, the poet Raymond Queneau. In his autobiography, *The Frog Prince,* Girodias explains how he succeeded in persuading a private banker to lend him money to start his publishing house by putting a notice in a newspaper; how he found a young man by the name of Laurent Rombaldi, about his age and as innocent as he was, who agreed to distribute his books; and through what subterfuge he found paper.

Girodias heard that a stock of thirty-five tons of paper were about to be taken over by the Germans, and got in touch with the owner, who first gave him one price, then raised it several times before agreeing to sell. Girodias meanwhile prevailed on a friend with a German accent to telephone the owner and threaten him with "*ennuis*" with the Kommandantur, if he did not immediately get rid of the stock of paper.[3] The source of the color film for the reproductions is not known. During the war, Editions du Chène published books on primitive art, on furniture, tapestry, jewelry, and a series of albums on modern painters, Bonnard, Matisse, Renoir. Girodias also published an album on the tricolor painters. And he commissioned the Picasso Album.

Five of the reproduced paintings in the Album mention Louise Leiris as their proprietor. Louise Leiris, the step-daughter of Daniel-Henry Kahnweiler, had taken over his gallery in 1941 to avoid aryanization. The gallery became, during the Occupation years, a center of backroom dealing in degenerate art. One of the paintings reproduced in the Album, the portrait of a *Seated Woman* (1939), apparently belonged to the French actress Madeleine Renaud. A still life with a bowl of fruit and a glass set on a black tablecloth and dated November 1941 belonged to the dealer, Jeanne Bucher. The other paintings illustrated in the Album belonged to the artist.

The paintings in the possession of the two dealers, and hence possibly offered for sale, were mostly dark and depressing still lifes, whose message was attenuated by a vague title. Typical was *Still Life,* now known as *Still Life with Dead Fowl* [or *with Dead Pigeon*], of 1942, showing a bird, belly up and head drooping from the table top, its stiff, striped gray wings evoking those of a downed airplane. Two other blandly entitled "still lifes" of April 1942 have now become known as *Head of a Bull on a Table,* two haunting paintings that Picasso made after the death of his friend Julio Gonzales (see Fig. 20). The works noted as "belonging to the artist" were portraits of women, seemingly emprisoned within an ominous oppressive space, their faces frequently distorted in a catatonic grin. Overall, and despite slight changes of mood from painting to painting, even the most casual peruser of the Picasso album could not help but sense that Picasso's point of view on contemporary reality diverged from the upbeat visual language officially approved in Paris in 1943.

The surrealist poet Robert Desnos, who wrote the preface, had met the publisher Maurice Girodias's right-hand man, André Lejard, through the publication *Arts et Métiers graphiques;* Desnos and Picasso had known each other slightly before the war. On Picasso's side, there was a certain friendliness vis-à-vis the young poet and, on Desnos's part, a boundless admiration for Picasso. In 1930, Desnos had written an article entitled "Bonjour Monsieur Picasso" for a special issue of *Documents* in homage to the artist. In the climate of the Occupation, friendships were formed among individuals who had rarely seen each other before the war. One met one's friends in the cafes and restaurants sympathetic to one's politics, preferably near one's home because transport was so complicated. As recalled by Françoise Gilot, differences of generations no longer counted. She evoked in an interview the ease with which a young woman like her was able to meet and become friendly with the most fascinating and prestigious people, explaining how she met Robert Desnos at a restaurant where she and a friend were also having dinner, and how Desnos invited them to end the evening at their place across the street to listen to jazz records (a rare opportunity at a time when jazz was considered a decadent form of music).[4]

The circumstances under which Desnos and Picasso came to be associated in the publication of this Album can only be surmised. Gilot remembers the periodic visits of Desnos to Picasso, whom she met in May 1943, and she particularly recalls a comment that the artist made about Desnos: "I do not understand why he writes in a collaborationist newspaper. For him, it is particularly dangerous."[5] At that time, Gilot ignored that Desnos, then a journalist at *Aujourd'hui,* was active in a resistance network.

During the Occupation years, Picasso often helped his friends survive by giving them works of his to sell (Eluard, Hugnet), by making gifts of drawings and prints (to the stateless members of the surrealist group Main à Plume), or by collaborating in poetry projects. In the case of Desnos, the result was *Contrée,* a book of poems illustrated by Picasso, and the Album. In an era when it is fashionable to criticize Picasso's wartime behavior, the following tribute from an unusual source, namely, the painter Henri Matisse, is worth quoting. "Picasso pays dearly for his exceptional qualities," Matisse wrote to his son, Pierre. "But he leads a dignified life in Paris. He works, he doesn't want to sell, and he makes no demands. He still has the human dignity that his colleagues have abandoned to an unbelievable degree."[6]

This being said, it showed courage to write positively about Picasso's art at a time when critics like Camille Mauclair, Mosdyk, and Vanderpyl felt free to demolish his art, and when the collabo painter Maurice de Vlaminck could lash at him in his memoirs, *Portraits avant Décès.* "He steals from past masters, and from his contemporaries. Nothing escapes him! A diletante . . . he does not draw a line without evoking Giorgione, Greco, Stenlein, Lautrec, Greek figurine and Greek masks, Forain, Degas, Cézanne, African and Oceanic sculpture. He orchestrates everying."[7]

The text by Robert Desnos that accompanied the Picasso Album is a difficult one, despite its author's ambition (confided to his diary) "to be perfectly clear, absolutely rigorous."[8] Like Sartre writing "let us remember here that an image is nothing more than a relationship *[un rapport],"*[9] Desnos repeatedly evokes the reciprocity of subject and object, container and contained: He describes Picasso's visual universe as "a universe in perpetual expansion and contraction, about which our ideas change and become more complete as it becomes more complete and reveals itself in a new aspect."[10] He suggests that our understanding of Picasso's canvases implies "the complicity of the author and that of the spectator . . ."[11] And he says of the individual works that "they are not, as has been said of other forms of art, a window open on to the world, but the entire world contained in a finite space."[12] (It seems that Desnos met Sartre through Picasso. The bookseller Alain Brieux, who lived with the Desnos in 1943, recalled a dinner hosted by Desnos and his wife Youki, attended by Sartre, Simone de Beauvoir, Picasso and Dora Maar, in the course of which an enormous ham was consumed.)[13]

Desnos evokes in passing the contrast between the content of Picasso's art and "other forms of art" when he writes: "One explains nothing if one speaks of taste, technique, colors or drawing. It is about that and about more than that."[14] He pointedly interprets Picasso's portraits combining the profile and the front view of the same person, as depicting the double faces of our contemporaries. "These faces in which profile and full face are united in unmistakable human resemblance, they are the faces of our contemporaries."[15]

And he conveys with unconcealed passion the yearning for life and for freedom that he sees surging from Picasso's oeuvre, feelings, he notes, that remain alien to those who do not aspire to freedom: "Thus all of Picasso's oeuvre manifests an exigency of freedom that is unmistakable. It is because of this exigency that it is a cry against death, because of this exigency that it is about glorious life worth living. It is for such reasons that it cannot satisfy the appetites of those who deny it [freedom] and thereby aspire to failure and to death."[16]

Shortly after the text was published, in February 1944, Desnos was visited by the Gestapo at his home, arrested, and sent to the French internment camp of Compiegne. He might not have been deported and later died of typhus in a concentration camp, if the collabo critic Alain Lobreaux had not described him to Nazi friends as a dangerous anti-Nazi.

The story of the Picasso Album epitomizes the climate of 1943 when, animated by new hopes, individuals united by a shared hatred of nazism and a desire to leave behind concrete evidence of their feelings, took risks that they might not have taken earlier, some of them paying with their life. But the Album is also important for its images, suggesting that the generic motif of still life and portraiture in Picasso's hands can convey a tragic subtext. It is also important for the essay by Robert Desnos, a prescient example of the influence of Sartre on a new generation of critics and of artists.

Breaks and Continuties in Postwar French Art

7

Wartime Gilt

French Furniture of the 1940s

As France continues to rethink its recent past, an exhibition outside Paris provided an unprecedented look at the decorative arts of this troubled and controversial decade. Boulogne, a Paris suburb bordering the Bois de Boulogne, is best known today for its elegant Art deco homes, for its right-wing politicians and, since last year, for a museum celebrating 1930s Return-to-Order painting and sculpture (Le Musée des années 30). Recently, Boulogne's Centre Culturel mounted an ambitious temporary exhibition, "Les Décorateurs des années 40," that sought to examine and rehabilitate a little-known period in the French decorative arts. Devoted to sumptuous-looking furniture and home accessories made in France shortly before, during, and immediately after World

First published in *Art in America*, September 1999.

War II, the show presented ensembles by 21 decorators who either opposed functionalism from the start – Gilbert Poillerat, Serge Roche, and Dolt (Pierre Dariel), among others – or who veered away from it in the 1930s and early 1940s – most notably, Jacques Adnet and Jean-Charles Moreux.

Spread over two floors of the Centre Culturel – a high-ceilinged modern building with a grand staircase and circular loggia – were many pieces of furniture never before seen by the public, some of them grouped to re-create their original setting, others deservedly alone in a bay of their own. Despite the straitened circumstances under which they were made, these objects emanate self-confidence, freely embracing unusual materials, bold forms, frank color and a lightheartedness that was emphatically out of tune with its context, particularly during the Vichy years (1940–44).[1] That this exhibition came about at all is in large part due to the new willingness of France to confront – in this case without contrition – the disasters of Vichy.

No doubt contributing to the upbeat feeling of the show was the kitsch character of many of the pieces, particularly those in wrought iron by Gilbert Poillerat and Raymond Subes. The former's baroque dining table on a hunting theme offers an especially arresting example of such flamboyance. This extraordinary piece, with its supports in the form of *bucrane* (deer skulls and antlers), knotted ropes and chains, and a tree branch – all in wrought iron – was fabricated during the war and finished with secondhand materials (Fig. 24). Although this table, with a design evocative of Nazi taste, was reproduced in the catalogue of the 1945 exhibition "Formes d'aujourd'hui," its whereabouts were long unknown. It recently turned up in the possession of Roche, whose bric-a-brac imagination rivaled Poillerat's own.

The use of wrought iron in the decorative arts of this period well illustrates the wartime scarcity of materials. This ordinary metal was often gilded, as in the legs of a marble-topped console by Poillerat, or treated like bronze to give the appearance of opulence, as in a pair of floor candleholders by Subes. Other times it was tempered with historical quotation, as in René Prou's pair of armchairs in white wrought iron with yellow cushions, where the curlicued armature ironically echoes a Louis XVI original.

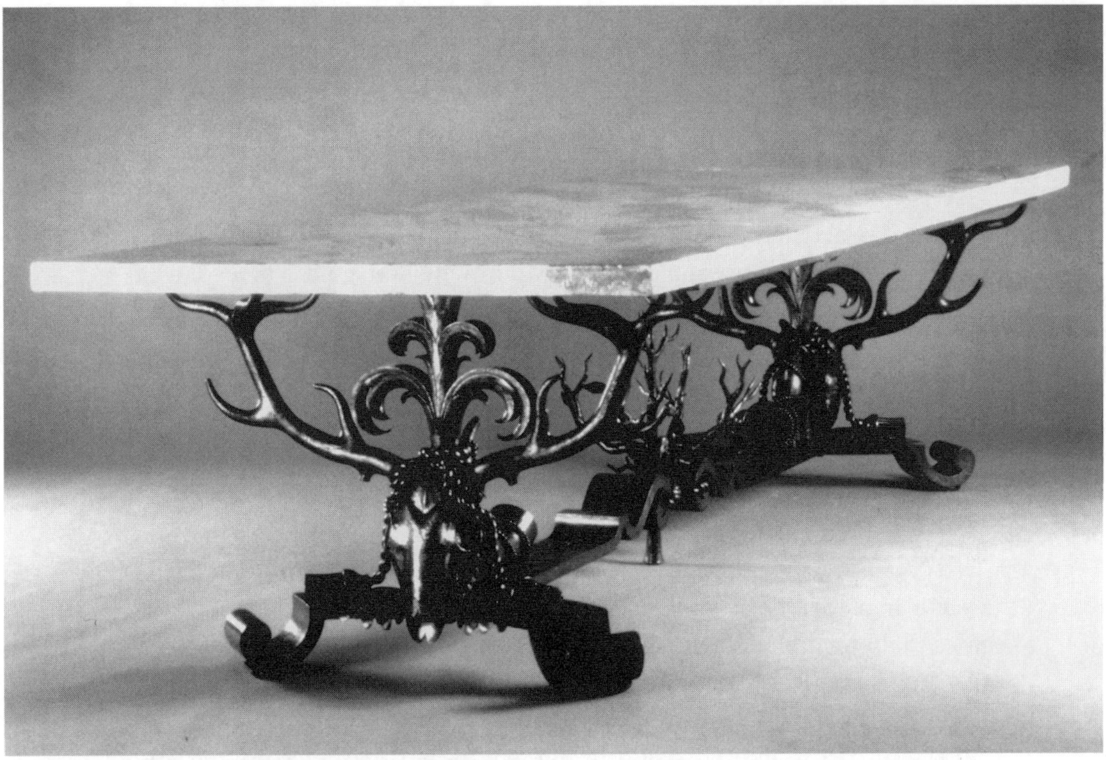

24. Gilbert Poillerat, Table with faux-marble top and wrought-iron legs, 1938–42. Galerie Yves Gastou, Paris (photo: Laurent-Sully Jaulmes).

The show offered many other quotations, from a mixture of periods and styles. Marc du Plantier's dining room draws from both Ancient Egypt (for the hieratic chairs) and Pompeii (for the murals, with their clothed and nude figures on a bare ground). The consoles and sideboards with aged mirror that both Roche and Dolt designed evoke a Baroque and decadent Venice. And the high-back seats adorned with Aubussson tapestry by André Arbus, Jacques Quinet and Adnet have a pompous classical French look reminiscent of the Louis XIV era.

Arbus flirted with a variety of French period styles, only to veer away from quotation after the war, when he produced for his daughter a combination desk and easel in blond sycamore, shown at the Salon des artistes décorateurs in 1947. His 1943 chest in sycamore with musical-instrument designs, parchment and gold leaf evokes a refined though unnameable past. Emilio Terry, lacking a precedent for his surreal variations on the common chair, claimed he had invented the Louis XVII style, named after the so-called lost dauphin, the young son and heir to the throne of Louis XVI who died in prison under mysterious circumstances during the Revolution.

Color played an important role in French furniture of the 1940s, and red was the color of choice for seats and sofas with curving, baroque backs in a variety of materials. Examples in the show included Maurice Jallot's rococo *causeuse* (settee-for-two) in tapestry, René Drouet's 1938 leather-and-wrought-iron banquette shaped like a pair of red lips à la Man Ray, Dolt's 1938 sofa in red satin, and Terry's 1948 lacquered-wood bridge chairs with curvaceous red and black backs shaped like the four playing-card suits. Red or tawny leather was the hallmark of sporty armchairs, a desk and telephone-table tops designed by Paul Dupré-Lafon, mostly dated after the war. Red leather appeared on sideboards and consoles, such as the 1942 *bar à liqueur* by Maxime Old, the 1945 console with leather doors and a wrought-iron base by the house of Dominique, and Adnet's rectangular sideboard cased in leather with gilded wrought-iron hinges by Poillerat, ca. 1939.

Throughout the 1940s, delirious figurative ornamentation – ranging from tassels, ropes and claws to palm leaves and figurines – was revived in French decorative art. A plain country-style eating table in light oak by Adnet from 1945 is transformed by the four white ceramic figures by Maurice Savin that serve as legs. No less striking is a 1948 ebonized wood console by Jean Pascaud supported by a pair of white stone caryatids signed Androusov (Fig. 25). And a blond oak coffer from 1940, sitting on top of an ornate wrought-iron base by Poillerat, is arrestingly embellished in front with a hunting-scene relief by Emmanuel Auricoste.

During the Vichy years in particular, the trace of an artist's hand was deemed especially important to fine furniture. Adnet revived the notion of the portable altar by inviting artists to create a trompe-l'oeil painting inside the doors of his desk-cabinets. Jule Leleu and Dominique called on artists to adorn the doors of their lacquered sideboards with landscape and other motifs of extraordinary detail. Jean Mayodon, the director of the Sèvres manufactures, contributed a pair of gilded ceramic mermaids to already ornate iron doors by Subes (Fig. 26).

This collective approach to the applied arts, with decorators, figurative painters, sculptors and ceramists entering into an ideologically motivated alliance, was highly valued by the architectural historian Louis Hautecoeur, a well-known opponent of modernism and functionalism, who became director of the Department of Fine Arts in Marshal Pétain's government. Pétain looked to the medieval guild system (renamed "Corporatism") as a model and, like his Nazi counterpart, Hitler, thought that such a system, bringing together craftsmen and artists, would reduce the "excessive" individualism of fine artists and resolve the problem of class conflict.[2]

According to the curators of the show, Bruno Foucart and Jean-Louis Gaillemin, the recent postmodern rehabilitation of historicism in both the fine and applied arts explains the rediscovery of these worthy predecessors after years of being excluded from the canon. "One had to wait for the eighties and the postmodernist crisis [for] the demise of the puritanical and naive vision that ascribes . . . virtue to the tube, lying to marquetry, honesty to glass, a reactionary politics to wood and democracy to metal," writes Gaillemin in the catalogue.[3]

The point is well taken. After Derrida's critique of Kant's esthetics, it is no longer possible to exclude overtly ornamented objects from the canon of the decorative arts.[4] Uncertainty as to what is and

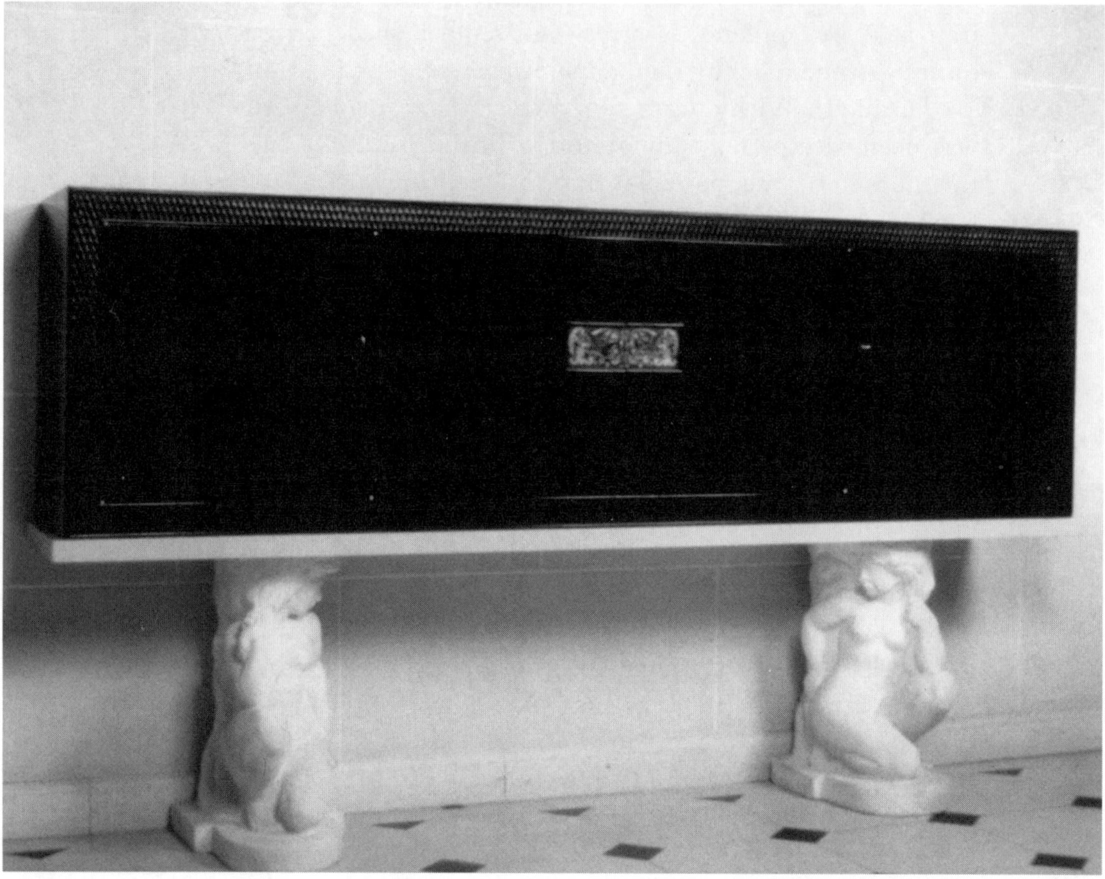

25. Jean Pascaud, Console in ebonized wood with sculpted base by Vadim Androusov, 1948. Private collection, Paris (photo: Poteau).

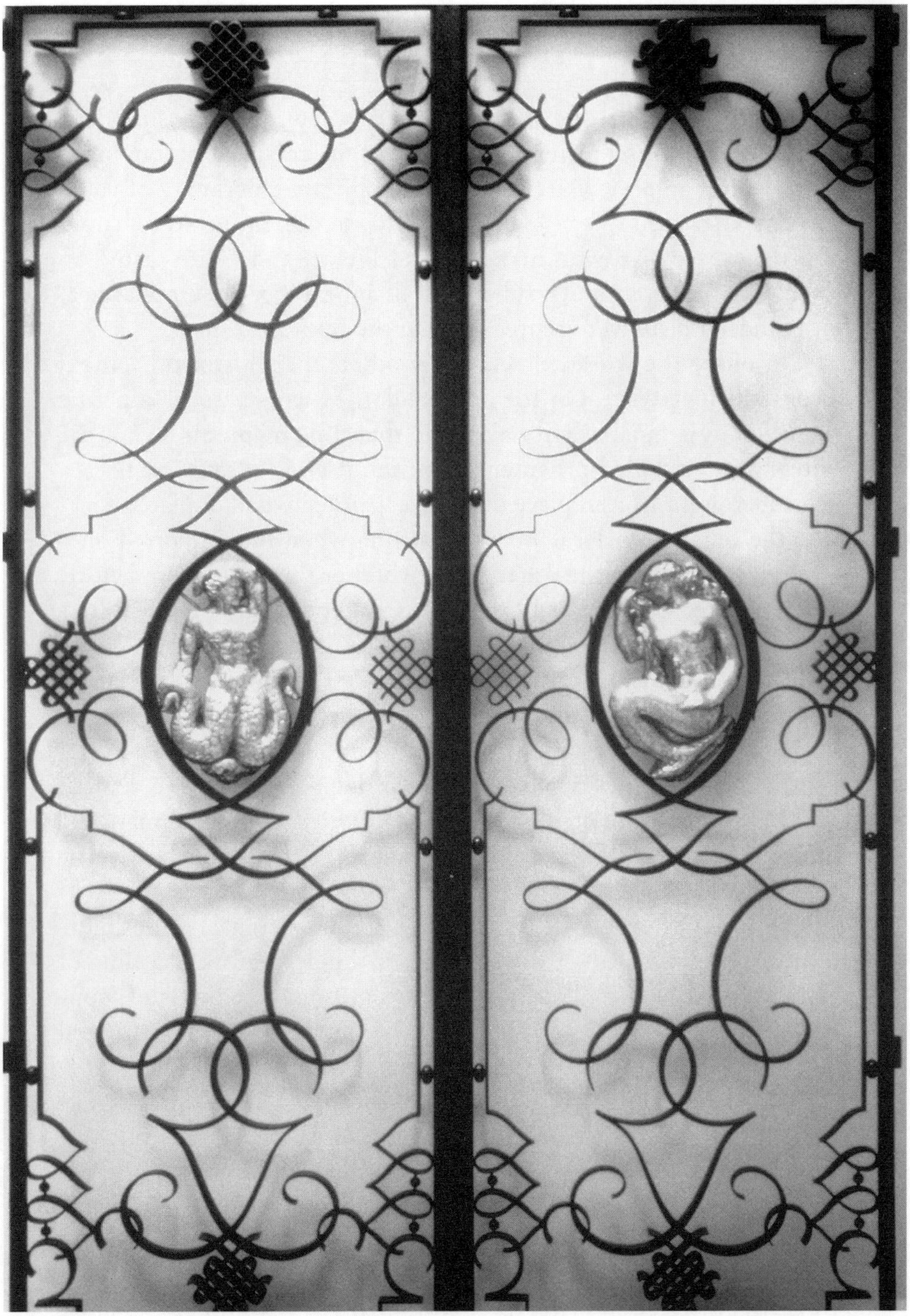

26. Raymond Subes, Bookcase doors with ceramic ornaments by Jean Mayodon, 1943. Private collection, Paris (photo: courtesy Editions NORMA, Paris).

is not essential in a work of art lies at the very root of postmodern discourse and consciousness. The objects in this exhibition make clear that it is impossible to establish an objective hierarchy of value between what used to be called "bad taste" in decorative arts, characterized by excessive workmanship and kitsch, and "elite taste," in which exquisite craft and a sober overall appearance are emphasized. Both kinds of taste were represented in the Boulogne show.

Curiously, the works in this show reflect their historical context in contradictory ways. On the one hand, the pieces bespeak a period when time was more readily available than fine materials, hence the abundance of detailed ornamentation; the use of "ersatz" materials, such as wrought iron in place of bronze, painted wood in place of lacquer; the reliance on local woods at a time when fine imported ones were unavailable. On the other hand, whether they date from before, during or after World War II, the works, while radiating fantasy, luxury and theatrically, evince little practical or monetary concern.[5]

In fact, despite the postwar need for new solutions in everyday design, these decorators continued to look either to rich private patrons or to the government for their clientele. They were encouraged by their ardent supporter, critic Waldemar George, to remain loyal to "the mark of a refined *esprit,* of which the Frenchman, the sensitive geometer, is the privileged keeper."[6] The French government commissioned works from them for a variety of purposes – as gifts to foreign leaders, as furnishings for new transatlantic liners and foreign embassies – thus bailing out the decorators at a time of rising international competition. They continued to enjoy such support until the so-called modernist 1950s caught up with them, and they began to languish, take up painting or do other things.[7]

Politics undoubtedly contributed to the 1940s decorators' lack of public exposure until recent times. Many of those whose work was represented in this show were born around the turn of century – Jacques Adnet (1900–1984), André Arbus (1903–1969), Paul Dupré-Lafon (1900–1971), Maxime Old (1910–1991), Jean Pascaud (1903–1996), Marc du Plantier (1901–1975), Gilbert Poillerat (1902–1998), Serge Roche (1898–1988), Raymond Subes (1893–1970) and others. Thus, they were in their 40s – and at the height of their powers – during the Occupation. Of the 21 decorators discussed in the exhibition catalogue, only Dolt closed up shop for good in 1940. He is quoted as saying: "I believe that war annihilates everything including the taste for interiors, however humble they may be. Our métier, having no reason to express itself, must go into hibernation."[8] The others, out of expediency or a sharing of the politics of Vichy, continued throughout the war years to satisfy the needs of the French state and of a well-heeled clientele.[9]

As a result, French decorative arts of the 1940s have long suffered not only from an association with an antifunctionalist viewpoint, as argued by the curators, but from their genuinely compromising association with Vichy and the Nazi presence in Paris for four of these years. This taint, however just or unjust it may be, partly explains why work of the 1940s, in the fine as well as the decorative arts, has remained in hiding for so many years. It may also account for the presentation of the exhibition in a venue off the beaten track, in a right-wing neighborhood.[10]

8

The Mature Richier, the Young César

Expressionist Confluences in French Postwar Sculpture

FOR A PERIOD during the postwar years in Paris, the sculpture of Germaine Richier (1902–1959) and that of César Baldaccini, known as César (b. 1921), were frequently confronted.[1] In 1959 they were both included in the important exhibition *New Images of Man* at the Museum of Modern Art in New York. Although of different generations, both sculptors used their thorough grounding in the building of classical figures to shape nonstereotypical human forms, either expressively figurative or partaking of the human and the animal realms, against the dominant trend of the time – abstraction. In light of César's mature oeuvre as a *nouveau réaliste,* this brief Expressionist encounter – useful in understanding the various attitudes of postwar Paris – calls for examination.

According to René Huyghe, Expressionism, which had been the major art practice before World War II, simply lost momentum during the Occupation years, and the plastic tendency – meaning formalism – came to the forefront.[2] How then was the expressive mode that was practiced in France perceived until its alleged natural demise dur-

First published in the *Art Journal,* Vol. 53, no. 4, Winter 1994.

ing World War II? And what factors allowed the formalist tendency to flourish? For the conservative French critic Bernard Champigneule, writing shortly before the outbreak of World War II, the sculptors who had once gravitated around Auguste Rodin and Emile Bourdelle had not followed in their masters' footsteps because they "wanted an art that was more rigorous, more concentrated, more general and more distant from the expressive"; Charles Despiau and Aristide Maillol were two sculptors who fit this description.[3] To Bernard Dorival, Expressionist painting between the wars had also become "more distant from the expressive" manner of George Rouault's earlier generation of French Expressionist painters.[4] The same author did explain that another wave of Expressionist art had emerged in the 1920s, "impure in its essence," "morbid," exhaling "a heady perfume," looking "tortured with anxiety," and in all these respects "different from the national model of this movement."[5]

The latter group was comprised mostly of Jewish artists of Montparnasse who formed the core of the Ecole de Paris: Chaim Soutine, Moïse Kisling, Amedeo Modigliani, Ossip Zadkine, Jacques Lipchitz, among others.[6] Although they did not in fact show a uniform Expressionist facture, Expressionism was the overall label under which they were placed. In the thirties tension between French and non-French artists increased to the point that few non-French artists were allowed to participate in the 1937 Paris Exposition Universelle.[7] The controversy over whether to turn Lipchitz's *Prometheus' Victory over the Vulture* from plaster to bronze after its display at the Pavillon de la Découverte of the Exposition Universelle, and the resulting victory of the anti-Lipchitz forces, added to the tension. "No highly placed protectors for Lipchitz," wrote Mady Menier. "Its enormous size condemned it to a mere plaster existence, and the immense Prometheus was destroyed."[8]

During the Occupation years in Paris, Nazi officers spying on the French art world made sure that no mutinous art was shown and that no work by a Jewish artist was ever on display, Expressionist or not. Classical sculpture by Maillol, Despiau, and their followers – Paul Belmondo and Hubert Yencesse, among them – became extremely popular, and its *juste milieu* sensibility was greatly admired by Hitler's favorite sculptor, Arno Breker.[9] As for Expressionist art per se, it became exemplary of decadence in art. Although not censored as such, it was rarely on display and prompted vulgar outbursts in the pro-Nazi press.[10] Because it was suppressed during the years of intense suffering in France, an Expressionist, humanistic art focusing on the battered body might understandably have exploded in the aftermath of war. (The horrific renderings of dismembered bodies by Otto Dix in Germany and the Surrealists in France after World War I come to mind as a precedent.) Yet this did not occur.

Starting around 1943, Jean Bazaine, Maurice Estève, and other painters who in 1941 had called themselves Painters in the French Tradition converted to tricolor abstraction.[11] From the testimony of Louis Leygue, a professor of sculpture at the Ecole des Beaux-Arts in Paris at the time, one learns that the pressure to turn to abstraction, when it began to look as if the Allies would win the war, also manifested itself in sculpture.[12] (The taste for abstraction of New York's Museum of Modern Art curator Alfred Barr, who had occasionally come to Paris on studio visits during the 1930s, was the most concrete link I can think of for this shift.) Thus, abstract art, or rather semiabstract art – innovative only in the eyes of a generation that had missed the first waves of European abstraction – became the dominant mode of art practice of the new, postwar Ecole de Paris. It was now read as the symbol of freedom and resistance vis à vis the classical representations associated with the tyranny of Nazi aesthetics.

The first text on sculpture to come out after the liberation of Paris, *La Sculpture en France depuis Rodin,* by Léon Gischia and Nicole Védrès, confirmed this point of view. Official classical sculpture was vehemently condemned, and the two tendencies within nonacademic sculpture were noted with differing degrees of enthusiasm: one type, which the authors did not bother to illustrate, was "perfectly abstract, geometric and anti-figurative"; the other type, "turned toward an interpretation and a transposition of existing forms," was abundantly illustrated by works in bronze, stone, or plaster, with the latest ones signed by Balthazar Lobo, Henri-Georges Adam, Etienne Martin, Emile-André Leroy, Juana Muller, and Henri Delcambre.[13] In each case, however, a figurative reference could be perceived through the abstract cubistic or biomorphic form. The only examples of Expressionistic figurative sculpture in the entire book – *Head* by Jean Fautrier and two skull images from the war years by Pablo Picasso – were found in a section titled "Sculpture by Painters."

The first truly innovative abstract sculpture to emerge in Paris after the war included a new parameter – movement. Referring back to Constructivism, with a nod to Marcel Duchamp's kinetic oeuvre and to Alexander Calder's mobiles, this work brought together artists of various nationalities who then lived in Paris. The gallery of Denise René has been given credit for unveiling this trend with the April 1955 show *Le Mouvement,* which included, besides Duchamp and Calder, the sculptors Robert Jacobsen, Jean Tinguely, Yaacov Agam, Pol Bury, and J. R. Soto (together with painter Victor Vasarely). Playful and grounded in the viewer's active participation, this new sculpture was a definitive farewell to Expressionism.

Of course, neither *La Sculpture en France depuis Rodin* nor Dense René's exhibition tells the entire story of sculpture in postwar Paris. However, the more Expressionist figurative sculptors of the postwar years – Alberto Giacometti, Picasso, Richier, and the young César – were considered "personalities whose itinerary escapes from the norm."[14]

What caused the Expressionist detour against predominant trends observable in the oeuvre of the mature Richier and that of the young César remains an enigma. The artists' answers have an authentic ring – Richier: "I made my compass lie . . ."; César: "I let my materials guide me" – but they hardly suffice.[15]

Had it not been for World War II, Richier might have had an eventless *juste milieu* career: sought after for her portrait busts in the 1930s, this former *élève particulière* of Bourdelle had from early on in her career her own studio and set of assistants.[16] Unlike another of Bourdelle's students, Giacometti, who proceeded to absorb the Cubist lesson and to move in and out of the Surrealists' orbit in the thirties, Richier remained a classical sculptor during the same period, specializing in statues of female nudes. Critics have compared her work from those years with Charles Despiau's, whose idealized sensitive heads had the same inward-turned expression and fine taut surfaces.

In June 1940, after the debacle of the French army, an armistice was signed between the French and the Germans, and Paris was occupied. Richier and her first husband, a Swiss sculptor also trained by Bourdelle, happened to be in Switzerland at the time and decided to remain there for the time being. The sculpture *June 1940,* a classical bust of a young man with one eyeball bulging out of his pained face, is more emotional than her previous work, and its title is indicative of a willingness on the part of Richier to introduce current events into her sculpture. *June 1940* marks not only the armistice, but the end of freedom and democratic processes in France with the arrival of Marshal Philippe Pétain. Another work, *The Toad* (1940; F. Guiter collection) depicts a classical female nude shown crouching on all four like a toad ready to jump and is Richier's first sculpture suggesting the "animal" side of humanity. *The Fencers* (1943; F. Guiter collection), two figures engaged in a duel, shows insistent tactility and evokes war.

Between 1944 and 1946 there was a notable change in her choice of sitters. (Throughout her career, Richier started out from a live model.) When in October 1946 Richier returned to Paris, Nardone, the model who used to sit for Rodin and was by then a fat old man, posed for her. Also during this time she created her first Surrealist hybrids, by using tree stumps and branches in lieu of body parts in her plaster casts (e.g., *The Forest Man,* 1945; F. Guiter collection) or by combining into one image the shape of an insect with that of a skinny, long-limbed female (*The Grasshopper,* 1944; F. Guiter collection). Inspired by the web of the spider, Richier spun a web of her own invention – with a few crisscrossing rods – around some of the large works that she completed after her return to Paris (*The Spider I,* 1946; *Man with Claws,* 1952; *The Ant,* 1953; all F. Guiter collection).

No more idealized classical bodies now. The animal forms, when present, were explicit, and the bronze surfaces had become rugged to the touch, pitted as if worked like heavy dough. Decaying debris from nature seamlessly integrated into the shape of the figures added to the uncanny look of Richier's new work. In regard to Richier's controversial commission for the church of Assy, *Crucifix,* 1950, art historian Sarah Wilson has noted that there appears to be a "fusion of body and bark," and in regard to *The Shepherd of Landes,* she writes that "the face is made from a brick pierced and rubbed smooth by the sea."[17]

A year after the 1947 International Exhibition of Surrealism, and three years before Giacometti's first postwar show, Richier's new imagery went public with a retrospective at the Maeght gallery in Paris. Among the haunting images seen at the exhibition was *The Thunderstorm,* 1947–48, with its "sister" image *The Storm,* 1948–49. These two larger-than-life-size bronzes (Fig. 27), opened at the back and with disturbing surfaces, marvelously reveal the possibilities of an Expressionist content in figurative sculpture. As if not comprehending their predicament, a woman and her male companion shamelessly display their ugly nude bodies, arms hanging awkwardly by their sides with branchlike endings in lieu of outstretched fingers. The woman is of nearly equal size and bulk to the man. Are they the Adam and Eve of the post-Holocaust era? Or escapees from the Last Judgment?

In the fall of 1956 Richier had another major exhibition in Paris, this time at the Musée National d'Art Moderne; included was *The Shepherd of Landes,* the frightening effigy in bronze of a tall decomposing body on stilts. She died of cancer on July 31, 1959, during her exhibition at the Musée d'Antibes.

While César's sculptures, unlike Richier's, tend to perpetuate the stereotypes of the passive victimized woman versus the aggressive predatory male, it is nevertheless easy to note a resemblance between Richier's postwar images and some of César's of the mid fifties: the same misshapen bodies; the same corroded, rugged surfaces; the same sense of a decaying body immobilized at an unexpected, seemingly unposed moment; the same allusion, in Peter Selz's words, to the "primeval and legendary creatures who are in the state of evolution along an imaginary philogenetic tree."[18]

Had it not been for World War II, César might never have become recognized as an artist. A Mediterranean like Richier, César grew up in Marseilles in a neighborhood of recent Italian immigrants. In 1940 Marseilles became home to many Parisian refugees who were stranded there after the armistice. Among them were Ecole des Beaux-Arts students who befriended the young César (a part-time night student at the Marseilles Ecole des Beaux-Arts) and who immediately sensed his sculptural gifts. After the Germans invaded the so-called free zone of France, his new friends persuaded him to leave with them in 1943 to attend the Paris Ecole des Beaux-Arts.

The school did not turn the uncouth youth with the strong *midi* accent into a gentleman, but gave him a thorough grounding in tra-

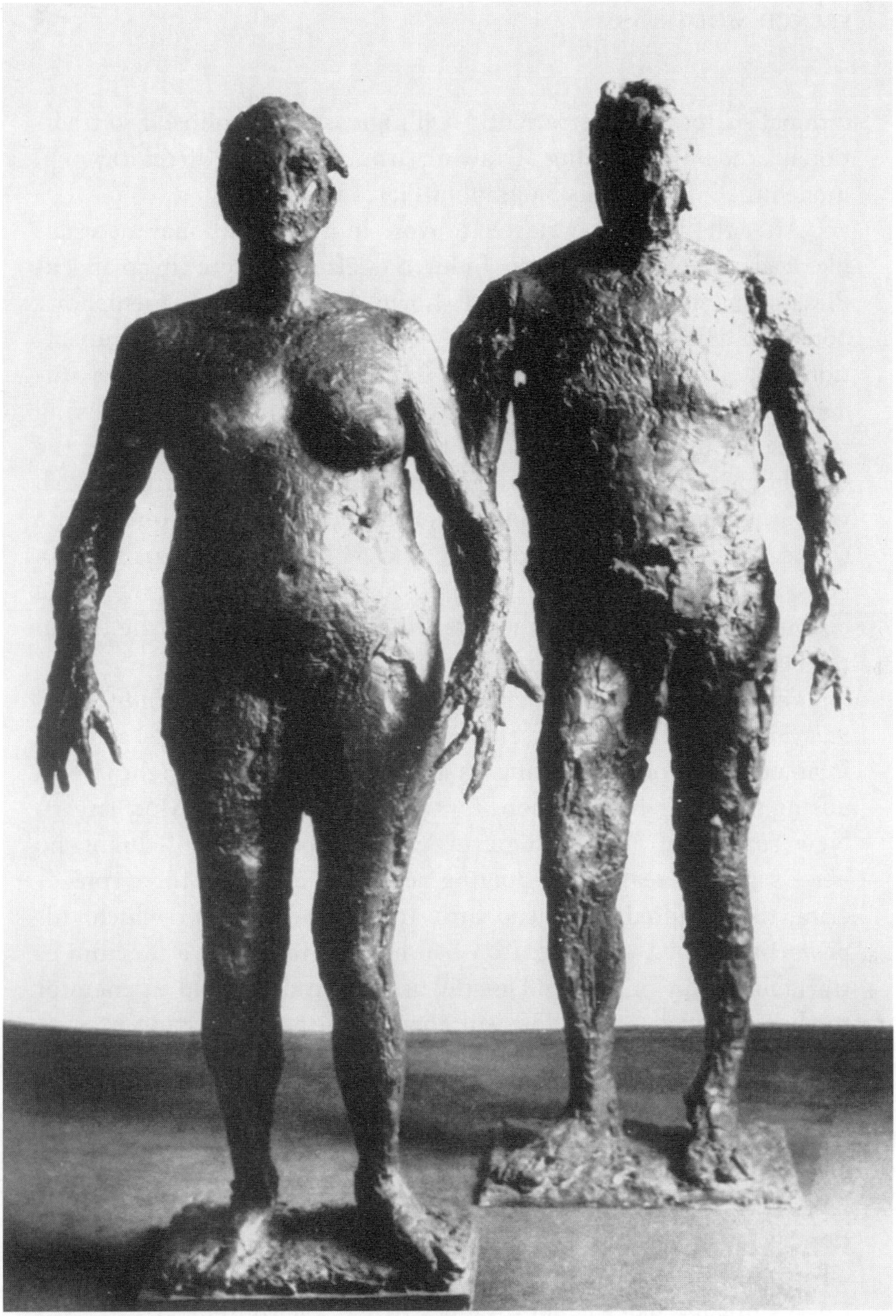

27. Germaine Richier, *The Thunderstorm (L'Orage)*, 1947–48. Bronze, height 74½ in. (right); *The Storm (L'Ouragane)*, 1948–49. Bronze, height 70 in. (left). Musée national d'art moderne, Centre d'art Georges Pompidou, Paris (photo: courtesy of the museum).

ditional sculpture. "He patiently, willingly, submits himself to traditional academic teaching. Drawing from a model, direct carving, modeling . . ." wrote his biographer Pierre Restany.[19]

After the war César started to work in unconventional materials like lead, wire, and scrap iron. Industrial leftovers were cheap and, as Picasso and the Surrealists had shown, had enormous metaphoric potential. His first nonacademic pieces were toylike witty inventions, few of which have survived. César remained on and off a student at the Ecole des Beaux-Arts for a total of thirteen years, living for a while in a studio next door to Giacometti. In 1954 he won the Collabo prize for a large see-through welded-iron structure of a fish with threatening open mandibles, precariously balanced on top of a tripod base. This piece, shown at Lucien Durand in Paris, gave a boost to César's reputation. A cat, a scorpion, a bat, a grasshopper, a bedbug, a mosquito, and other predatory creatures joined the fish in the bestiary of César's animal works.

Parallel to the animal series were the nudes. *Seated Nude, Pompeii* (Fig. 28), a life-size skeletal figure in welded metal rods, arrested in an odd position as if sitting on air, alludes to bodies caught in lava during the Vesuvius eruption. *Torso* (1954; Museum of Modern Art, New York), with its missing arm, two stumps in lieu of thighs, no head, sagging breasts, and bulging belly, was a tour de force considering the hundreds of cheap little iron corners out of which this powerful image was made. Iron had become for César a medium as tractable as clay or plaster. He now used arc welding and a generator to shape, as well as join, hot softened metal parts. Starting in 1955 the bestiary and the human figures sometimes merged into strange mutated creatures.

Gunther Metken has noted differences in the work of Richier and that of César from this time, stating: "Unlike Germaine Richier, he [César] does not make a detour through a technique of reproduction – plaster, lost wax – but lets the iron evolve and express itself on its own."[20] Yet it is evident that regardless of varying technique, César's images, like Richier's, radiate expressive content.

According to the curators of *Paris Post War: Art and Existentialism 1945–1955*, it was the mood of the postwar years in Paris that gave form to those uneasy images: "The psychology of the postwar period, deeply bound up in the simultaneous desire for both caesura, continuity and catharsis, was reflected in contemporary art and

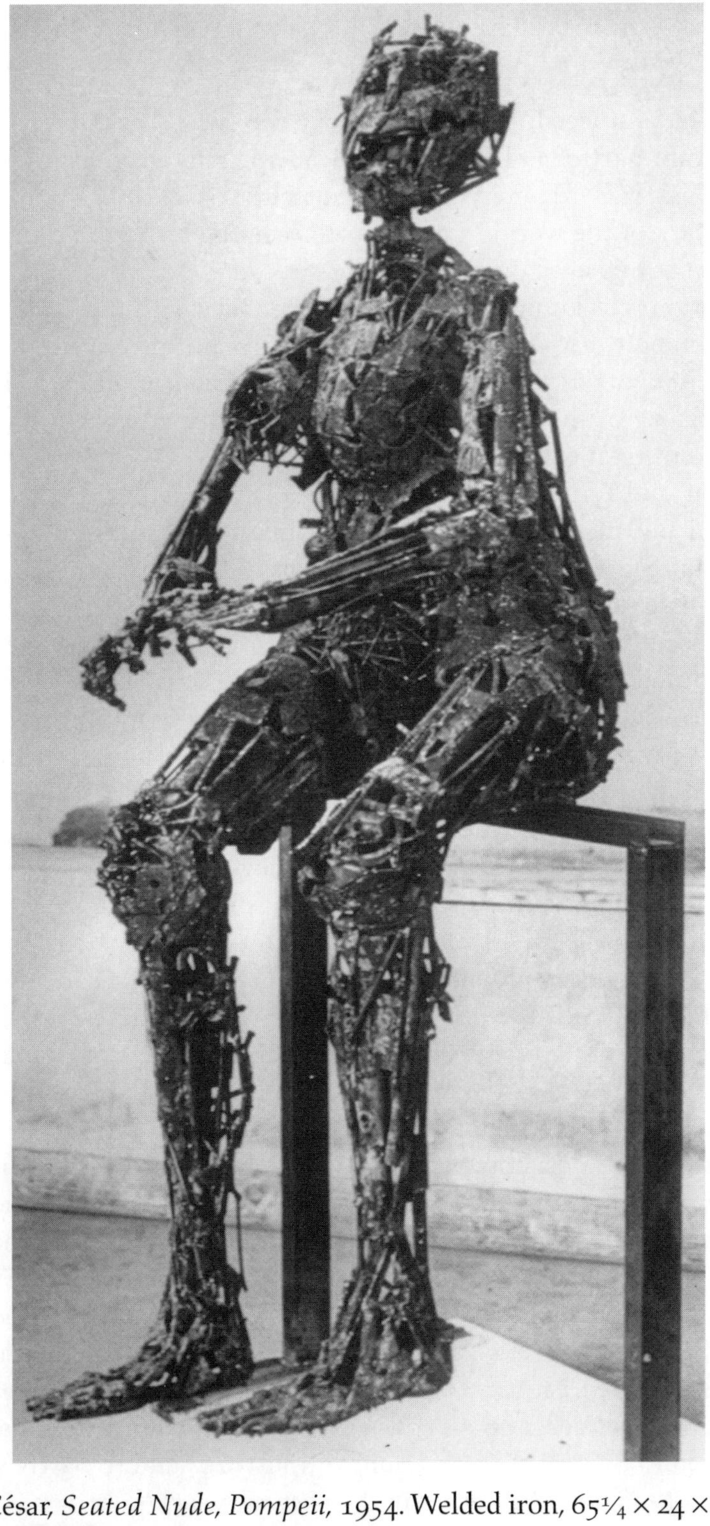

28. César, *Seated Nude, Pompeii,* 1954. Welded iron, $65\frac{1}{4} \times 24 \times 33$ in. Private collection.

thought."[21] Indeed, like characters in the novels of Albert Camus, Jean Paul Sartre, and Simone de Beauvoir, the creations of Richier and César can remotely suggest existentialist clichés, such as "the absurdity of the world," "notions of becoming rather than the fixity of being," and even "nausea."[22]

Nothing is known about Richier's contacts with the "existentialist" sculptor par excellence, Giacometti, who also spent the war years in Switzerland and whom she had befriended in Paris. In fact, the history of the exiled sculptors' community at work in Switzerland during the Occupation years – Richier, Giacometti, Marino Marini, and Fritz Wotruba – has yet to be researched. César, on the other hand, has talked about his erstwhile neighbor at the corner of rue du Moulin Vert and rue Hipolyte-Maindron in the 14th arrondissement, and how he became fascinated with wire armatures after seeing Giacometti working on his. But in an interview César said: "Alberto liked skinny women, and I like fat ones."[23] He also acknowledged other stylistic influences on his work: primitive art, Pablo Gargallo, Julio González, Richier herself, and of course Picasso.

In comparison Richier did not leave many clues about her move away from *juste milieu* classicism: "I believe I found my way when I grew tired of analyzing forms. . . . When something no longer interests you, you want to move on to something else," she told her niece.[24] It has been proposed that Richier's second husband, René de Solier, a Surrealist writer whom she met in 1946, helped her to change her outlook by introducing her to the Paris intellectual milieux of the late forties and early fifties.

Indeed, as the intelligentsia regrouped after years of muzzling and isolation, and as the horrors of the Nazi regime came to the surface, much soul-searching was going on in Paris. Foremost were questions of ethics: a position of pessimist existentialist humanism on the one hand and a desperate search for new myths on the other. Heady discussions took place around Sartre and around the recently returned André Breton at the Café des Deux Magots. Richier, it seems, shuttled between the two mentors. And her most steadfast supporter (besides de Solier) was Georges Limbour, whose name is attached to Surrealist publications in the 1920s and to Sartre's publication *Les Temps Modernes* in the postwar years.[25]

As for César, he conveys in conversation the feeling that his conversion from academicism to the new work came to him naturally not from Sartre but from asserting his cultural and social "otherness" (what Sartre would call his existential being). He traded the long white coat, the well-lit atelier, the clay and the plaster of the bourgeois sculptor for the industrial setting in which he felt more at ease with himself:

> You don't understand. My friends, Albert Féraud, Nadar, they came from solid bourgeois milieux. People with my kind of background were unheard of in art school. I did not like to read. I was brought up on popular culture, the street, American films, slang. . . . I am a manual type: first I worked with clay; then I worked with metal because it was cheap. . . . And you don't do the same things when you change materials. . . . I made my first welded piece in Draguignan at a friend's car repair shop. Then for several years I worked in a factory at Villetaneuse.[26]

But if César's departure from academicism had to do with a consciousness of his existential otherness (and anticipates his predilection for popular culture typical of Pop artists and *nouveaux réalistes*), and if Richier's abandon of *juste milieu* classicism had to do with the intellectual climate of postwar Paris, why were their Expressionist figurative phases such an atypical trajectory?[27]

There was shortly after the liberation a small group of Communist artists whose resistance record had been without blemish and who also vehemently opposed abstract art. André Fougeron, Boris Taslitzky, and Edouard Pignon sought to impose an Expressionist version of Soviet social realism on the Paris art world. With the exclusion of Communists from the French government in May 1947, however, Communist ideology lost ground, and the Communist voice in artistic matters waned, to the advantage of abstract art.[28] The controversy concerned mostly painting, and I have found no evidence that either Richier or César were involved politically or aesthetically in these controversies.

More likely is the impact of their work on Picasso's 1944 *Man with a Sheep,* a ghostly white plaster form frequently photographed in the artist's studio before being cast in bronze. Picasso, who became a Communist in September 1944, had also refused abstraction throughout his artistic career. *Man with a Sheep* is an uncanny image. Here, there is no desire to shock the viewer with the Surrealist conceit of irrational conjunctions. The meaning of the religious icon of an adoring shepherd bringing his live offering to the newborn Christ has been subtly subverted. The human and the animal species are made to appear reversible: the restive lamb destined for slaughter has become "human," and the shepherd is shown as the dehumanized agent of the cruel acts.

In retrospect, after the events of Auschwitz and Hiroshima, the Surrealist poetic imagination seemed lame. Nazi cruelty had surpassed all that was imaginable. Representing the Holocaust poetically was said to be an impossible task. Yet that was what Picasso, Richier, Giacometti, and the young César tried to do, using the figure in a new expressive way. In the case of Richier and César, this obsession with the expressive human body did not last. In her last years Richier occasionally collaborated with abstract painters and herself veered toward a more abstract vision (she even began to paint her bronzes in bright enamels). As for César, with his *nouveau réaliste* takeoff in 1959 – the *Compressions* – he allowed his viewers to understand that the years of mourning were over. Abstract art apparently suited the ambiguities of the postwar years better than disturbing figurative effigies with open-ended meanings. Mute about the carnage caused by Hitler and his acolytes, abstract art managed to exude a good conscience because of its formal vanguardism.[29]

9

Pierre Restany

Postwar Remnants of Cultural Pétainism Exposed

IN THE FOLLOWING PAGES, I examine how in the context of a debate over the Americanization of French everyday life, one critic expressed his conviction that it was far more urgent for French society to shake up old habits than to rant against the dehumanizing effects of technology. I explore Restany's student background in a postwar intellectual Paris awash in Marxism, Heideggerianism, and existentialism. And I show how in the context of a Paris artworld trying to recover international preeminence with French-made postcubist abstraction still reeling from Pétainism, Restany took up the cause of the monochromist Yves Klein and homed in on artists who drew inspiration from the leftovers of the new consumer society, calling them *nouveaux réalistes.* The reemergence into the Parisian limelight of Marcel Duchamp just as General de Gaulle came out of retirement to lead the Fifth Republic in 1958, and the issues raised by this congruence, end this chapter.

One of the first French industries to recover after World War II was the automobile industry. In 1945, the Renault company launched the 4 chevaux (it was the pièce de résistance of the Automobile salon in 1946); then in 1948 the Citroen 2 CV appeared on the market. Neither car was speedy, nor shapely. But after a hiatus

First published in *Yale French Studies,* December 2000.

of five years when no French cars were built, and few circulated, the availability of these small, awkward, and relatively cheap new cars changed many things in French people's life as well as in the French landscape.

By 1955, the car had become so ubiquitous as to stir alarm – not among the general public, but in a young and marginal figure of the postwar era in France, Guy Debord, about to launch the Situationist International. Whereas the automobile was sold as a promise of higher quality of life, freedom, and escape for the masses, for Debord, the democratization of car ownership was a bad thing. The masses want automobiles not for convenience and mobility – public transport is just as efficient – but to imitate the rich, who, the media tells them, are happy because they drive a car. That, at least, is what we read in Debord's "Introduction to a critique of Urban geography," dated September 1955 in the translation by Ken Knabb.

> This present abundance of private cars is nothing but the result of the constant propaganda by which capitalist production persuades the masses . . . that the possession of a car is one of the privileges our society reserves for its privileged members. . . . Such pathetic illusions of privilege are linked to a general idea of happiness prevalent among the bourgeoisie and maintained by a system of publicity that includes Malraux' esthetics as well as the imperatives of Coca Cola – an idea of happiness whose crisis must be provoked on every occasion by every means.[1]

By the end of the fifties, the automobile had entered the fray of art. César Baldaccini, known as César (1921–1998), who had achieved success with expressionist sculpture in rusty welded iron parts, such as *Torso* (1954) now at the Museum of Modern Art in New York, veered off course when he discovered near Paris an arsenal of abandoned car carcasses and the American-made machines that compressed them. On several occasions Restany – whom he had known since 1954 – accompanied him there. At the Paris Salon de Mai of 1960 César displayed three large parallelepipeds of contorted metal made from crushed car carcasses, each weighing a ton (Fig. 31).

"Ce fut un beau scandale [It was some beautiful scandal]," writes Restany, recalling with glee the jaundiced faces of the Salon hierarchy, whose sense of decorum and good taste these mammoth ready-mades challenged.[3] The acclaimed welder had not only succumbed to the temptation of modern technology and substituted a powerful machine for the welder's hand-held torch, he had given up shaping his sculpture in a subjective evocative manner by presenting his work as it came out of the process of compression – a generic cube. The publicity engendered by the Salon de Mai event reached far beyond the usual coterie of artworld afficionados. César became a celebrity.

Impressed by the new *compressions,* Restany invited the sculptor to join the *nouveaux réalistes,* a group in formation that shared Restany's conviction that a page must be turned on "an artistic milieu saturated with formal recipes and material compromises [les compromis de la matière]."[4] The group was to include during its three-year existence Yves Klein, Jean Tinguely, Niki de Saint Phalle, Raymond Hains, François Dufrène, Jacques Mahé de Villeglé, César, Arman, Spoerri, Christo, Martial Raysse, and Mimo Rotella. The *nouveaux réalistes* became in the early sixties a group to contend with, assisted by Restany's immense energy and talent at promoting their careers. He curated exhibitions, including some in New York, wrote monographs about them, gave lectures worldwide, and published several theoretical texts on the new-realist phenomenon.

Who is this now older statesman of French criticism, recently honored in France with exhibitions and other accolades? Born in French Catalonia in 1930 and raised in Morocco, the son of a prosperous wine merchant, Restany came to Paris in the late forties to prepare for the Ecole Normale Supérieure at the Lycée Henri IV (with the secret ambition of becoming a poet). According to his biographer, young Restany quickly tired not only of the lycée regimen but of the ambient intellectual terrorism of postwar Paris:

> Sartre reigns as the uncontested mentor of young people, he is the idol of a whole generation. . . . Marxism pervades thinking and one cannot escape. . . . Away from Marxism, there is no salvation. Either one deals with Communism, or one is a bastard, and an imbecile. . . . As a Gaullist he [Restany] learns to shut up. . . . He feels close to Albert Camus."[5]

There is little denying that intellectual power was in the hands of the left in France after the liberation, even if the French left was itself fragmented. In his book on postwar French intellectuals, the historian Tony Judt reveals the complexity of leftwing allegiances in the postwar years, depending on whether the issue at hand was how to punish French writers who had collaborated, or how to remain pro–Soviet Union after the revelations of the Moscow trials, or whether Algeria should remain French, to cite only these major points of dissension. Judt also claims that in the early fifties there was an anticommunist option with moral coherence, led by the sociologist-historian Raymond Aron, "but in the political and cultural context of these years, it [Aron's option] also placed one outside of the mainstream of intellectual life."[6]

With his biographer, Restany is reticent to reveal his sources. "Like other students at Khagne, he read Husserl and Heidegger."[7] In the tortuous political climate alluded to above, one can only surmise young Restany's positions: He probably shared Camus's existentialism, his forgiving stance toward wartime collabo writers, and perhaps also the famed novelist's ambivalence toward the idea of an independant Algeria. Although Restany never mentions Aron as a mentor, his anticommunist politics and interest in developing a sociological approach to contemporary art may well have been influenced by the Gaullist historian and sociologist. It is clear that the budding neo-dadaist did not swallow piecemeal what the academic establishment had to offer. He did not finish Normale, and at twenty-one, began a lifetime of foreign travels, in particular to Italy, and of intellectual and artistic discovery on his own.

Much of Restany's theorizing about the extraordinary in the ordinary, about the presence of art in the banal reality of urban everydayness, in the use of what he calls "le materiau de la sociologie urbaine"[8] suggests a familiarity with Henri Lefebvre's *Critique de la vie quotidienne.*[9] But Restany never showed a trace of anti-Americanism, the fashionable stance in the French fifties adopted by Lefebvre, by the situationists and by Marxists in general. In fact throughout the fifties, while the French art press generally put down exhibitions in Paris galleries of recent American art, including Jackson Pollock and Jasper Johns, Restany game them a closer look and encouraged his artist friends to do the same.

Becoming an art critic is rarely something calculated. The activity usually begins modestly and anonymously with visits to galleries, meeting artists, following them to their studios and – particularly in Europe – writing catalogue essays for their exhibitions, all the while making ends meet through other means. Throughout the fifties, as the ex-Normalien's reputation grew and he expanded his horizons beyond Paris to the rest of Europe, Restany made his living as press attaché and speech writer for a series of French government functionaries. His contacts with French officials proved very useful when the artists he championed wished to do things such as hire guards of the Republic in full regalia (Yves Klein in 1958), fill a gallery with garbage (Arman in 1960), and obstruct a Paris street with oil barrels (Christo in 1961–62).

He not only acted as a facilitator and media person, offering his ideas to the artists who interested him, but his experience as press attaché taught him how to catch the attention of the media, a talent that the situationist Guy Debord never forgave him for. I personally remember the proto-dadaist evening he engineered one night in Brussels in 1965 on behalf of his *nouveaux réalistes,* in the course of which he spoke out in a state of true or feigned drunkenness, terrorizing some in the audience with rude comments on their physique, on their art or on their politics, while the rest of the audience laughed.

What was the Paris artworld when Restany joined it in the early fifties? In an interview with the author, Restany described the postwar situation as follows:

> In 1952, Pollock came over for the Venice Biennale and was in Paris for his show at Studio Facchetti. But nobody paid attention because the European public was not ready to buy American art and because Paris was making a big screen trying to keep a hegemonous situation. . . . They [the big Paris mafia] wanted to press the idea that there was a kind of abstract key to the reading of Cubism. They tried to invent a parallelism between Abstract Expressionism and the post-cubist abstract line – Villon, Poliakoff, de Stael [Fig. 29], and so on.[10]

He then named the Galerie de France, founded in 1942; the Galerie

Charpentier, a hotbed of collaboration during the war; and the Salon de mai as spaces "totally integrated into that promotional system."[11]

This abstract key to the reading of cubism had begun during the Occupation years, when a number of middle-of-the-road "painters in the French tradition" as they had called themselves in 1941 (Jean Bazaine, Maurice Estève, Alfred Manessier, Gustave Singier, and others), veered toward postcubist *bleu-blanc-rouge* abstraction in early 1943. (By then, the winds of victory had shifted.)[12] At its best, this type of painting revealed the scaffolding of cubist representation with or without a figure or landscape enmeshed in the image. "Freedom" allegedly symbolized by this cubist abstraction lacked some key ingredients – improvisational freedom of line, and an expressive *matière* considered un-French and degenerate at that time.[13]

Some twelve years after Paris was liberated, Ecole de Paris painting, at least according to an exhibition held at galerie Charpentier under that name in 1956, continued the postcubist tradition inaugurated in 1943.[14] The cover of the catalogue featured a freehand hard-edged composition picturing a bird inside a cage by the French cubist abstractionist Jacques Villon, in yellow, blue, and pink, overlayed by an armature of radiating lines. The exhibition included a few paintings by figurative traditionalists who had seen their reputation ascend at the end of the thirties, such as Christian Caillard, Maurice Savin, and Roger Limouse,[15] as well as works by artists whose emergence dated from the Vichy years – the painters in the French tradition mentioned above. It also included a Bonnard-influenced painting by Raymond Legueult, a participant in the propaganda trip to Nazi Germany of 1941, and a favorite of the anti-Semitic art critic Lucien Rebatet.[16]

Restany's testimony suggests that after the Liberation, the idea of art as a national endeavor excluding un-French influences remained operative. Or, put in another way, although philosophical power may have clearly shifted to the left in France after the war, on the art front there was more continuity than discontinuity with the recent rightwing nationalistic past. The choices made by the powerful Galerie Charpentier confirm this view.

Yet, as normalcy returned to Paris, as major figures of the artworld who had been prevented from showing their work during the

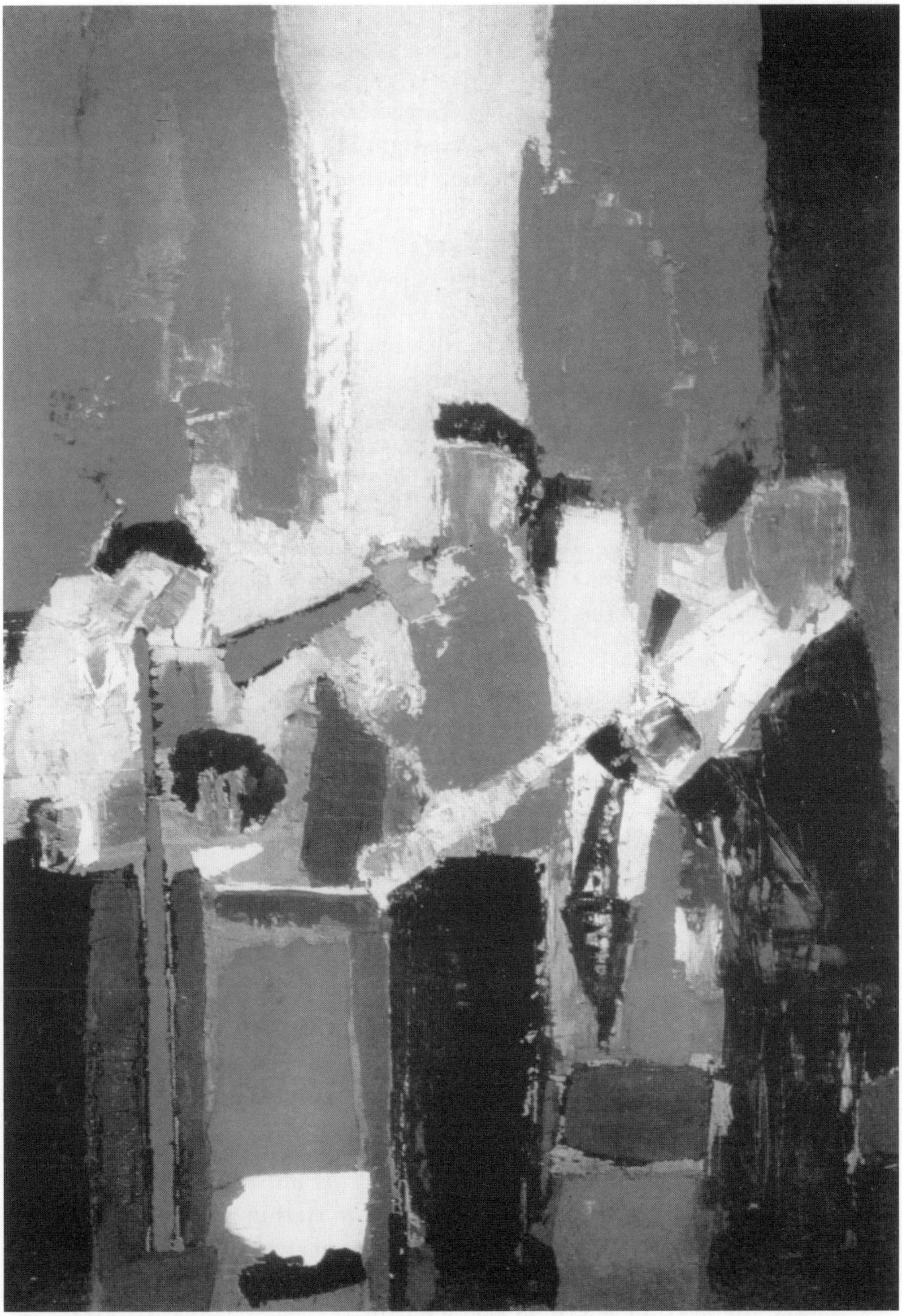

29. Nicolas de Stael, *The Musicians,* 1953. Oil on canvas, 162 × 114 cm. Private collection, Paris.

Occupation years emerged from their silence, as exiled artists made their way back to France, there were signs of change. Even the Charpentier 1956 exhibit acknowledged this change: Marc Chagall, Max Ernst, and Pablo Picasso were each represented by a painting, as was Hans Hartung (Julio Gonzales's son in law and a Resistance fighter who had lost a leg in the Spanish Civil War), whose gestural abstractions had begun to receive attention in Paris in the late forties.

Indeed, although power clearly remained in the hands of galleries that displayed Ecole de Paris painting and sculpture, new energy emerged in marginal new galleries, feeding on varieties of artistic practices and stimulating critical controversies. Denise René, who had worked in the Resistance during the war, specialized in "cold" geometry (Victor Vasarely, Soto, Dewasne); the "hot" abstractionists Hans Hartung, Pierre Soulages, Camille Bryen, and the CoBra group show at Colette Allendy and Lydia Conti; American artists show at the Facchetti studio gallery; Iris Clert would join the fray in 1956 by exhibiting Yves Klein, Jean Tinguely, Armand Arman, and others.

The gallery of René Drouin, the most important outpost of postwar vanguardism, was a special case. It had been started in 1939 by Leo Castelli with the architect-designer René Drouin, who kept it open during the Occupation years. It had shown Fautrier in 1943, put a work by Dubuffet in a group show in July 1944, and it continued to represent these artists in the fifties. A rarely mentioned exhibition at that gallery in 1959 was by the Italian situationist Giuseppe Pinot-Gallizio. Painted cloth draped all over the gallery's interior was sold by the yard in a new-realist vein that went unrecognized by Restany.

"When I started to write in the early fifties," Restany told me, "it was impossible in Paris just like in New York not to take some kind of position." Within the small milieu of postwar French art criticism, he could choose between Michel Tapié de Celeyran, the advocate of Fautrier and Dubuffet and in general of *l'art autre,* Michel Ragon who rallied around the lyrical abstractionists, Hartung, Soulages, and the CoBra group; Michel Seuphor, who remained loyal to "cold" abstractionists; and Charles Estienne, the foremost enemy of the new American art.[17] Or he could side with the *Internationale Situation-*

iste led by Guy Debord, who swore the end of art as it was known and practiced in bourgeois societies, and that briefly counted among its members the French *affichist* Maurice Dufrène, the CoBra member Asger Jorn, the Italian Pinot Gallizio, the Dutch Constant Nieuwenhuys.[18]

Restany's model of a critic was Tapié de Celeyran. A descendant of Toulouse Lautrec, Tapié was known for his picturesque eccentricities (he drove a Ferrari, smoked cigars, and played in a jazz band), but also for his global vision of art (he traveled frequently to the United States). "His concept of l'art autre imposes itself and remains a historic point of reference," Restany told his biographer.[19]

What did Tapié contribute to the postwar debate on art that Restany considered "a historic point of reference"? He used the dadaist Duchamp's indifference to beauty as an artistic paradigm. In his 1952 text on *l'art autre,* Tapié assailed all art that brings pleasure to its onlooker through notions of beauty, form, space, and aesthetics. He claimed that "today's productions exist *outside* of these notions, with a total indifference toward these notions." Up until Dada, he explained, all the isms had been revolutionary only superficially. Between 1920 and 1940, he went on, there were no first-rate revelations except for the surrealist phenomenon, and now, leaving Picasso aside, Picabia and Marcel Duchamp were the only relevant artists.

Yet, he asserted, contemporary productions suggested that the example of Dada has not been heard except by a few rare individuals. Individuality, not movements, mattered now, and especially individuals who were not "prisoners of their past" but of their "becoming." Tapié's text then turned into a vertiginous whirl of words – "dynamic drunkenness," "the transfinite extasy of beauty, mystery, eroticism, mysticism. . . ," a rhetorical *flonflon*[20] after which Restany often modeled his own prose. Finally Tapié named the artists involved in this new *informel,* or *informe,* mode.[21] Preeminent were Jean Fautrier and Jean Dubuffet, but the list was long and included Henri Michaux, Georges Mathieu, Pierre Soulages, Jackson Pollock, Alfonso Ossorio, Mark Tobey, Hans Hartung, Camille Bryen, Hans Hofmann, William de Kooning, among contemporary painters, and Germaine Richier, Leonard Baskin, Reg Butler, Edouardo Paolozzi, and Claire Falkenstein, among the sculptors.[22]

To distinguish himself from Tapié, and as a means of moving to center stage, Restany sided for Mathieu and Hartung against Soulages, despite the fact that all three painters were among Tapié's favorites. But, more important, he sided with Fautrier against Dubuffet. If Restany's reasons for not liking Dubuffet were more political than artistic – "Dubuffet's demagogical impulse irritated me"[23] – his choice was far from accidental.

For one thing, Fautrier had proved himself a humanist in his artistic response to the Occupation years, by bearing witness to the Nazi killings of innocent victims in a series of paintings entitled *Hostages* (1943–45). This Duchamp lookalike had an unusual background for an artist. He had been raised in London by a single wealthy mother, and when the Depression hit in the thirties, he had moved to the Alps, become a ski instructor and run a nightclub at a ski resort. He returned to Paris during the Occupation and, abandoning the figurative mode of his earlier years, invented new ways of making paintings, using powder, plaster, glue and thick paper support. He applied this new method to the *Hostage* paintings, which evoked more than they represented – squashed faces, and brutalized bodies. It is these works that had led Tapié to his notion of *l'art autre.*[24]

But another aspect of Fautrier emerged after the war, raising an interesting dilemma and preparing Restany not only for the antics of Yves Klein but those of other artists he was going to defend under the name of *nouveaux réalistes.* Starting in 1950, Fautrier scandalized the Paris artworld by exhibiting "originaux multiples" [original multiples], works that suggested the possibility of mass-producing art in such a way that the word *original* lost meaning.[25] This rarely talked-about phase of Fautrier's oeuvre challenged the authenticity of the artist's gesture as a direct expression of feeling, and threatened the value system of the art establishment. Had he read Walter Benjamin?

"I will no longer paint," Fautrier said to Jeanine Aeply, at whose workshop he prepared the works, "I will create my oeuvre directly with mechanical processes."[26] Fautrier abandoned the production of original multiples when Aeply closed her workshop, but the idea had been thought-provoking enough to make Restany realize that after

Fautrier "there was not going to be a second generation of gestural painters."[27] If it made no difference whether an artwork was produced by hand or by mechanical means, authenticity based on physical gesture was at risk. The same conclusion was reached in New York by the neo-dadaist Robert Rauschenberg when he presented two nearly identical gestural paintings *Factum I* and *Factum II* in 1955.

What were going to be Restany's choices?

Restany's first discoveries, Laubies, Bertini, Bellegarde, Halpern, Peter Brunig, Hundertwasser, and Delahaye, whom he brought together in January 1957 at Galerie Kamer under the title *Espacesz Imaginaires*,[28] hardly became household names. Even so, they were interesting artists, whose friendship led to new contacts not only in Paris but in Germany and Italy. In Yves Klein (1928–62), however, Restany found his match, a visionary who "charmed and stimulated [him] by this unbelievable and audacious character."[29] After they met in December 1955, Restany agreed to write the essay for Klein's first exhibition at Colette Allendy.

In the conservative artistic context of the French fifties, Restany was the only critic ready to take a chance on an artist who dared to exhibit monochrome paintings of different colors (soon the artist settled on a single color – a deep resonant blue) without the trace of a hand or evidence of personality. How did Restany justify his enthusiasm? The critic explained how Yves Klein's monochrome "propositions" took art beyond the art of painting, beyond Malevich's square ("there is no black square nor white ground"), beyond the integration of art into architecture ("One cannot suspect him of a decorative intent"), beyond vibration as a sign of life. Thus emptied of associations with previous vanguards, Yves Klein's propositions focused uniquely on color ("the uniform expression of a certain tonality") and raised the possibility that *there lay the spiritual in art*.[30] There is no question that Restany showed an early appreciation for dematerialized conceptual art.

This analysis, still assuming the possibility of transcendence in art through the experience of color alone, did not entirely break with the tradition of abstract painting. Restany chose to ignore in Klein the dadaist prankster and publicity seeker who, a year before he met Restany, had produced a catalogue of nonexisting paintings and who in the summer of 1955 sent friends to the opening of the Salon des Réalités Nouvelles (which had refused his work) with requests to be directed to his paintings.[31] The critic realized that in order to establish Klein's legitimacy as an artist in Paris in 1955, the Duchampian affinities must be kept silent.

Yet as the fifties approached their end, a number of artists – Klein, Tinguely, Raymond Hains, César, Arman, and others, stopped looking for abstract solutions to the problem of art making in an era of mechanical reproduction. They appropriated ideas from the contemporary real in a somewhat Duchampian manner: Klein claimed to be capturing the world's cosmic energy via blue powder and blue sponges (Fig. 30). César and Arman were displaying the garbage and other leftovers of the society of consumption, either compressed (César, Fig. 31) or accumulated inside plastic boxes (Arman, Fig. 32); Raymond Hains and his friends Villeglé and Dufrène were focusing on billboard advertising, Christo on the packaging aspect of objects of consumption, Tinguely on the mechanical instrument of reproduction itself with his drawing machines called *Metamatics.*

By the end of the fifties, Restany knew these artists well, and he was the first critic to appreciate their work and to read a connection among them. He sensed that if this art was going to thrive, he would have to distinguish their realism from old-hat realism. So he plumbed the Duchampian connection. Restany related the hands-off presentation of fragments of urban and industrial everyday life to Duchamp's appropriation of banal objects in his ready-mades: "By the sole fact of this appropriating gesture, the object transcends its insignificant, banal, everydayness and is liberated: it attains its full expressive singularity."[32]

Bolstered by Duchamp's enthusiasm for technology, Restany maintained that it was wrong to read the new-realist sensibility other than as a celebration of the modern everyday: "Now, lots of people in Europe and America have tended to consider *nouveau réalisme* as a kind of critical approach toward the consumistic society at the end of the fifties. It may appear that way today but it is a totally distorted vision."[33] The only disagreement he had with Duchamp was on the visual qualities of the ready-made. He claimed that seen in retrospect, the ready-made, long considered aestheti-

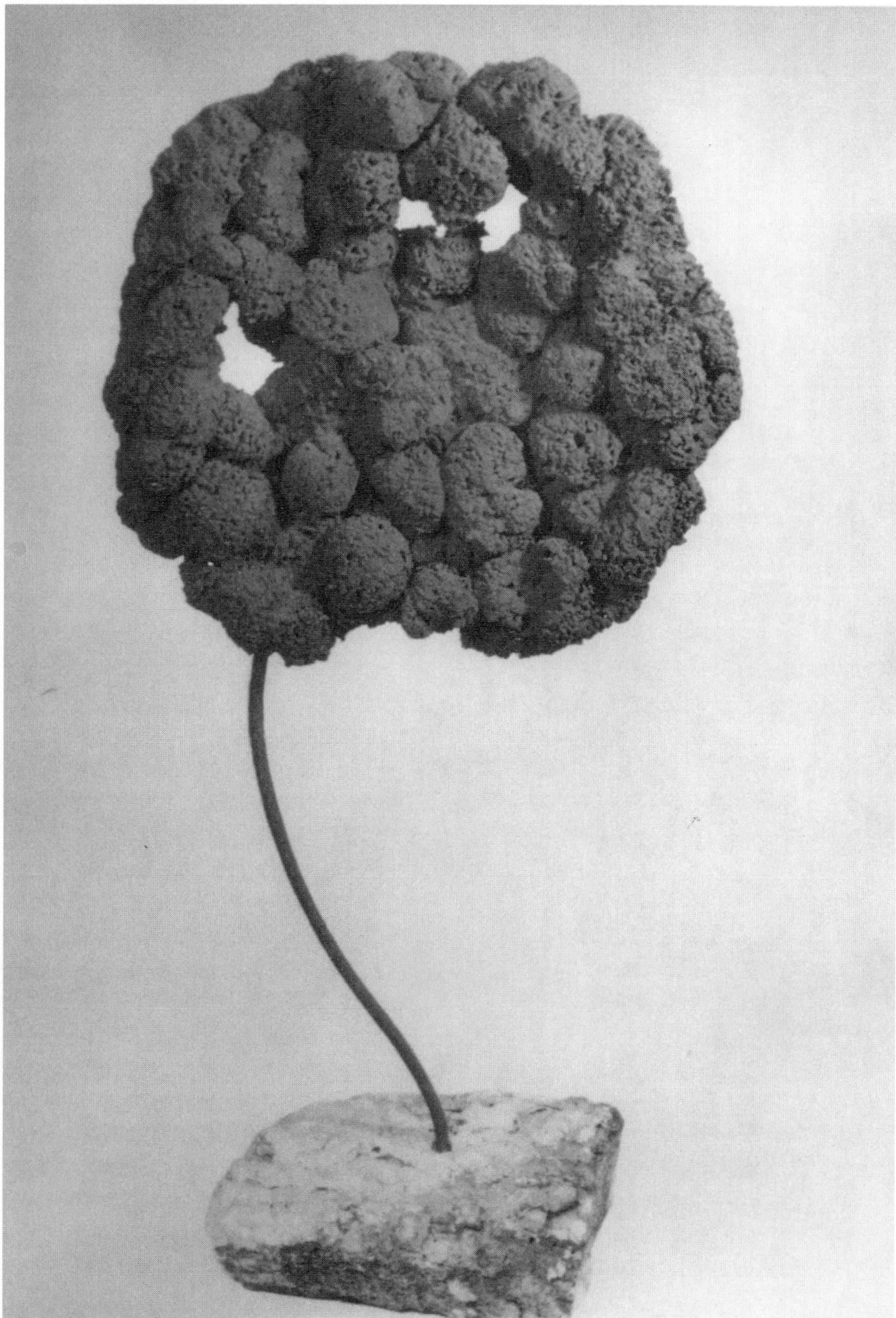

30. Yves Klein, *Untitled, Blue Sponge,* 1959. Sculpture. New York, Guggenheim Museum.

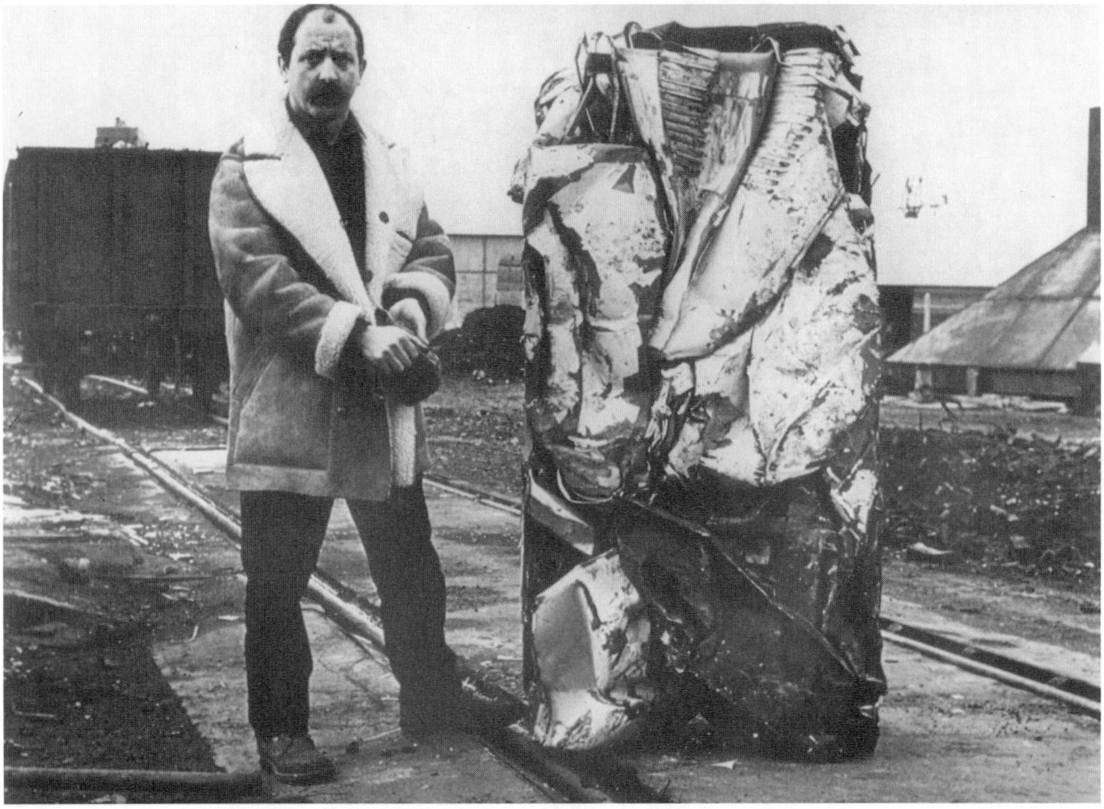

31. César with Sunbeam compression, c. 1960 (photo: courtesy Denyse Durand Ruel).

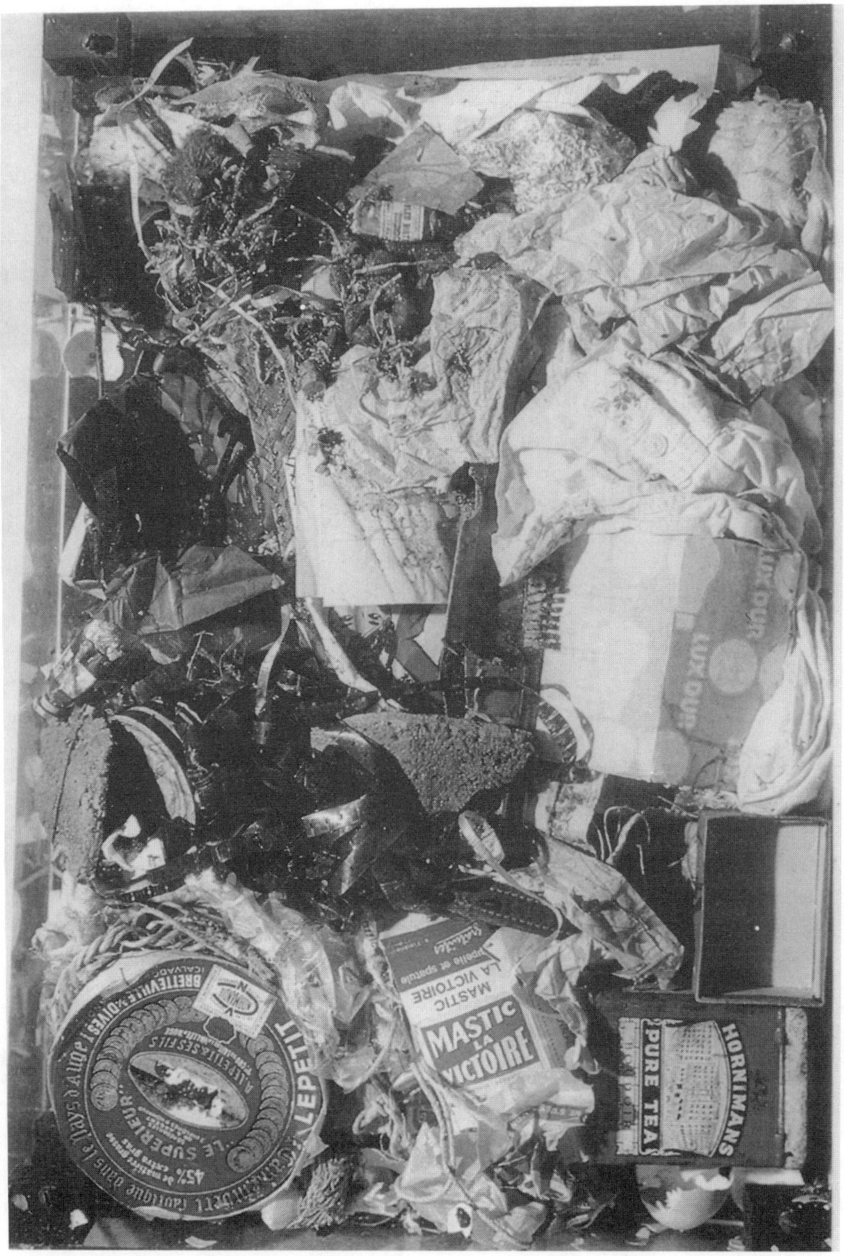

32. Arman, *Bourgeois Garbage,* 1959. Collection of the artist.

cally neutral, was in fact beautiful: "As Robert Motherwell noted very judiciously on the subject of the first ready-made of 1914, it is obvious thirty-five years later that the bottle rack selected by Duchamp had a far more beautiful shape than most pieces of sculpture executed as such in 1914."[34]

The figure of the artworld that Restany invoked, Marcel Duchamp, had left France for the United States in the midst of World War II in 1942 and made only occasional visits to Paris in the late 1940s and early 1950s. At that time, his brother, the postcubist painter Jacques Villon, was more talked about than he was. Besides the aforementioned Michel Tapié, only the very marginal *lettrists* led by Isidore Isou were Duchampian *avant la lettre.* However, as publications concerning Duchamp's art and his writings began to appear in French, as their author made more regular visits to the French capital, agreed to interviews and book signings, and even curated exhibitions, the inventor of the ready-made could no longer be ignored.[35] In December 1959, he was seen at the opening of a surrealist exhibition he and Breton organized in Paris. He had missed the opening of the 1947 surrealist show. In October 1959, according to Restany's biographer, Duchamp attended and juried a performance by Tinguely at the home of Iris Clert, also attended and juried by Restany and Jean Arp.[36]

Asked in an interview whether he felt like a role model for the new generation, Duchamp replied:

> People say that. . . . I suppose every young generation needs a prototype. In this case, I play that role. I'm delighted to. But it doesn't mean any more than that. There is no glaring resemblance between what I have done and what they're doing now. Furthermore, I did as few things as possible, which isn't like the current attitude of making as many as you can, in order to make as much money as possible.[37]

Indeed, in retrospect, Restany's legitimation of new realism through the Duchampian model appears more and more problematic. The attitude of the new realists toward work and money has been without question different from Duchamp's.[38] As for the celebratory tenor of new-realist work alleged by Restany, it does not always coincide with the visual experience: César's car compressions, to take that example, hardly connote the celebration of the modern everyday that Restany insisted on seeing. There is in the act of compressing the leftovers of car accidents something that puts a damper on the euphoria of owning a car, and there is a more general comment on the economics of space in the very act of reducing large things to their minimum bulk. Read in this light, César's compressions act as a warning, rather than mere promotion of the *société de consommation.* As for the seductive though lethal blue powder used by Klein as a symbol of cosmic energy, it is perhaps an allusion to the inevitable pollution including acid rain that comes with industrialization. Klein's sad-looking "flowers" drenched in blue powder suggest such an interpretation.

Benjamin Buchloh even intimates that industrialized death is detectable in the archetypal images of Arman, and he takes that artist's accumulations of leftover dentures, reading glasses, gas masks, and doll's limbs as cases in point. His analysis of Arman's work as straddling the recent past and the predictable future is worth quoting verbatim: "Anticipating another form of the industrialization of death, Arman's immobile arrangements stare at an emerging ecological catastrophe resulting from an ever-accelerating and expanding consumer culture and its increasingly unmanageable production of waste."[39]

The situationists had already formulated their criticism of the new realists as follows: "New Realism, drawing heavily on the form of dadaism (but not its spirit) is an apologetic trashcan art. It fits quite well in the margin of pseudo freedom offered by a society of gadgets and waste."[40]

To conclude:

Duchamp's reemergence in Paris in the late fifties oddly coincided with a turning point in French politics – de Gaulle's election to the presidency of the Fifth Republic in 1958 and the attendant promise of stability, prosperity, and hopes for peace in Algeria. De Gaulle, the anticommunist Resistance hero who had been in retirement since 1946, enacted a new constitution, giving the president a seven-year mandate and far more authority than former presidents of France had ever had. In the late fifties, the ascendancy of the left seemed to be ebbing, at least on the political and economic front, in favor of a non-Fascist non-Pétainist conservatism.

Small wonder that Restany and many of his noncommunist contemporaries – a generation that had lived and suffered through the war years as preteens and teens – did not see the late fifties through the evils of consumerism but through the opportunities it presented, rarely through the memory of the Holocaust but more often through a joy at being alive, not through a yes or a no to an independent Algeria, but through a determined yes to de Gaulle's Fifth Republic and no to the postwar remnants of cultural Pétainism.

The situation of art in Paris after the war has been the subject of several postwar exhibitions in Paris and in London. Two of them offer a narrative that is worth comparing to the one offered in this text. In 1987, the French curator, Bernard Ceysson, organized a mammoth exhibition at the museum of modern art in Saint-Etienne on art in Europe 1945–53 with the subtitle "Les années décisives."[41] With a clearly stated anti-American art agenda, he tried to show that postwar European art was ready for a bold takeoff that American power had aborted in 1953. According to Ceysson, as soon as the war was over, a page was turned and creativity began again furiously, animated by a variety of aesthetic and philosophical viewpoints, including existentialism.

In 1993, the Tate gallery organized an important exhibition called *Paris Post War: Art and Existentialism, 1945–55*.[42] There, the accent was on the mood of existentialism that pervaded the postwar years in artists ranging from Fautrier to Giacometti. That exhibition also took as its premise that a page was turned as soon as freedom had come back, and that the pain that had been felt but not expressed during the Occupation years was brought to the surface in postwar art. Both points of view propose that art in France after the war was in radical discontinuity with Pétainist culture.

Restany describes another narrative: a conservative xenophobic French artworld, reluctant to let go of the privileges it had obtained under the Vichy regime of Marshal Pétain during the Occupation years 1940–44. In this narrative, new realism was necessary to undercut the power of an artistic milieu steeped in values derived from the recent past, a milieu where it was thought that French-made postcubist abstraction could compete with the new American art. In this reading, the influence of Pétainist culture lingers long after France is liberated, and the change of artistic outlook that takes place in the late fifties coincides with the reappearance of Duchamp in the French artistic consciousness, and of de Gaulle in the French political consciousness. An incompatible mix, it was bound to explode sometime and did in May of '68.

Epilogue

Hitler Equals de Gaulle in a May '68 Poster

May '68 is remembered in Paris not only for street riots, the occupation by students of public buildings including the Sorbonne and other signs of student unrest, but for the sudden appearance on the walls of the French capital of hundreds of incendiary posters. Created by art students and *engagés* artists ensconced at the Ecole des Beaux-Arts and the Ecole des Arts Décoratifs, these mostly black and white images in a variety of exhortatory modes concentrated their attacks on the then French president Charles de Gaulle, the very individual who, between June 1940 and the Liberation of France in 1944, had symbolized resistance to Vichy and to the Nazis.

One such poster, a photography-based serigraphy pictured Hitler in uniform holding a mask of de Gaulle and wearing an armband with the general's emblem – the cross of Lorraine – in place of the Nazi swastika (Fig. 33). Such an image would hardly be worth looking at were it not for the fact that, like all the posters that came out of the student-run presses, its style and content were discussed at length by student committees and a consensus reached prior to distribution.

Furthermore, a far better-known poster from May '68 in which the French police, the CRS (Compagnies Républicaines de Sécurité), are analogized to Hitler's death camp guards and elite military corps, the SS (Schütz Staffel), also resonates with the period of the Occupation. Thus the poster equaling Hitler to de Gaulle conveys more than the confused memory of a lonely lunatic. It speaks for a generation that has minimal information on the Occupation in France, has not itself experienced or studied nazism, does not discriminate between various forms of authoritarian behavior, and trivializes the brutality of fascism. It also speaks of a trend against singularizing the crimes of Hitler and hence the Holocaust.

In the next pages, I will look at the image in the context of a newly politicized consciousness in young artists' ranks, and of the invasion of the university by death-of-the-subject philosophy. I will then show how an antifascist visual text can also foster a politics of banalization. And I will conclude by suggesting that such a vision tends to leave fascist-type politics and culture ready to rise again. As put by Jean Pierre Le Goff, "far from combating the real danger that the rise of the extreme right constitutes, this vision [born of May '68] sustains a dangerous confusion."[1]

According to Catherine Millet, French art chronicler of the period, by the late sixties a number of young artists were condemning art-for-art's-sake and the Duchampian stance of moral indifference (Fig. 34) in response to the Vietnam war and to the Cuban and Chinese revolutions. New realism comes under fire. During the May '68 events, the promoter of new realism, Pierre Restany, is run out of the Sorbonne as a pro-capitalist Gaullist. American Pop art is also under attack for its alleged political neutrality: "Pop art," writes Millet," becomes the illustration of American imperialism." In Paris, at the Salon de la Jeune Peinture, *new figuration* – art that deals critically with political and social issues – is promoted against American Pop art. In large-scale allegories such as Erro's *American Interiors* (Fig. 35), the generic American home is invaded by heroic-looking Vietcong guerrillas. "Visual artists like all intellectuals participate in the formidable political mobilization of the time," Millet writes, though she concedes that the message of the art is not always clear.[2] Typical is Erro's indiscriminate visual roster of famous men, ranging from Jackson Pollock to Adolf Hitler, seen in a recent retrospective of this icelandic-born artist at the Galerie Nationale du Jeu de Paume in Paris.[3]

The influence of *maîtres à penser,* French theoreticians like Louis Althusser, Gilles Deleuze, Jean Francois Lyotard, Michel Foucault, and Roland Barthes, "who attempt to make the artist emerge

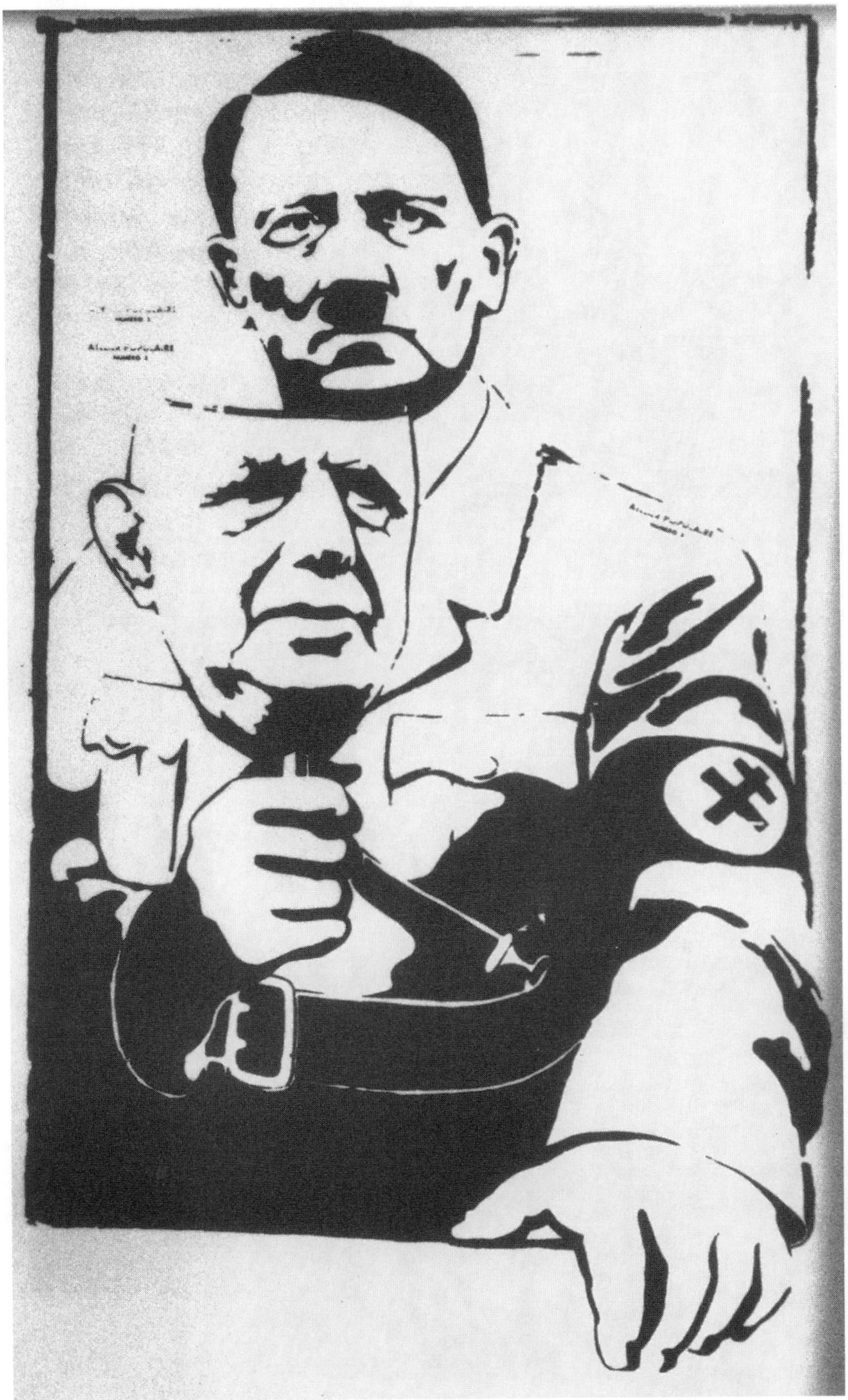

33. Anonymous poster, *General de Gaulle* (mask), 1968 (photo: J. Pavlovsky/Rapho).

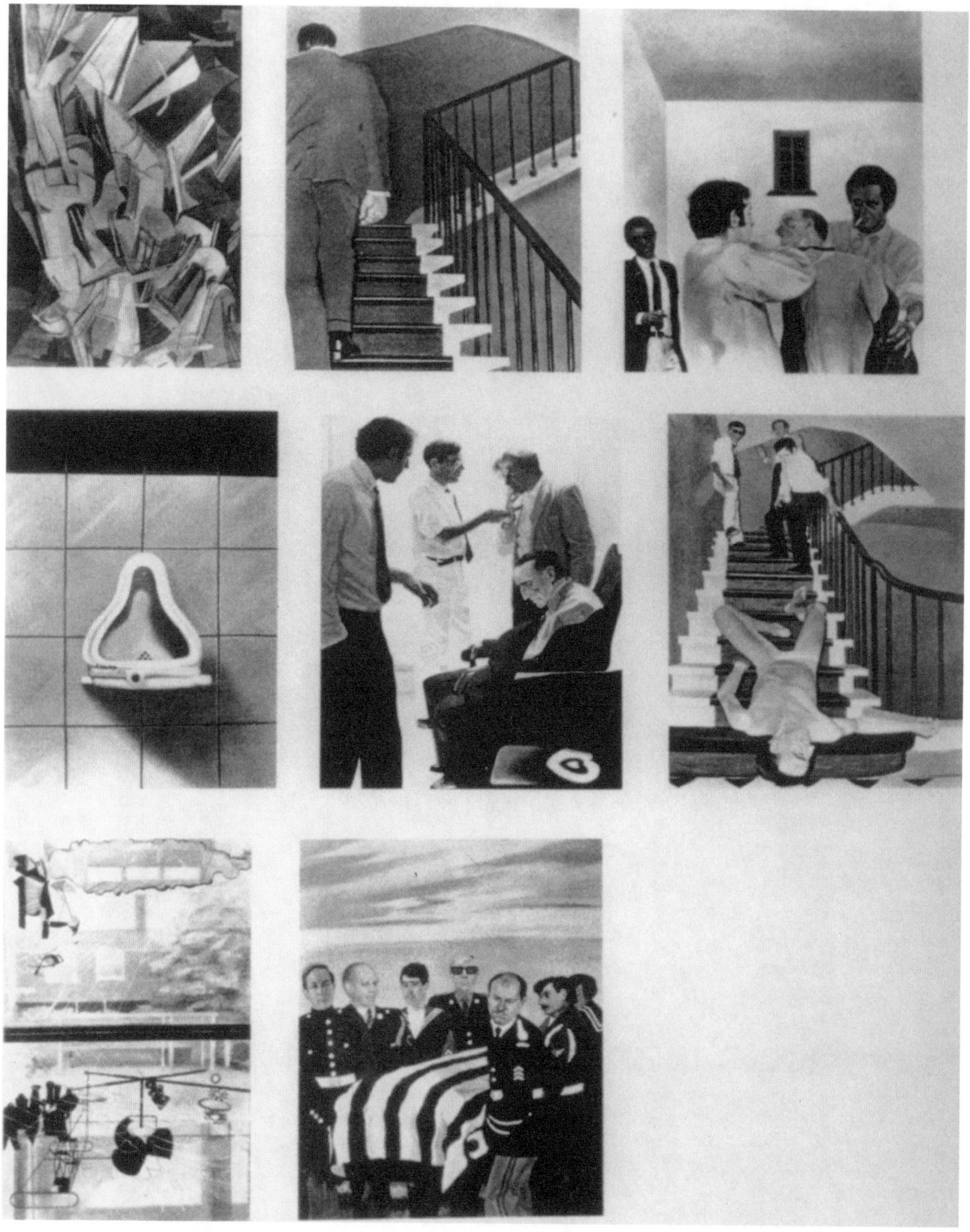

34. Gilles Aillaud, Eduardo Arroyo, Antonio Recalcati, *To Live or to Let Die. Or The Tragic Ending of Marcel Duchamp,* 1965. Dimensions and location unavailable.

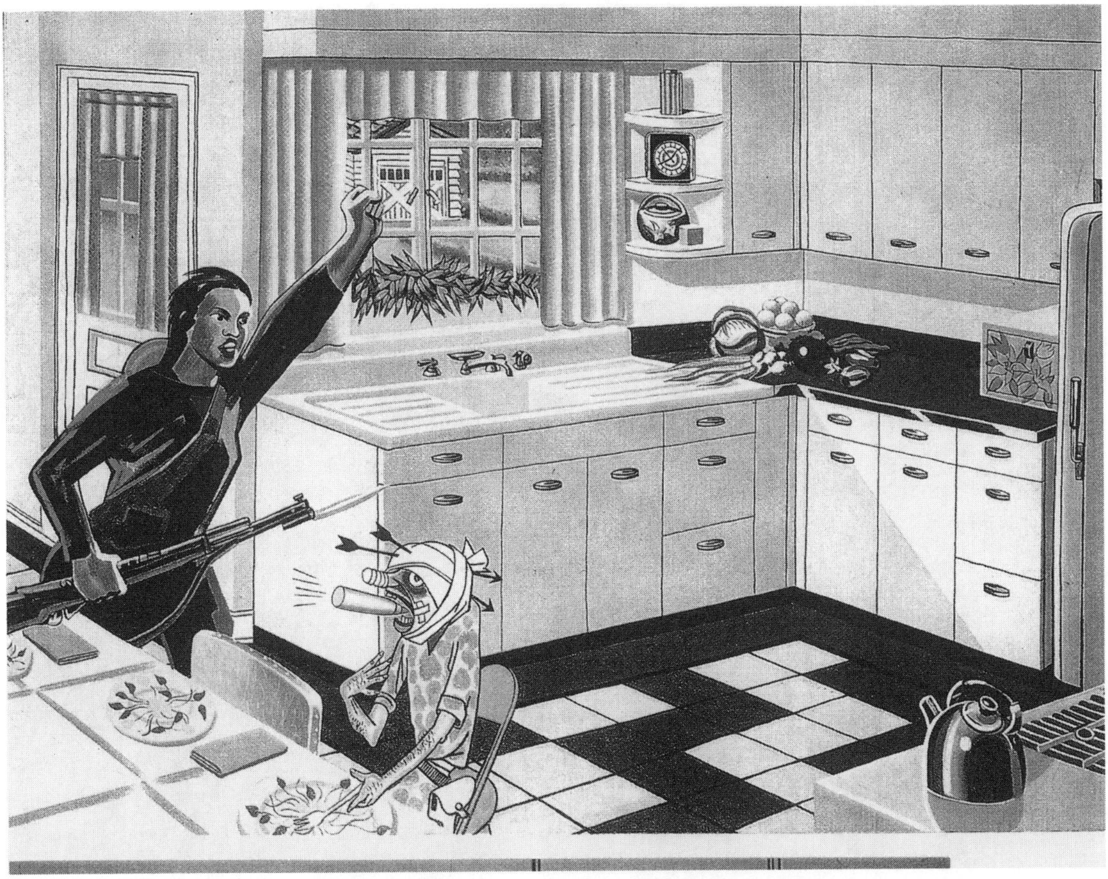

35. Erro, *American Interior no. 1*, 1968. Private collection, Caracas (photo: courtesy of the Musée du Jeu de Paume, Paris).

from his ivory tower," is also at its peak.[4] In a phase of death-of-the-author thinking among philosophers, artists respond through unsigned collective work ("Les Malassis"), through an impersonal Pop art style (Bernard Rancillac, Gérard Fromanger, Gilles Aillaud), through "detourning" well-known original photographs or paintings toward a legible political message (the situationist strategy). The May '68 artist is recruited within this milieu. He/she too wants legibility to prevail over aesthetic criteria. When the Hitler-equals-de-Gaulle poster passes muster, it is assumed that its antifascist message will be clear, monosemic.

In May '68, fascism is understood in student ranks as almost all forms of authoritarianism – the parent, the employer, the teacher, the policeman, and many other embodiments of power. Yet it is not applied to the Pétain regime. Despite that regime's fascistic policies, a "complexity" argument distinguishes it from fascism. On the other hand, as the elected president of the Fifth Republic since 1958, de Gaulle was indeed a figure of power and hence, in the parlance of May '68, a fascist. By then, de Gaulle's resolute stance against the enemies of democracy during World War II has been supplanted by the memory of more recent events: the General's "condoning" the French army's recourse to torture during the Algerian war and the way he went about ending the Fourth Republic and establishing the Fifth in 1958. This "blemished" image explains why the French Resistance hero could serve in 1968 as a symbol of fascism.

In point of fact, however, it was not General de Gaulle but Marshall Pétain who was an accomplice to Hitler's crimes. Pétain, not de Gaulle, was the French counterpart of Hitler. *Mis en abyme* behind the antifascist statement is an anachronistic comparison that transposes the ideological and political antagonists during Vichy, banalizes Hitler, and trivializes fascism. Through a structuralist amalgam, the author of the poster has equalized in appearance a French hero and an antihero, and has thus equated a Nazi and an anti-Nazi. By expanding the meaning of fascism beyond its antidemocratic, anti-Semitic essence, the poster has banalized the real Hitler and his uniquely heineous fascism.

To this day, there is great reticence on the part of the actors of May '68 to come forth and explain their images and themselves. In 1988, an exhibition took place on May '68 in Paris, and interviews with some of the artists involved were included in the catalogue. Asked about the de Gaulle/Hitler poster, one of the artists involved in poster making, Gérard Paris-Clavel, refused to name the author, though he conceded that it had been made at the Ecole des Arts Décoratifs. He said that in 1968 they thought it was superb, and admitted in retrospect that it was *lamentable.* He also confirmed that the Ecole des Arts Décoratifs was the headquarters of the situationist group.[5]

In a recent conversation, another participant, who prefers anonymity, defended the same poster by saying that of course it was anachronistic and wrong but antifascism was the overwhelming theme of May '68, the capitalist state was considered fascist, the police were violent, and the insurgents feared an invasion by *Occident,* the violent fascist group led by the son of Georges Prade, a leading collaborator. What the artists interviewed have refused to discuss is the other agenda readable in the poster – namely, the banalizing of Hitler and of fascism.

According to Claude Singer, the author of *Vichy, l'université et les Juifs,* banalizing started soon after the end of World War II. Singer quotes professor Vladimir Jankelevich, noting, when the first amnesty laws were promulgated in 1951,"there are no more guilty nor innocent, the trials for collaboration fade away, and with that, the evidence of shame and treachery."[6] For Singer, a strategy that makes an amalgam of all the victims of Hitler's crimes suits not only the former collaborators and French governments after the war but also resisters and Jews, who, he writes, "contribute to erase the specificity of their destiny under Vichy so as to facilitate their return within the great French family."[7]

The "banalization" that had taken place right after the war in France, however, had tended to give those who had lived in France during the Vichy years a uniformly heroic image (a Resistance image inspired by de Gaulle's). As of 1968, however, the representation of the everyman was that of a nonhero. Put in philosophical terms, as of 1968, structuralist theory exculpated an allegedly unstable self and pointed to the social, the unconscious, the forces of history and of ideology as responsible for an individual's (good or bad) decisions during the Occupation.[8] The Hitler/de Gaulle poster certainly accords with a view in which all – including the best and the worst – are seen in the same light, and the fascist reality of Vichy is ignored.

Thanks to a pro-banalizing mainstream in France, a number of bureaucrats and politicians with far from clear records of behavior during the Occupation (including François Mitterand, Tixier Vignancourt, Georges Pompidou, and not to forget Maurice Papon) carried on their careers and achieved success. As for the new generations, they have been saved from humiliation over their parents' less than pure behavior during Vichy.[9] But banalizing has unexpected consequences: The trivializing of fascism has allowed true fascists to operate overtly in French politics and culture. A text by Joseph Algazy documents the resiliency of fascist and Vichyite tendencies and individuals in the immediate postwar years.[10] Then, rising in the late sixties was a new intellectual right, *la nouvelle droite* and its neofascist enterprise called GRECE (Groupement de Recherche et d'Etudes pour la Civilisation Européenne), led by Alain de Benoist.

Despite Pierre-André Taguieff's claim in *Sur la Nouvelle Droite*[11] that its pro-Europe stance distinguishes the politics of this new right from that of Jean Marie Le Pen, this group is overtly proto-fascist. De Benoist's mentor was Lucien Rebatet (a name that has come up repeatedly in these pages), the polemicist of *Je suis partout,* condemned to death by a Liberation tribunal, whose sentence was commuted to life imprisonment in 1947, then reduced to "residence surveillée," and who was back in circulation writing for *Rivarol* and other extremist publications in the sixties.[12]

Notes

Introduction. Art, Nationality, and National Tradition in France from 1937 to 1968

1. Ralph Schor, *L'Antisémitisme en France pendant les années trente* (Paris: Complex, 1992); Gérard Noiriel, *Les Origines républicaines de Vichy* (Paris: Hachette, 1999); Pierre Laborie, "Vichy avant Vichy," *l'Opinion française sous Vichy* (Paris: Seuil, 1990).
2. See Frances Stonor Saunders, *The Cultural Cold War: The CIA and the World of Arts and Letters* (New York: The New Press, 2000). See also Giles Scott-Smith, *The Politics of Apolitical Culture,* forthcoming at Routledge, 2001. See Serge Guilbaut, *How New York Stole the Idea of Modern Art: Abstract Expressionism and the Cold War* (Chicago: University of Chicago Press, 1983), and Bernard Ceysson, *L'Art en Europe: Les Années décisives 1945–1953* (St-Etienne: Musée d'Art Moderne, 1987).
3. Marc Ferro, "Le film: Une Contre-analyse de la société," in *Faire de l'histoire, Nouveaux Objets,* Jacques Le Goff and Pierre Nora, eds. (Paris: Gallimard, 1974), 322. All translations are by the author unless otherwise noted.
4. Donald Preziosi, *Rethinking Art History: Meditations on a Coy Science* (New Haven and London: Yale University Press, 1989), 11.
5. See Germain Viatte in "Paris: Les Chemins de l'art et de la vie," *Paris–Paris 1937–1957* (Paris: Centre Georges Pompidou, 1981), 28.
6. See Patrick Weiser, "L'Exposition internationale: L'Etat et les beaux arts" in *Paris–Paris, 1937–1957* (Paris: Centre Georges Pompidou, 1981), 56.
7. Viatte, "Paris," 28.

8. Jean Laude, "Problèmes de la peinture en Europe, et aux Etats Unis (1944–1951)," *Art et Idéologies* (St-Etienne: CIEREC, 1978), 17–18.
9. Sarah Wilson, "Paris Post war: In search of the Absolute," *Paris Post War Art and Existentialism 1945–55*, 47.
10. Jean Laude, *Problèmes*, 16.
11. Ceysson, *L'Art en Europe*, 12.
12. See Gisèle Sapiro, *La Guerre des écrivains 1940–1953* (Paris: Fayard, 1999). See "Les Dossiers de la famille Tournier," *L'Express*, January 7, 1999, 33–37.

1. Collaboration Foretold. French Art of the Present in Hitler's Berlin

1. This had been known previously as the Königlichen Akademie der Künst.
2. A recent biography of Samuel Beckett that includes Beckett's German diaries from 1936–1937 shows that process in action and reveals the conditions under which Beckett was able to see works by modern artists while traveling through Germany. See James Knowlson, *Damned to Fame: The Life of Samuel Beckett* (New York: Simon and Schuster, 1996), chap. 10.
3. This exhibition has yet to be examined in the context of French Popular Front propaganda-through-art politics. For that purpose, scholars have generally used a corpus of images provided by the Paris *Exposition Internationale des Arts et Techniques* and art exhibitions at various venues in Paris in 1937. It has also been neglected by students of Nazi art in favor of *Entartete Kunst* and *Grosse Deutsche Kunsthausstellung*, exhibitions organized exclusively by the Germans and comprising for the most part art made by German artists. It is brought up by Berthold Hinz, "La peinture durant le IIIième Reich et l'antagonisme de ses origines," in Gérard Regnier, ed., *Les réalismes 1919–1939*, exh. cat., Centre Georges Pompidou, Paris, 1981, 123–24, as an example of the "secret continuity" between vanguardism and genre painting in the French conception of art, in contrast with Nazism, which exploited an alleged antagonism between the two for political reasons; it is mentioned in passing by Dawn Ades, "Paris 1937: Art and the Power of Nations," in Ades et al., *Art and Power: Europe under the Dictators 1930–1945*, exh. cat., Hayward Gallery, London, 1996, 62; in Michèle C. Cone, *Artists under Vichy: A Case of Prejudices and Persecution*

(Princeton: Princeton University Press, 1992), 166–67, the show is discussed as suggesting a predisposition toward collaboration on the part of participating artists, since twelve of the thirteen "travelers" to Nazi Germany in 1941 had been in the Berlin show of French art in 1937.

4. See Serge Tchakhotine, *Le viol de foules par la propagande politique* (Paris: Gallimard, 1939).
5. Ernest Pazet, quoted in Pascal Ory, 524.
6. Jean Zay, *Souvenirs et solitude* (Paris: Julliard, 1945), 375.
7. The catalogue was entirely and exclusively in German, using the Gothic script that Hitler had revived. A copy of it can be consulted at the Frick Library in New York under "Berlin, Royal Academy."
8. Ory, 524. Those were the words used by Léon Blum in the preface to the catalogue for the exhibition at the Palais National des Arts in 1937, which the French premier called "his" exhibition.
9. *Ausstellung Französischer Kunst der Gegenwart*, exh. cat., Preussische Akademie der Künste, Berlin, 1937, 19.
10. The names of Alfred Courmes and Pierre Ladureau do not appear in the index of artist participants in the 1937 International Exhibition catalogue, *Cinquantenaire de l'exposition internationale des arts et des techniques dans la vie moderne* (Paris: Institut Français d'Architecture/Paris Musées, 1987).
11. The French state lent seventeen works from its national collections at the Musée du Luxembourg, among them *Landscape* (no. 297) by Maurice Utrillo, *Landscape* and *Still Life with Grapes* (nos. 308 and 310) by Maurice de Vlaminck. The Louvre sent thirteen, and the Musée de la Ville de Paris only two, including *Mandolin and Vase* (no. 35) by Georges Braque. As Robert Rey, the curator, knew these artists personally, I suspect that they were aware of the event.
12. According to a German critic of the exhibition, few of the works were recent, and few came from the artists themselves. See Von Fritz Hellwag, "Ausstellung Französischer Kunst der Gegenwart/Preussische Akademie der Kunst zu Berlin," *Kunst* 75 (Aug. 1937): 334. *Kunst*, then edited by Paul Kirchgraber, predated the Nazi period but had had to adjust to the new policy banning art criticism.
13. According to information provided to the author by John Elderfield's office at the Museum of Modern Art, New York, in a telephone conversation of February 4, 1997, the 1914 painting had been put aside for the Russian collector Sergei Shchukhin, but the advent of World War I in Aug. 1914 and then the Russian Revolution had caused the painting to remain in the artist's studio through 1937. The painting appears in a

photograph of Pierre Matisse's living room in John Russell's recent *Matisse* (New York: Abrams, 1999).

14. There is also the possibility that some of the lenders were Jewish.
15. See the anonymous foreword to André François-Poncet, *The Fateful Years: Memoirs of a French Ambassador in Berlin 1931–1938*, trans. Jacques LeClercq (New York: Harcourt, Brace, 1949), vi. "As a historical figure, André François-Poncet belongs to the era of appeasement. . . . He was aware of the unqualified abhorrence of war which, up to Munich, held its sway over both his own country and allied Britain."
16. Ibid., v.
17. Ibid.
18. Ibid., 279.
19. In Bernadette Contensou, ed., *Paris 1937: L'art indépendant*, exh. cat., Musée d'Art Moderne de la Ville de Paris, 1987, 14, the date of January 20, 1937, is given for the first meeting relative to a sister exhibition in Paris, *Maîtres de l'Art Indépendant 1895–1937* at the Petit Palais, suggesting that the two shows were organized in tandem.
20. Ministère des Affaires Etrangères, Archives Diplomatiques (AD), Oeuvres Françaises à l'Etranger, Box 513, letter of Jan. 28, 1937, headed "Ambassade de France à Berlin," and signed "André F. Poncet."
21. Prior to the Third Reich, German painting had been far from weak. However, Hitler himself was dissatisfied with the new German painting, as compared with the new German sculpture.
22. It is possible that the Arno Breker retrospective at the Musée de l'Orangerie in June–July 1942 had something to do with the broken promise of 1937.
23. The exhibition of contemporary Polish art is interesting in light of the German-Polish accord signed Jan. 26, 1934.
24. See Stephanie Baron, *Degenerate Art: The Fate of the Avant-Garde in Nazi Germany*, exh. cat. Los Angeles County Museum of Art, Los Angeles, 1991, 9.
25. AD, Box 513, letter of Mar. 4, 1937, headed "Ministère de l'Education Nationale. Beaux Arts," signature illegible.
26. Ibid.
27. AD, Box 513, letter of Mar. 11, 1937, headed "Ministère de l'Education Nationale. Beaux Arts," signature illegible. "I approved the principle of a French exhibition in Berlin for the Spring, in spite of certain difficulties that we will meet in the gathering of the works, in the first place because national museums must keep their most important works during the [Paris] Exposition, also because of the desire of art dealers

not to empty their galleries during that time, and last because of the lack of enthusiasm shown by collectors toward our requests."

28. AD, Box 513, telegram of Mar. 4, 1937, headed "Ministère des Affaires Etrangères."
29. Louis Hautecoeur, *Les beaux arts en France: Passé, avenir* (Paris: Picard, 1948), 267.
30. See n. 27 above.
31. AD, Box 513, letter of Mar. 23, 1937, headed "Association Française d'Expansion et d'Echanges Artistiques," and signed "R. Brussel."
32. AD, Box 513, note of Mar. 24, 1937, headed "Le Ministre des Affaires Etrangères. Service des Oeuvres Françaises à l'Etranger," and signed "S. Marx."
33. See n. 25 above.
34. Ibid. The name Huyghe was crossed out and that of Robert Rey, who accepted the assignment, written above his.
35. Robert Rey, *La Peinture moderne ou l'art sans métier* (Paris: Presse Universitaires de France, Que-Sais-je, 1941).
36. Lucien Rebatet, "Peinture moderne," *Je Suis Partout*, Feb. 14, 1942.
37. Robert Rey, *Contre l'art abstrait* (Paris: Flammarion, 1938).
38. AD, Box 513, letter of Apr. 13, 1937, headed "Ministère de l'Education nationale."
39. AD, Box 513, telegram of June 5, 1937, 19:10, headed "Berlin Affaires Etrangères."
40. AD, Box 513, letter of June 8, 1937, headed "ambassade de France à Berlin," and signed "André F. Poncet."
41. Ibid.
42. Chapelain-Midy, born in 1904, was one of the painters that Bernard Dorival grouped within the generation of 1930. "Thus these painters," he wrote, "hope to give painting a large audience and put an end to the divorce of the artist and his public"; Dorival, *Les étapes de la peinture française contemporaine* (Paris: Gallimard, 1954), 257. He won the Carnegie Prize in 1938.
43. For more on the German response to Maillol, see H. Eckstein, "Maillol," *Kunst* 75 (Jan. 1937): 107–15.
44. See n. 39 above.
45. Hellwag (as in n. 12), 339.
46. Ibid.
47. Ibid. For more on Hellwag's review of the show, see Cone, 166–68.
48. AD, Box 513, telegram of Aug. 1937, headed "Berlin Affaires Etrangères," and signed "François Poncet."
49. François-Poncet, 213.

50. Göring collected modern French art in secret, and Goebbels was among the ideologues who had proposed that German Expressionism become the model of new Nazi art.
51. See Stephanie Baron (as in n. 24), 12. In the cultural wars that raged in the first years of the Nazi regime, Goebbels had lost to Alfred Rosenberg, the partisan of *völkisch* art – art for and of the people – finally siding with Hitler on the issue of a racial Germanic tradition as the essence of the new German art.
52. Berthold Hinz, "Degenerate and Authentic," in Ades et al. (as in n. 3), 331.
53. See n. 40 above.
54. Ibid. From the *Bourse Gazette:* "What is striking is that the painters represented in this exhibition remain loyal to the tendency of 'l'art pour l'art' whose native land is France. The French do not paint to express a philosophical idea but for the pleasure of the eye and to decorate life with a decor in good taste. For us Germans, on the contrary, it is essential that life always have something to do with philosophy." From the *Lokal Anzeiger:* "French art is not a philosophical art. It does not show a philosophy in paint, but painting which comes out of a philosophy of life, fixed once and for all." From the *National Zeitung:* "If one wishes to characterize the evolution of contemporary French painting, one can say that it has generally turned away from abstraction, from doctrinaire tendencies, from fashion, to give itself over fully to the natural play of forms and colors."
55. See Romy Golan, *Modernity and Nostalgia: Art and Politics in France between the Wars* (New Haven: Yale University Press, 1995).
56. A portrait of Mme Othon Friesz was in both exhibitions.
57. Robert Rey, foreword to *Ausstellung Französischer Kunst der Gegenwart* (as in n. 9), 14.
58. Raymond Escholier, "Préambule," in *Maîtres de l'art indépendant 1895–1937*, exh. cat., Petit Palais, Paris, 1937, 5.
59. Bernadette Contensou, "Autour de l'Exposition des Maîtres de l'art indépendant," in Contensou (as in n. 19), 13.
60. Escholier (as in n. 58), 6.
61. "Une esposition d'art français à Berlin," *Cahiers d'Art* 12 (1937), 62. Despite this proclamation, Matisse and Lèger, both *Cahiers d'Art* artists, had works in the Berlin show.
62. *Le Temps*, July 1, 1937.
63. Zay (as in n. 6), 375.
64. François-Poncet, 213.
65. Ory, 945, n. 46.

66. See Sonia Combe, *Archives interdites* (Paris: Albin Michel, 1994); and idem, "Today's French Historical Research," *Telos,* no. 108 (Summer 1996): 149–64.
67. Whether Matisse's knowing participation in the Berlin exhibition was exceptional or not, it raises the question of vigilance with respect to the context in which artists exhibit their work during their lifetime. See "Un entretien avec Umberto Eco," *Le Monde,* Oct. 5, 1993, on that subject. Whether the show as a whole reveals an attitude of cooperation on the part of the artists who participated depends, of course, on the knowledge they had of the circumstances and conditions of the 1937 event. So far, the best evidence of this attitude is that when, in 1941, a trip was organized for artists by the Nazi Propaganda Office, all twelve French artists who agreed to go on the trip had been part of the Berlin show. See Cone, 168.
68. René Remond has repeatedly maintained that good history interprets the past in terms of what was known at the time and without the benefit of hindsight. Such an argument has enabled the Vichy epoch to remain clouded in ambiguity. Before judging the appropriateness of the Berlin show Professor Rémond would ask us to situate the exhibition in the appeasement atmosphere of the time. But would that condone the absence on racial and xenophobic grounds of so many major artists then working in France and who considered France their (adopted) "homeland"? See also chapter 2, note 1.
69. Eugen Weber, *La France des années trente: Tourments et perplexités* (Paris, Fayard, 1995), 13.
60. Jean-Baptiste Duroselle, *La décadence 1932–1939* (Paris: Imprimerie Nationale, 1979), 294.
71. What an exhibition aiming at the defense and illustration of French culture in 1937 ought to have been about is worth pondering. If indeed the fear of imminence of war were part of the collective unconscious on both sides of the border, then images conjuring the memory of World War I would have been appropriate.
72. In *The Fateful Years,* 205, François-Poncet writes of the French athletes at the Olympic Games: "They cut a good figure as they marched smartly by. As they neared the stand, on a given order, they gave the Olympic salute, raising their right arms horizontally on a line with their shoulders. The crowd mistook this gesture for the Hitlerian salute. Believing it a chivalrous homage to the Third Reich and its leader, they gave vent to a wholly mistaken enthusiasm." Why, if that was the case, did the British and the Americans not give the same "salute" when they went by the official stand?

73. Jane Clapp, *Art Censorship: A Chronology of Proscribed and Prescribed Art* (Metuchen, N.J.: Scarecrow Press, 1972), 255.
74. This information is taken from *Paris 1937* (as in n. 19).

2. Decadence and Renewal in the Decorative Arts Under Vichy

1. The most influential *porte-parole* of the "complexity" point of view is René Rémond, who has taken to task the conclusions and the methodology of Zeev Sternhell, a well-known authority of French fascism. An exemplary duel occurred when Sternhell criticized French historians (including Rémond) for continuing to present Vichy as "a conservative, paternalist regime under the enemy's boot, nothing more than a regrettable bout of fever," while Sternhell contends that "the [Vichy] system put in place in July 1940 was no less violent than the Mussolini's dictatorship" (Sternhell, "Ce passé qui refuse de passer," *Le Monde* [21 September 1994]). Among Rémond's methodological criticisms was the commonplace argument that hindsight is twenty-twenty vision. For Rémond, the good [objective] historian "interrogates the past starting from the preoccupations of the time, and must not abuse the advantage [he has] of knowing how it came out" (Rémond, "La Complexité de Vichy," *Le Monde* [5 October 1994]). It is only because democracy won out in 1944–45 that de Gaulle's early resistance stance looks right to us and not Pétain's accommodation with . . . fascisms. In June 1940, given the military debacle and the demoralized state of France, the initiatives of Pétain made sense to a vast majority of the French citizenry, not de Gaulle's minority voice. From this point of view, Pétain's role appears in a complex, ambiguous, and uncertain light. So does the young, ambitious Mitterand, measuring his options and choosing first Pétain and then the Resistance.

   When a longtime supporter of the "complexity" thesis, Claire Andrieu, wrote that when such a premise was "pushed to extremes . . . [it] might lead to the erasure of the difference between the Resistance and Collaboration" (*Esprit* [December 1994], 208), she was also accused of practicing bad history by the editor of *Esprit,* Joel Roman.
2. J. P. Azéma and François Bédarida, eds., *Vichy et les français* (Paris: Fayard, 1992), 252. This book published the proceedings of an international colloquium. See also chapter 1, note 68.
3. Ibid., 254.
4. Ibid., 260.

5. Ibid., 368.
6. Ibid., 359.
7. Ibid.
8. Christian Faure, *Le Projet culturel de Vichy* (Lyon: CNRS, 1989), 270–71. Faure notes that the celebration of folkloric productions was Pétain's own idea: "the fact that they are in effect folkloric, is due to his personality. He calls upon peace, the tradition of ancestors, continuity. The hostility of Pétain against industrialization, the city and consequently intellectuality, comes out of conceptions that identify with a farm society under threat and with corporatism confronted with capitalism. It thus opposes the city to the country."
9. Ibid., 120. For more on the social policies of Vichy see Jean Pierre Le Crom, *Syndicats, nous voilà: Vichy et le corporatisme* (Paris: L'Atelier, 1995).
10. Faure, *Le Projet culturel de Vichy,* 270.
11. Faure, *Le Projet cultural de Vichy,* 272.
12. Quoted in *Le Nouvelliste* (2 May 1941).
13. Quoted in *Métiers de France* (May 1942), 1.
14. *Tables Royales, Versailles* (Paris: Direction des Musées Nationaux, 1994), n.p.
15. Faure, *Le Projet culturel de Vichy,* 17.
16. *Artistes et Artisans* (Paris: Service de l'artisanat, 1942), 63. This publication was a transcription of six lectures given during the national selection of artisans exhibition in 1942.
17. Ibid., 62–63.
18. Ibid., 71–72.
19. Ibid., 51.
20. Ibid., 78.
21. Yvonne Brunhammer, "Les Années 1920–1930," in *Les Réalismes* (Paris: Centre de Culture Georges Pompidou, 1980–81), 344. See also Nancy Troy, *Modernism and the Decorative Arts in France* (New Haven: Yale University Press, 1991).
22. Brunhammer, "Les Années," 350–51. See also Viviane Jutheau, *Jules et André Leleu* (Paris: Vecteurs, 1989).
23. *Beaux Arts* (15 May 1925), 17.
24. Guillaume Janneau, "La réorientation de Sèvres," *Beaux arts de France,* vol. II (December 1942–January 1943), 96.
25. Chantal Gastinel-Coural, *La République dans ses meubles* (Paris: Musée des Arts Décoratifs, 1993), 14.
26. Ibid., 15. His eventual partner was André Groult.

27. In the 1930s, Dufy was among the artists with Matisse, Rouault, Leger, Derain, Miró, and Le Corbusier that Madame Cuttoli called upon when she undertook to revive tapestry-making and to create her own workshops. The San Francisco Museum of Art had a show of these tapestries. See *Beaux arts* (13 January 1939), 1.
28. Guillaume Janneau, "Nouveaux Cartons pour les Manufactures Nationales de Tapisserie," *Beaux arts de France* (October–November 1943), 38.
29. Marcelle Brunet and Tamara Préaud, *Sèvres des origines à nos jours* (Fribourg: Office du Livre, 1978), 311.
30. Janneau, "La réorientation de Sèvres," *Beaux arts de France* (October–November 1943), 96.
31. Jacqueline du Pasquier, "Robert Lallemant, Homme et artiste à multiples facettes," in *Céramique de Robert Lallemant* (Orléans: Musée des Beaux Arts, 1993), 7–15.
32. Interview in *Comoedia* (5 August 1944).
33. Brunet and Préaud, *Sèvres des origines à nos jours,* 320.
34. Ibid., 328.
35. A Fay-Halle and V. Guillaume, *Porcelaines de Sèvres au XXème siècle* (Paris: Editions de la Réunion des Musées Nationaux, 1987), 23.
36. Brunet and Préaud, *Sèvres des origines à nos jours,* 328. "It was an ashtray with the equestrian statue of Charlemagne holding a scepter, and on the reverse, a legend saying that the Great Reich, split by the sons of the Emperor, has just been reunified by the Fuhrer." I should add that in the opinion of the curators of a 1987 exhibition of Sèvres porcelain at the Louvre, these models were not considered of sufficient quality to be included in the show as "they are not works of art"! Fay-Halle and Guillaume, *Porcelaines de Sèvres,* 23. Access to them has been denied to the author.
37. Troy, *Modernism and the Decorative Arts in France,* 208.
38. Louis Hautecoeur, *Considérations sur l'art d'aujourd'hui* (Paris: Librairie de France, 1929), 112.
39. André Vignoles, *Jean Mayodon céramiste* (Paris: Galerie Landrot, n.d.), n.p.
40. Camille Mauclair, "L'architecture va-t-elle mourir?" in Yvone Brunhammer and Suzanne Tise, *Les Artistes Décorateurs 1900–1942* (Paris: Flammarion, 1990), 84.
41. Bibliothèque Nationale Yd 2 1843 (27) and photos 8 May 1944.
42. Janneau, "L'artisanat des métiers d'art," *Beaux arts de France* (June–July 1943), 284.
43. The old argument of a relationship between decadence and "splendid

isolation" goes back to Croce, as explained by Richard Drake in "Decadence Decadentism, Decadent Romanticism. Toward a theory of Decadence," *Journal of Contemporary History* (January, 1982), 85.

44. See in particular *Art et Artisanat*, no. 7, 35, on the necessity to reserve the execution of official sculpture to French practitioners; see ibid., no. 9, on adding the word "Français" to the name of the "Union des artistes dessinateurs."
45. Anonymous editorials, *Beaux arts* (7 October 1938–January 1939).
46. Brunhammer, "SAD, Société des artistes décorateurs," *Les Années UAM 1929–1958* (Paris: Musée des Arts Decoratifs, 1988), 128–31.
47. Brunhammer, "Pour ou contre l'ornement," *Les années UAM*, 119–21.
48. Mary McLeod, "Urbanism and Utopia: Le Corbusier from Regional Syndicalism to Vichy," Ph.D. diss., Princeton University (Ann Arbor: University Microfilms International, 1985), 421.
49. Troy, *Modernism and the Decorative Arts in France*, 208.
50. Janneau, *Decoeur* (Paris: Moreau, 1923), n.p.
51. Janneau, *Le Luminaire* (Paris: Moreau, 1925), n.p.
52. Louis Hautecoeur, Guillaume Janneau and Louis Chéronnet, *L'art décoratif: Le mobilier moderne* (Paris: Comoedia-Charpentier, 1942), 16.
53. Janneau, *Meubles nouveaux* (Paris: Moreau, 1943), n.p.
54. Brunhammer, "Pour ou contre l'ornement," 121.
55. See Solange Goguel, *René Herbst* (Paris: Editions du Regard, 1990). "Under the initiative of Robert Mallet-Stevens, René Herbst, Louis Barillet, and Raymond Templier, proposals were addressed to members of SAD and UAM for a regrouping, under the name of Société des Artistes Décorateurs Modernes, with René Herbst, a UAM member, as Vice-President."
56. Hautecoeur, Janneau, and Chéronnet, *L'art décoratif*, 5–6.
57. Ibid., 15.
58. "Les achats et commandes de l'Etat aux artistes en 1941," *Beaux arts de France* (October–November 1942), 25.
59. "Les achats et commandes de l'Etat aux artistes en 1942," *Beaux arts de France* (April–May 1943), 214.
60. Brunhammer, *Les réalismes*, 352.
61. Pierre du Colombier, "Décorateurs et artisans," *Beaux arts* (27 June 1942).
62. Janneau, *Ferronerie d'art d'aujourd'hui* (Paris: Moreau, n.d.), n.p.
63. Deborah Silverman, *Art Nouveau in Fin-de-Siècle France* (Berkeley: University of California Press, 1989), 132.

64. See Michèle C. Cone, *Artists under Vichy* (Princeton: Princeton University Press, 1992), 80–81.
65. Troy, *Modernism and the Decorative Arts in France*, 227.
66. Olga Raggio, Introduction to "The Decorative Arts under Louis XIV," *Metropolitan Museum of Art Bulletin* (Spring 1989), 1.
67. Jacques Soulillou, *Le Décoratif* (Paris: Klincksieck, 1990), 17.
68. Eugen Weber, "Decadence on a Private Income," *Journal of Contemporary History* (January 1982), 1.
69. Zeev Sternhell, *Neither Right nor Left: Fascist Ideology in France*, trans. David Maisel (1986; reprint, Princeton University Press, 1995), 294.
70. According to Griffin, *The Nature of Fascism*, 35, all forms of fascism share the need to make believe that their contemporaries are "living through or about to live through a 'sea change' . . . in the historical process." Change is necessary because "the perceived corruption, anarchy, oppressiveness, iniquities or decadence of the presence, rather than being seen as immutable . . . are perceived as having reached their peak and interpreted as the sure sign that one era is nearing its end and a new order is about to emerge." Combine the conjuring up of core myths with populist ultra-nationalism, and you have a fascist minimum or "palin-genetic ultra-nationalism."

3. Lucien Rebatet. Anti-Semitic Art Criticism During Vichy

1. Julia Kristeva, *Powers of Horror: An Essay on Abjection*, trans. Léon Roudiez. New York: Columbia University Press, 1982, p. 1.
2. Ibid., p. 180.
3. See Robert Belot, *Lucien Rebatet, Un Itinéraire fasciste* (Paris: Seuil, 1994), p. 235.
4. Lucien Rebatet, "Le Salon des Tuileries," *Je suis partout*, June 23, 1941.
5. Rebatet, "La Critique des Livres: Peintres modernes," *Je suis partout*, April 11, 1942.
6. See Centre de Documentation Juive Contemporaine, XVCI–80, pp. 59–63.
7. C. Laville, "A quoi reconnaît-on les juifs?" *Cahier jaune* 1 (November 1941).
8. Cited in Kristeva, *Powers of Horror*, p. 181.
9. Michael Marrus, *The Politics of Assimilation: A Study of the French Jewish Community at the Time of the Dreyfus Affair*. Oxford: Clarendon Press, 1971, pp. 85, 196.

10. See J. Marquès Rivière, "Pourquoi une exposition juive?" CDJC, XIg–118, pp. 11–30.
11. Robert de Beauplan, "L'Exposition Antijuive," *L'Illustration*, September 1941, from typewritten document, CDJC, DLVI–18.
12. F. Vinneuil [alias Lucien Rebatet], "Un grand et ravissant chef d'oeuvre," *Je suis partout*, May 6, 1938.
13. Curiously, there was a lot of interest in film in the anti-Semitic camp; Rebatet wrote film reviews in the 1930s; Robert Brasilac and Maurice Bardèche coauthored *Histoire du cinéma*. Paris: Denoel, 1942.
14. See Jean Perrin, "La femme vampire dans la poésie romantique anglaise," in *Les Vampires*, ed. Antoine Faivre and Jean Marigny. Colloque de Cerisy. Paris: Albin Michel, 1993.
15. Kristeva, *Powers of Horror*, p. 178.
16. See Christian Delporte, *Les Crayons de la propagande*. Paris: CNRS, 1993, p. 129.
17. CDJC, XIb–546.
18. For more on the organic metaphors of Rebatet's art criticism, see my *Artists under Vichy: A Case of Prejudice and Persecution*. Princeton University Press, 1992, ch. 2.
19. Rebatet, "Entre le juif et le pompier," *Je suis partout*, February 14, 1941; "n'aurait certainement pas pu morde sur nous avec cette facilité."
20. Jean Goens, *Loups-garous, vampires et autres monstres: Enquètes médicales et littéraires*. Paris: CNRS, 1993, p. 71.
21. Zeev Sternhell, *Ni Droite ni gauche: L'Idéologie fasciste en France*. Paris: Seuil, 1983, p. 289.
22. Louis Hautecoeur, *Considérations sur l'art d'aujourd'hui*. Paris: Librairie de France, 1929, p. 72.
23. René Huyghe, *Les Contemporains*. Paris: Tisné, 1949, p. 108; Bernard Dorival, *Les Etapes de la peinture française contemporaine*. Paris: Gallimard, 1946; Louis Hautecoeur, *Littérature et peinture du XVIIème au XXème siècle*. Paris: Armand Colin, 1942, p. 306.
24. Rebatet, "Le Salon des Tuileries," *Je suis partout*, June 23, 1941.
25. Kristeva, *Powers of Horror*, p. 183.
26. Ibid., p. 2.
27. Goens, *Loups-garous*, p. 75.
28. Rebatet, *Les Décombres*. Paris: Denoel, 1942, p. 20.
29. For Kristeva, *Powers of Horror*, p. 178, the anti-Semite is in a *"rage against the symbolic"* (namely, Jewish monotheism) that leads him to "the attempt to substitute *another Law* for the constraining and frustrating symbolic one," something she names *"material positivity . . ."*

It is "a full tangible reassuring and apply substance [which] will be embodied in the Family, the Nation, the Race, and the Body." (Kristeva's italics).

30. Goens, *Loups-garous,* p. 67.
31. Ibid., pp. 83–4. The most thorough bibliography on vampires and vampirism is found in Goens, *Loups-garous.* Faivre and Marigny, *Les Vampires,* also contains many references. A history of the original "vampire" from central Europe and its successive metamorphoses is found in Denis Buican, *Les Métamorphoses de Dracula: L'Histoire et la légende.* Paris: Edition du Felin, 1993. Film versions are discussed in Lotte H. Eisner, *L'écran démoniaque.* Paris: Eric Losfeld, 1990; and in Francis Courtade, *Cinéma Expressioniste.* Paris: Henri Veyrier, 1984. Although these are French-language books, their bibliographies include titles in other languages.

4. "Abstract" Art as a Veil. Tricolor Painting in Vichy France

1. Jean Bazaine, born in 1904 in Paris, began to show his painting in 1930 with Jean Fautrier, Goerg, and Marcel Gromaire. During the 1930s, he occasionally wrote in *Esprit,* the review representing the views of Emmanuel Mounier. Besides having been the leading light of "bleu blanc rouge" painting, he is known for his work in stained glass at Assy and in Paris at the Church of St.-Severin.
2. *Comoedia,* edited by René Delange, came out regularly during the entire Occupation period. In addition to giving the major literary figures of the Occupation a platform, the review published art criticism and interviews with living artists, including one with Paul Cézanne's son.
3. Until January 10, 1943, all galleys were brought to the press office of the German army for inspection. Disobedience entailed the temporary suspension or the interdiction of the publication. After that date, self-censorship was imposed. It is significant that the article on "peinture bleu blanc rouge" appeared after the new system took effect. However, the guidelines for self-censorship forbade publication of anything "that might be harmful to the prestige of the German Reich, that might be damaging to order and calm in the occupied territories, or that might endanger the safety of the occupying forces"; *Histoire générale de la presse française,* ed. C. Bellanger, Paris, 1975, IV, 13–15.
4. J. Bazaine, "La Peinture bleu blanc rouge," *Comoedia,* 30 Jan. 1943, 1–6: "Une nation ne choisit pas au hassard son drapeau. Il y aurait

beaucoup à dire sur cette sorte de cristallisation colorée des instincts profonds d'un peuple."

5. Ibid.: "Ce sera peut-être aujourd'hui, à travers la rigueur subtile de quelques ton purs, de créer une réalité si jeune, si fraiche, si obsédante, qu'elle s'imposera à son tour comme une réalité quotidienne."
6. B. Dorival, *Les Etapes de la peinture française contemporaine 1911–1944*, 6th ed., Paris, 1946, 296: "Après l'armistice de 1940, un seul parti restait aux Français, semble-t-il: ressaisir toutes leurs forces et aller de l'avant. . . . Et c'est ce qu'ils firent, dès 1940. . . . Une fois de plus, la peinture participait à la vie de la conscience française. . . . La Peinture alla de l'avant."
7. P. Francastel, *Nouveau dessin, nouvelle peinture*, Paris, 1946, 14: "Et combien, parmi ceux qui se piquent d'aimer les arts, soupçonnent qu'il se prépare, en ce moment même, en pleine catastrophe, une évolution importante de la peinture?"
8. R. Huyghe, *Les Contemporains*, Paris, 1949, 108: "Le crise latente se précipite, et, dès 1941, la peinture française, en pleine occupation, répond à l'envahisseur en railliant toutes ses forces d'audace."
9. R. Huyghe, "Letter from Paris," *Magazine of Art*, Nov. 1945, 272. See also Huyghe (as in n. 8), 110: "Il faut bien dire que les intellectuels, aux côtés du peuple, furent à l'avant garde de la Résistance et qu'ils y jetèrent âprement toutes leurs forces."
10. H. Rousso, *Le Syndrôme de Vichy*, Paris, 1987, 20–21: "Les Français semblent refouler cette guerre civile, aidés en cela par l'établissement d'un mythe dominant: le résistancialisme. Le terme . . . désigne un processus qui a cheché: primo la marginalisation de ce que fut le régime de Vichy et la minoration systématique de son emprise sur la société française . . .; secondo, la construction d'un objet de mémoire, la 'Résistance, dépassant de très loin la somme algébrique des minorités agissantes que furent les résistants . . .; tertio, l'assimilation de cette 'Résistance' à l'ensemble de la nation, caractéristique notamment du résistancialisme gaullien."
11. See Introduction, note 2.
12. T. J. Clark, "Jackson Pollock's Abstraction," *Reconstructing Modernism: Art in New York, Paris, and Montreal, 1945–1964*, ed. S. Guilbaut, Cambridge, 1990, 211.
13. Ibid., 239.
14. See Dorival (as in n. 6); Huyghe (as in n. 8).
15. J. Bazaine, "Tour d'horizon," *Nouvelle Revue française*, Aug. 1941, 225.

16. Interview with the author, May 5, 1984.
17. S. Wilson, "Les Jeunes Peintres de tradition française," in *Paris–Paris, 1937–1957*, exh. cat., Centre d'Art et de Culture G. Pompidou, Paris, 1981, 107.
18. The Témoignage group first exhibited together at Galerie Matières in Lyons in 1938, then in Paris at Galerie Matières et Formes in 1939. Both galleries were run by Marcel Michaud. Several issues of a review entitled *Le Poids du monde* were published, including a manifesto written in May 1939. Gaston Diehl describes the Témoingnage group in an unpublished manuscript, "Le Nouvel Art contemporain, 1925–1944."
19. For an account of the political history of the review *Esprit*, see M. Winock, *Histoire politique de la revue "Esprit" 1930–1950*, Paris, 1975.
20. G. Severini, *Témoignages: 50 ans de réflexion*, Rome, 1963, 248–249: "En conclusion nous sommes contre: l'éclectisme, la confusion des genres, les 'procédés,' les 'stylismes,' les esthétismes, les académismes et toutes les lâchetès spirituelles.

    "Nous sommes pour: l'authenticité et la pureté, toutes les formes de beauté riches d'un contenu spirituel, la franchise, la probité, la sincérité absolue, aussi bien envers nous-mêmes qu'à l'égard de l'art et de tous les problèmes, même d'ordre social, politique ou économique qui pourraient se pôser.

    "Car nous ne sommes pas indifférents à ces problèmes (nous ne croyons plus à la tour d'ivoire de l'art), mais nous tenons à préciser que, nos bases communes étant des vérités éternelles, et le travail que nous nous proposons visant surtout les valeurs absolues, nous entendons garder notre liberté spirituelle en dehors et au dessus du contingent."
21. Although Bazaine had not been awarded the Prix de Rome, the reward for the art student who, having completed the Ecole des Beaux Arts curriculum, won first place in the two-tier final competition, he had received another award, the Blumenthal Prize. Established by an American couple in the 1920s, this prize went to promising young artists with a background less classical than that provided by the Ecole des Beaux Arts. Many of its recipients had studied at the Ecole des Arts Décoratifs, and were exhibiting at the Salon des Tuileries.
22. H. Bouchard, "Le Passé de nos salons" (date uncertain – March 1941?), Paris, Musée-Atelier Bouchard MS fr. 12. He was also implicated in the purge of public sculpture undertaken at the behest of the Germans, in the course of which many monuments in bronze were removed

from public places and melted down. Henri Bouchard (1875–1960) was the archetypal figure of the artist-bureaucrat. A Prix de Rome winner, he made his living by teaching at the Ecole des Beaux Arts and benefited from state commissions throughout his career. His *Apollo,* a sculpture commissioned for the new Palais de Chaillot, still stands there.

23. Interview with the author, May 5, 1984.
24. L. Namer, "La Politique artistique du gouvernement de Vichy. Hommes et structure," *Mémoire de maîtrise,* Ecole Nationale des Sciences Politiques, Paris, 1983, 266.
25. Ibid., 270.
26. Z. Sternhell, *Ni Droite ni gauche: L'Idéologie fasciste en France,* Paris, 1983, 305: "Il est difficile de voir dans ce texte un appel à la Résistance." The person of Emmanuel Mounier has been so haloed in France because of his moral rectitude, his sincerity, and the fact that he did join a Resistance network during World War II, that few historians have been willing to admit that Mounier erred on the side of Vichy at the beginning of the regime. See, in particular, Winock (as in n. 19).
27. Bazaine had adopted the point of view of his mentor, Emmanuel Mounier, that having to submit your writing – or your curatorial activities – to censorship was no reason to abstain from publishing or from organizing exhibitions. "I do not believe in a policy of absence, of waiting, of prudence," he had written in the *Nouvelle revue française,* Aug. 1941, 225.
28. The charge that the movement toward abstraction took place in expectation of the arrival of a new set of "occupiers," the Americans, whose taste allegedly ran to abstract art, was made at the time by the malevolent collaborationist critic Lucien Rebatet.
29. V. Bosson, *Jean Bazaine,* Paris, 1975, 42.
30. Galerie Jeanne Bucher, June 10–July 4, 1941 (Bazaine, Pignon); Galerie Friedland, Jan. 18–Feb. 14, 1942 (Bazaine, Estève, Gromaire, Lapicque, Lhote, Pignon, Tal Coat); Galerie de France, Feb. 6–March 4, 1943 (Bazaine, Borès, Fougeron, Gischia, Lapicque, Le Moal, Manessier, Pignon, Robin, Singier, Villon).
31. Most of the collections of art belonging to the French State, and a few important private collections, had been transferred to hiding places in the French provinces before the war had been declared. The Palais de Tokyo was barely finished when the war broke out, and thus had never served as a permanent museum.
32. The Action Française Artistique à l'Etranger was a branch of the Min-

istry of Foreign Affairs. It had a tradition of sponsoring exhibitions of French art for viewing abroad as part of public relations efforts by the French government. See chapter 1.

33. L. Rebatet, "Les Révolutionnaires d'arrière garde," *Je suis partout*, Oct. 29, 1943: "[Ils] forment à eux cinq la plus remarquable collection de l'erreur, du rabaclage laborieux de Cézanne, de Picasso, de Rouault, de Lhote, du trognon avorté, de l'arbitraire et de l'impuissance."
34. J. M. Campagne, "L'Art 'nouveau' d'accommoder les restes," *Les Nouveaux Temps*, Feb. 17, 1943: "La farce de l'abstraction a assez duré. Si dans certains milieux, on a intérêt à la prolonger, que l'on ne la qualifie pas de Renaissance avec majuscule."
35. *Aujourd'hui*, although begun in September 1940 with the high expectation of being an independent voice under the editorship of Henri Jeanson (formerly of the *Canard enchaîné*), changed its editor and viewpoint when Georges Suarez replaced Jeanson after the latter was fired for refusing to publish an article favorable to the meeting between Pétain and Hitler in Montoire. See *Histoire générale de la presse française* (as in n. 3), IV, 47.
36. *Le Rouge et le bleu* was founded in November 1941 by Charles Spinasse, a former minister in the government of Léon Blum who had turned collaborator. The journal lasted only until Aug. 22, 1942 and, with a mere 3,200 subscribers, it represented only a minor voice.
37. *Confluences*, a literary periodical, came out of Lyons and was edited by René Tavernier, who published the writings of Resistance poets.
38. P. Strecker, "Considérations sur le Salon d'Automne," *Pariser Zeitung*, French ed., Oct. 24, 1943.
39. A. Speer, *Inside the Third Reich: Mémoirs*, New York, 1970, 184.
40. K.E. Silver writes in *The Circle of Montparnasse: Jewish Artists in Paris 1905–1945* (New York, 1985): "one estimate is that approximately eighty artists from Montparnasse died in the Holocaust." The overall number of artist-victims is unascertainable.
41. For the law concerning French citizens who had left France, see "loi du 23 Juillet 1940 relative à la déchéance de la nationalité à l'égard des Français qui ont quitté la France," *Journal officiel*, July 24, 1940.
42. See the letter from Christian Zervos to Alfred Barr dated Mar. 28, 1945. Alfred H. Barr, Jr. Papers, Picasso VIII B 3, Museum of Modern Art, New York.
43. Georges Huisman became Directeur Général des Beaux Arts in 1934. He presided over the commission in charge of choosing the artists who were to decorate the new structures then being built for the Paris

World's Fair of 1937 – principally the Palais de Chaillot and the Palais de Tokyo.

44. Jean Cassou started his bureaucratic career in the Socialist government of Léon Blum, working under Jean Zay, Minister of Education. Two years later, he became Associate Curator at the Musée du Luxembourg, which was then headed by Louis Hautecoeur. He is the author of an autobiography, *Une Vie pour la liberté*, Paris, 1981.
45. Henri Focillon was invited to teach at Yale University. He did so until his death in 1943.
46. See my *Artists under Vichy. A Case of Prejudice and Persecution*, chap. 7, Princeton University Press, spring 1992, and chapter 6.
47. On the issue of Picasso's alleged indifference to the plight of Max Jacob, see the interview of John Richardson by Barbara Rose, "Picasso Biographer Tracks the *Enfant Terrible*," in *The Journal of Art*, IV, 2, Feb. 1991, 73. "Rose: 'There is also a story about Picasso allowing the Jewish poet Max Jacob to be dragged off by the Gestapo when he was the one person who could have saved him.' Richardson: 'Not true. As someone who had every reason to steer clear of the Nazis, Picasso was the last person who could have saved Jacob.'" This is also the view I espouse (as in n. 46).
48. See the letter from Juan Larrea to Alfred Barr. Alfred H. Barr, Jr. Papers, Picasso VIII B 3. See also M. Fauré, *Histoire du surréalisme sous l'occupation*, Paris, 1982.
49. See J. Debu-Bridel, "Edouard Pignon raconte la bataille du Front National des Artistes," in *La Résistance intellectuelle*, Paris, 1970.
50. The other admired ancestors, according to the catalogue, were: Daumier, Apelle de Colophon, Poussin, Delacroix, the Flemish masters, Botticelli, Carpaccio, Cézanne, Bazzi di Vercelli, Fra Angelico, Bosschaert, Chardin, Maître de mon Village, Breughel, Chassériau, Mathieu le Nain, Cranach, Louis Le Nain, Seurat, Poussin, Chardin, Lisseuhiun, Pol de Limbourg, the masters of the School of Fontainebleau, Aeschylus, and "The Ancients."
51. See N. Nadjinicolaou, *Histoire de l'art et lutte des classes*, Paris, 1973, 92.
52. Clark (as in n. 12), 176.
53. L. Nochlin, "Return to Order," *Art in America*, Sept. 1981, 76.
54. B. Buchloh, "Figures of Authority, Ciphers of Regression," *Art after Modernism: Rethinking Representation*, ed. B. Wallis, New York, 1984, 107.
55. Nochlin (as in n. 53), 76.
56. "'Degenerate Art': The Fate of the Avant-Garde in Nazi Germany," the

exhibition seen at the Los Angeles County Museum in 1991, demonstrated that the majority of the works of art brought together for the original exhibition of Degenerate art in Munich in 1937 were figurative; a number of them (by Otto Dix, Max Beckman, Karl Hofer, among others) were in the *Réalismes* show reviewed by Nochlin (as in n. 53).

57. S. de Beauvoir, *La Force de l'âge*, Paris, 1960, 478.
58. The first author to make distinctions among French "collaborators" was Stanley Hoffmann. See his "Vichy et la Collaboration," *Preuves*, July–Sept. 1969, 61–63, 70–71, 73–74. More elaborate distinctions can be found in D. Veillon, *La Collaboration*, Paris, 1984.

5. Jean Paulhan and His Artist Friends

1. See Tony Judt, *Past Imperfect: French Intellectuals 1944–1956* (Berkeley: University of California Press, 1992), 26; Frédéric Badré's new biography of Paulhan, *Paulhan le juste* (Paris: Grasset, 1997); see also John Culbert, "Slow Progress: Jean Paulhan and Madagascar," *October* 83 (winter 1998).
2. The *Bleu Blanc Rouge* painters are discussed in chapter 4. Romantic realists included Roland Oudot, Maurice Brianchon, and Raymond Legueult, whose middle-of-the-road approach to painting was neither thoroughly academic nor thoroughly vanguard. Lucien Rebatet, the notorious critic of *Je suis partout*, coined the expression "Between-the-Jew-and-the-Pompier" to signify middle-of-the-roadism. Pompier art was the vulgar way of referring to the academic milieu, while Jewish art stood for extreme vanguardism foreign to the French sensibility.
3. Jean Paulhan, *Choix de lettres II 1937–1945: Traité des jours sombres* (Paris: Editions Gallimard, 1992), 331. In a 1937 letter in the same vein, Paulhan had called *Guernica* "fairly uninteresting," 37.
4. For a history of representations of death in the western world, see Philippe Aries, *Essais sur l'histoire de la mort en Occident du Moyen Age à nos jours* (Paris: Editions du Seuil, 1975).
5. See Michèle C. Cone, "Picasso's War in Occupied Paris," *Artists under Vichy: A Case of Prejudice and Persecution* (Princeton, N.J.: Princeton University Press, 1992), 133–34.
6. [Pierre] Drieu la Rochelle, "La peinture et les siens," *Comoedia*, 23 April 1941.
7. Paulhan, *Choix*, 224.
8. Jean Paulhan, *Braque le patron* (Paris: Mourlot, 1945; Geneva and Paris: Trois Collines, 1946).

9. *Jean Paulhan/Jean Grenier: Correspondance 1925–1968* (Quimper: Calligrammes, 1984), 145.
10. Fernand Mourlot, *Gravés dans ma mémoire* (Paris: Laffont, 1979), 117.
11. Ibid., 120.
12. All three works are referenced in André Berne-Joffroy, *Jean Paulhan à travers ses peintres* (Paris: Musées Nationaux, 1974), nos. 471, 463, and 467.
13. Paulhan, *Choix*, 264.
14. John Golding, Sophie Bowness, Isabelle Monod-Fontaine, *Braque: The Late Works* (New Haven and London: Yale University Press, 1997), 9.
15. Ibid.
16. Ibid., 3.
17. Ibid., 40.
18. Paulhan, *Choix*, 25.
19. Ibid., 96–97.
20. Lucien Rebatet, "Révolutionnaires d'arrère garde," *Je suis partout*, 29 October 1943.
21. See Bouvier on Braque's sculpture, *Comoedia*, 29 August 1942, and Bazaine on Braque in *Comoedia*, 5 June 1943.
22. Mourlot, *Gravés*, 127. In fact, the Nazi intellectual Gerhard Heller liked Braque's paintings, and one of them had been on view in an exhibition of modern French art held in Nazi Berlin in 1937. See chapter 1.
23. René Drouin and Leo Castelli had started the gallery in 1939 and, after Castelli's departure for the United States, Drouin reopened it alone. His first director, a collaborationist, was Georges Maratier; his second director, an active resister, was Gildo Caputo. Paulhan was the *éminence grise* of the gallery.
24. Paulhan, *Choix*, 337.
25. Gerhard Heller, *Un Allemand à Paris* (Paris: Editions du Seuil, 1981), 116.
26. Jean Paulhan, *Fautier l'enragé* (Paris: Blaizot, 1949).
27. The first to identify this postwar sensibility was the French critic Michel Tapié de Ceyleran. Against formalism and against any kind of Franco/French particularism, he placed Dubuffet as well as Fautier in the company of American, English, Dutch, and Canadian artists who, he felt, had rejected tradition and worked from a neo-Dadaist position of artistic tabula rasa. See chapter 9.
28. The catalogue of the 1943 Drouin exhibition provides only a list of the exhibited works, and one illustration with no caption, in addition to the Paulhan text.

29. See Marcel-André Stalter, "Fautrier, du permanent au fugace" in Suzanne Pagé, ed., *Jean Fautrier* (Paris: Paris-Musées, 1989), 42–43.
30. Berne-Joffroy, *Jean Paulhan à travers ses peintres,* 218.
31. For details see Jean-Paul Ledeur, "Fautrier, la chair de l'émotion," in Pagé, *Jean Fautrier,* 42–43.
32. Ibid., 95–96.
33. Paulhan, *Choix,* 322.
34. Ibid., 323.
35. Lucien Rebatet, "Les arts et les lettres," *Je suis partout,* 25 November 1943.
36. Jean-Marc Campagne, interview with the author, 16 June 1984. He brings up *"la spiritualité juive," "le paysage mental juif," "les particularismes juifs."*
37. This link is rarely acknowledged by Soutine scholars, as Romy Golan observes in "Blind Alley: The Reception of Soutine in France after World War II," in *Soutine,* exh. cat. (New York: The Jewish Museum, 1998). My thanks to Romy Golan for her valuable advice and for making her text available.
38. Jean Paulhan, *Fautrier l'enragé* (Paris: Editions Gallimard, 1962), 48.
39. The portrait is reproduced in André Verdet, *Jean Fautrier* (Frieburg: Limmer Gallery, 1981).
40. Jacqueline Cousin, Dossier Fautrier, *Cahiers bleus,* 1975. Reprint 1989, 83.
41. The name Garde ("keep" but also "nurse" in French) was given to Gerda Groth by Soutine. The artist decided to "keep" Groth after spending an evening with her, and let her become his "nurse."
42. Mlle Garde, "Mes années avec Soutine," *L'Oeil,* January 1956, 27.
43. Elie Faure quoted in *Soutine* (Paris: Orangerie des Tuileries, 1973), 14.
44. Paulhan, *Choix,* 343.
45. Ibid., 317. Masson was the French surrealist painter.
46. Ibid., 329. Roland Oudot and Maurice Brianchon were romantic realists whose best work was designing sets for the Paris Opera productions. See note 2.
47. Paulhan, *Choix,* 311.
48. Maurice Tuchman in Maurice Tuchman, Esti Dunow, and Klaus Peris, *Chaim Soutine (1893–1943),* catalogue raisonné, vol. 1 (Cologne: Benedikt Taschen Verlag, 1993), 16. Tuchman speaks of a transcendental motif in the invisible presence of wind in the late landscapes, whereas I read a memory of windblown steppes in the late landscapes peopled with children.

49. Mlle Garde, "Mes années," 29.
50. See Michael Marrus and Robert Paxton, *Vichy France and the Jews* (New York: Basic Books, 1981), 250–55.
51. Ibid., 236.
52. The collector Pierre Lévy tells in his memoirs that Max Kaganovitch, a refugee dealer in Lyons, continued to sell his work. See Pierre Lévy, *Des artistes et un collectionneur* (Paris: Flammarion, 1976), 185.
53. Mlle Garde, "Mes années," 31.
54. Paulhan, *Choix*, 311. An article entitled "Contre les peintres d'aujourd'hui," signed Maurice Sachs, praising Soutine, had appeared in the July 1934 NRF.
55. Ibid., 353. Georges Limbour had been a friend of Dubuffet since the 1920s, when both circulated among the surrealists.
56. Jean Dubuffet, *Bâtons rompus* (Paris: Minuit, 1986), 7.
57. Ibid., 8.
58. Ibid. It was not a funeral but a mass held at Eglise St.-Roch.
59. Berne-Joffroy, "Eléments biographiques," *Jean Paulhan à travers ses peintres*, xi.
60. Jean Paulhan, *Les Fleurs de Tarbes ou la terreur dans les lettres* (Paris: Editions Gallimard, 1941), 35.
61. Ibid. Such deconstruction of language evokes Artaud's ideas in the Theatre of Cruelty – the elimination of dialogue from the theatre, and the recourse to gestures, howls, and incantations instead.
62. Paulhan, *Braque le patron*, 22.
63. Culbert, "Slow Progress: Jean Paulhan and Madagascar," 89.
64. Paulhan, *Choix*, 342.
65. Berne-Joffroy, "Eléments," xx.
66. Quoted in Frances Morris, *Paris Post War: Art and Existentialism* (London: The Tate Gallery, 1993), 144.
67. Rebatet, "Révolutionnaires d'arrière garde."

6. The Picasso Album. A Landmark of Artistic Resistance

1. Pierre Seghers, *La Résistance et ses poètes* I, 1940–1944 (Paris: Marabout, 1978), 236.
2. Interview with the author by telephone, October 10, 1984.
3. Maurice Girodias, *The Frog Prince: An Autobiography* (New York: Crown, 1980), 375–84.
4. Françoise Gilot, interview with the author, March 15, 1984.
5. Ibid.

6. John Russell, *Matisse Father and Son* (New York: Abrams, 1999), 231.
7. Maurice Vlaminck, *Portraits avant décès* (Paris: Flammarion, 1943), 184.
8. Robert Desnos, *Ecrits sur les peintres* (Paris: Flammarion, 1984), 182.
9. Jean-Paul Sartre, *L'Imaginaire* (Paris: Gallimard idées, 1940), 20.
10. Desnos, *Ecrits,* 174.
11. Ibid. 179.
12. Ibid.
13. Interview with Alain Brieux, December 10, 1984.
14. Desnos, *Ecrits,* 175.
15. Ibid., 178.
16. Ibid., 177.

7. Wartime Gilt. French Furniture of the 1940s

1. Of Jacques Adnet, the critic Louis Cheronnet is quoted as saying: "In a harsh epoch that seems to be guided by materialist exigencies, disorder and hatred, he contributes the merry and confident music of a French heart." Bruno Foucart and Jean-Louis Gaillemin, *Les Décorateurs des années 40,* Paris, Editions NORMA, 1998, p. 67.
2. See chapter 2.
3. Foucart and Gaillemin, p. 57.
4. The question of ornament is discussed in Anne-Marie Sankovitch, "Structure/Ornament and the Modern Figuration of Architecture," *Art Bulletin,* December 1998, p. 704.
5. These designers' most loyal clients were fashion houses. During the Occupation years, Marcelle Alix called on André Arbus to redecorate her shop. See Foucart and Gallemin, p. 78.
6. Waldemar George, in *Formes d'aujourd'hui,* Galerie de l'orfèvrerie Christofle, 1945, n.p.
7. Jean Charles Moreux was named chief architect for French national palaces and chateaux in 1944, and the French state commissioned him to redecorate French embassies and to preside over renovations of the Louvre. Foucart and Gaillemin, p. 152.
8. Quoted in Foucart and Gaillemin, p. 92.
9. Jules Leleu suffered from his activities during the war. His name appears in the *Journal Officiel* (June 15, 1956) among those condemned by the Comité national d'épuration à l'encontre des peintres, décorateurs, sculpteurs et graveurs. He was forbidden to exhibit and to sell for one year, starting Sept. 1, 1944. This measure did not affect him materially, as it was retroactively applied.

10. Philippe de Villiers and Charles Pasqua are right-wing politicians from the Hauts-de-Seine region that includes Boulogne, as is Jean-Marie Le Pen from neighboring St. Cloud.

8. The Mature Richier, the Young César. Expressionist Confluences in French Postwar Sculpture

1. See Alain Jouffroy, "I'Ouragane oubliée," *Connaissance des arts* 320 (October 1978): 94. Richier and César are discussed together again in a text by Pierre Restamy, "L'Objet de la chair," in Daniel Abadie, *Les Années cinquanie,* exh. cat. (Paris: Musée national d'art moderne, Centre d'art Georges Pompidou, 1988), 234–36.
2. René Huyghe, *Les Contemporains* (Paris: Pierre Tisné, 1949), 108.
3. Bernard Champigneule, *L'Inquiétude dans l'art d'aujourd'hui* (Paris: Mercure de France, 1939), 166.
4. Bernard Dorival, *Les Etapes de la peinture contemporaine, 1911–1944* (Paris: Gallimard, 1946), 186.
5. Ibid., 189.
6. "Ce ne sont donc que quelques étrangers – juifs principalement – qui peuvent être classés dans l'Ecole de Paris." Ibid., 187.
7. See *Paris 1937: Cinquantenaire,* exh. cat. (Paris: Musée d'art moderne de la ville de Paris, 1987), for lists of participants. See Kenneth Silver and Romy Golan, *The Circle of Montparnasse,* exh. cat. (New York: Jewish Museum, 1985), for discussions of l'école française versus l'école de Paris.
8. Mady Menier, "A propos de la sculpture dans la section française de l'expo de 1937," *L'Art face à la crise* (St. Etienne: Université de St. Etienne, C.I.R.E.C., 1980), 101.
9. See Michèle C. Cone, *Artists under Vichy: A Case of Prejudice and Persecution* (Princeton, N.J.: Princeton University Press, 1992), chaps. 2 and 4.
10. Lucien Rebatet, "Les Arts et les lettres," *Je suis partout,* November 25, 1943.
11. See chapter 4.
12. Louis Leygue, interview with author, Paris, July 6, 1984.
13. Léon Gischia and Nicole Védrès, *La Sculpture en France depuis Rodin* (Paris: Le Seuil, 1945), 104. Gischia, a painter, had exhibited in 1941 among the Painters in the French Tradition and had himself become more "abstract." Védrès was a critic and art historian.
14. Restany, "L'Objet de la chair," 234. For further discussion on the pre-

carious status of Expressionist art, see Jean-Luc Duval, "Expériences singulières," in *L'Art en Europe 1945–53*, exh. cat. (St. Etienne: Musée d'art moderne, 1987), 86–94.

15. Françoise Guiter (Richier's niece), interview with author, September 30, 1993. César, interview with author, June 16, 1993.
16. A regular exhibitor at the Salon d'Automne and the Salon des Tuileries since 1928, Richier won the prestigious Blumenthal prize in 1936. She had her first solo show that year at Galerie Kaganovitch and a year later received a sculpture prize for her contribution to the Exposition Universelle in Paris.
17. Sarah Wilson, "Paris Post War: In Search of the Absolute," in Frances Morris, *Paris Post War: Art and Existentialism 1945–55*, exh. cat. (London: Tate Gallery, 1993), 42.
18. Peter Selz, *New Images of Man*, exh. cat. (New York, Museum of Modern Art, 1959), 50.
19. Pierre Restany, *César* (Paris: La Différence, 1988), 30.
20. Gunther Metken, "La Fin de l'âge du fer?" *Revue de l'art* 12 (1971): 49.
21. Wilson, "Paris Post War," 25.
22. Morris, introduction to *Paris Post War*, 18–19.
23. César, interview.
24. Guiter, interview. Guiter is preparing the catalogue raisonné of Richier's oeuvre and supplied me with corrected dates for some of the works and exhibitions.
25. For the Surrealist/existentialist debate, see Jacqueline Chenieu-Gendron, *Le Surréalisme et le roman 1922–1950* (Lausanne: L'Age d'homme, 1983), 322–28. An interesting take on the Surrealist/existentialist alternative is also offered by Martica Sawin in her important book on the Surrealists in exile. She shows that *Labyrinthe*, published in Switzerland shortly after the liberation of Paris, became a key source of information on both Surrealism and existentialism.

    Limbour's first article on Richier, "Quelques sculptures de Germaine Richier," appeared in *Action*, September 5, 1947. He noted her presence at the last Salon de Mai and compared her "insects" with those in paint by André Masson. Other texts by Limbour on Richier include: "Visite à un sculpteur," *Derrière le miroir* 13 (Paris: Galerie Maeght, 1948); "Forêts en bronze," *Action*, November 30, 1948; "Le Pouce de Germaine Richier," *France Observateur*, November 1, 1956; "Personnages imaginaires," *Lettres nouvelles*, June 17, 1959; and the preface to *Germaine Richier*, exh. cat. (Paris: Galerie Creuzevault, 1959). I thank Guiter for making these articles available.

26. César, interview.
27. César's friend Albert Féraud, an excellent sculptor in his own right and a winner of the Prix de Rome for sculpture, also became a welder, an "action" sculptor in stainless steel. Among César's contemporaries many became welders, but César was the only one to make figurative images with that technique.
28. See Denis Milhau, "Présupposés théoriques et contradictions du nouveau réalisme socialiste en France au lendemain de la seconde guerre mondiale," and Alain Giry, "La nouvelle abstraction et la critique de l'Humanité, 1945–1949," *Art et idéologies, l'Art en Occident, 1945–1949* (St. Etienne: Université de St. Etienne: C.I.R.E.C., 1978). See also Serve Guilbaut, *How New York Stole the Idea of Modern Art* (Chicago: University of Chicago Press, 1983), 130–31.
29. Not much has changed to this day: while attempts to deal with memory in a representational manner (e.g., the movie *Schindler's List* and the Holocaust Memorial in Washington) remain controversial, ambiguous nonrepresentational memorials to the Holocaust, warning of but also connoting the impossibility of memorialization, pass muster much better at least with the intellectual elite.

9. Pierre Restany. Postwar Remnants of Cultural Pétainism Exposed

1. Ken Knabb, ed. and trans., *Situationist International Anthology* (Berkeley, Calif.: Bureau of Public Secrets, 1981, 1989), 5.
2. See chapter 8.
3. Pierre Restany, *César* (Paris: La Différence, 1988), 70.
4. Pierre Restany, *Le Nouveau Réalisme* (Paris: 10/18, 1978), 34.
5. Henry Perrier, *Pierre Restany: L'Alchimiste de l'art* (Paris: Cercle d'art, 1998), 22.
6. Tony Judt, *Post Imperfect, 1944–1956* (Berkeley: University of California Press, 1992), 117.
7. Perrier, *Pierre Restany*, 22.
8. Restany, *Le Nouveau Réalisme*, 46
9. Henry Lefebvre, *Critique de la vie quotidienne* (Paris: Grasset, 1947).
10. Michèle C. Cone, "The Late Fifties in Europe: A Conversation with Pierre Restany," *Arts Magazine*, vol. 64, January 1990, 67.
11. Ibid., 68.
12. See chapter 4.
13. See chapter 5.

14. See *Art et Style,* vol. 41, 1956, with an introduction by Raymond Nacenta, director of the Galerie Charpentier.
15. See chapter 1.
16. See chapter 3.
17. Perrier, *Pierre Restany,* 44–46.
18. Michèle C. Cone, "Metro, Boulot, Dodo," in Lynn Gumpert, ed., *The Art of the Everyday* (New York: New York University Press, 1997), 48–49.
19. Perrier, *Pierre Restany,* 44.
20. In the words of Yves Alain Bois in *L'Informe Mode d'emploi* (Paris: Centre Georges Pompidou, 1996), 130.
21. For the difference between *l'informe* and *l'informel,* see Yves Alain Bois and Rosalind Krauss, *L'informe mode d'emploi.*
22. Michel Tapié de Celeyran, *Art autre* (Paris: Gabriel Grand, 1952), n.p.
23. Cone, "The late Fifties," 69.
24. Suzanne Pagé, curator, *Fautrier* (Paris: Musée d'art moderne de la ville de Paris, 1989). See also chapter 5.
25. These objects were shown at Galerie Billet Caputo with an introduction by Jean Paulhan in 1950, then at Galerie de la Nouvelle Revue Française in 1953, and at the Hugo Gallery in New York in 1956. See *Fautrier* catalogue, Galerie di Meo, 1986, 52. Of course it can be argued that Duchamp initiated the idea of the multiple.
26. Jeanine Aeply, "Les Originaux multiples," in *Cahier Bleu,* Dossier Fautrier (Paris: Librairie Bleue, Fall 1975, 1989), 55. See also Aeply, "Les Originaux multiples," *Nouvelle Revue Française,* September 1975, 118–21.
27. Cone, "The Late Fifties," 69.
28. Perrier, *Pierre Restany,* 64.
29. Ibid., 48.
30. See catalogue essay quoted in Perrier, *Pierre Restany,* 51–52.
31. Nan Rosenthal, "Assisted Levitation: The Art of Yves Klein," *Yves Klein* (Houston: Institute for the Arts, Rice University, 1982), 100–104.
32. Restany, *Le Nouveau Réalisme,* 45.
33. Cone, "The Late Fifties," 69.
34. Restany, *Le Nouveau Réalisme,* 28. For Duchamp's objections to this aesthetic rehabilitation of the ready-made, see Alice Goldfarb Marquis's biography of Duchamp, *Marcel Duchamp: Eros, c'est la vie* (Troy, N.Y.: Whitston, 1981), 324.
35. See Jean Schuster, "Marcel Duchamp, vite," *Le Surréalism, Même,* no.

2, Spring 1957, 143–45; Alain Jouffroy, "Marcel Duchamp," *Arts, Lettres Spectacles*, no. 694, October–November 1958, 12; Michel Sanouillet, ed., *Marchand du Sel: Ecrits de Marcel Duchamp* (Paris: Terrain Vague, 1958); Robert Lebel, *Sur Marcel Duchamp* (Paris: Trianon, 1959).

36. The event seems to have taken place in 1958.
37. Pierre Cabanne, *Dialogues with Marcel Duchamp*, trans. Ron Padgett (New York: Da Capo paperback, 1971), 95. Another view of Duchamp's attitude toward money is given in Marquis, *Marcel Duchamp*, 324: "John Cage found Duchamp extremely interested in money; he resented being thought a poor businessman."
38. Although Duchamp also made multiples, César casting his original iron pieces from the fifties into bronze multiples confirms Duchamp's judgment.
39. Benjamin Buchloh, "Plenty of Nothing, from Yves Klein's Le Vide to Arman's Le Plein," *Premises: Invested Spaces in Visual Arts, Architecture and Design from France 1958–1998* (New York: Guggenheim Museum, 1998), 97.
40. Ken Knabb, *Situationist International Anthology*, 144.
41. See Bernard Ceysson, Jacques Beauffret, and Jean Luc Daval, *L'Art en Europe: Les Années décisives 1945–1953* (Paris: Skira, Musée d'art moderne de Saint-Etienne, 1987).
42. Frances Morris and others, *Paris Post War: Art and Existentialism 1945–1955* (Tate Gallery, 1993).

Epilogue. Hitler Equals de Gaulle in a May '68 Poster

1. Jean Pierre Le Goff, "Ce fascisme qui n'en finit pas d'arriver," *Mai 68: L'Héritage impossible* (Paris: La Découverte, 1998), 190.
2. Catherine Millet, *L'Art Contemporain en France* (Paris: Flammarion, 1987), 66.
3. See Sarah Wilson,"Erro: L'Extase materiel," in *Erro* exh. cat. (Paris: Galerie Nationale du Jeu de Paume, 1999), 55.
4. Millet, 95.
5. Geneviève Dreyfus-Armand and Laurent Gervereau, *May '68: Les Mouvements étudiants en France et dans le monde* (Paris: BDIC, 1988), 192–97.
6. Claude Singer, *Vichy, l'université et les Juifs* (Paris: Les Belles Lettres), 1992, 343.
7. Ibid. 340.

8. See Ron Rosenbaum, *Explaining Hitler* (New York: Random House, 1998), p. xiii, for a development of this view.
9. It is not to condemn a child for his parents' deeds to observe that someone like Jean-Pierre Azéma, the Vichy historian whose father is described in Pierre-Marie Dioudonnat's *Je suis partout 1930–1944* (Paris: La Table Ronde, 1973, 443) as a volunteer in the Waffen SS as of December 1943 and a member of the Wallonie SS brigade in the spring of 1944, must have welcomed the idea that his father was guilty of no crimes except that of having been seduced by the wrong ideology. See also Henry Rousso on another Waffen SS, Christian de la Mazière, *The Vichy Syndrome* (Cambridge, Mass.: Harvard University Press, 1991), 105.
10. Joseph Algazy, *La Tentation néo-fasciste en France de 1944 à 1965* (Paris: Fayard, 1984).
11. Pierre-André Taguieff, *Sur la Nouvelle Droite* (Paris: Descartes, 1994).
12. Robert Belot, *Lucien Rebatet, un itinéraire fasciste* (Paris: Le Seuil, 1994). "La nouvelle droite est née. Or toute nouvelle qu'elle soit, cette droite a besoin de se référer à quelques 'valeurs' sûres. Lucien Rebatet en est une pour elle. Que vénère-t-on en lui? Le non-conformiste de *Rivarol* qui sait dire sa vérité à la droite des collines inspirées et de l'ordre moral, l'oracle des *Décombres* qui a prophétisé, avant beaucoup, le déclin des nationalismes. Et l'auteur des *Deux Etendards* qui a annoncé la mort du Dieu judéo-chrétien. Alain de Benoist, qui aura des contacts avec Rebatet, reconnaîtra sa dette . . ." (388).

Index